The Presence of Christ in the Church

The Presence of Christ in the Church: Explorations in Theology

Lawrence J. Welch

Sapientia Press
of Ave Maria University

Sapientia Press
of Ave Maria University
5050 Ave Maria Blvd.
Ave Maria, FL 34142
888–343–8607

Cover Design: Eloise Anagnost

Cover Image: Christ Pantokrator, 6th C. Image. Icon written by Ruth Ballard.

Printed in the United States of America.

Library of Congress Control Number: 2012934653

ISBN: 978-1-932589-59-7

Contents

Preface

THE ESSAYS in this book take up the subjects of the Magisterium, the priesthood, and theological anthropology. The sacramental presence of Christ in the Church—in her teaching authority, in holy orders, and in the human person—is the underlying unity of these essays. Each of them supposes that a sound theological presentation of these things must be based on an understanding of a sacramentally real presence of Christ to the Church. This means, for example, that the infallible teachings of the ordinary universal magisterium—part of the sacramental continuation of the teaching authority Jesus shared with the apostles—must be approached as first and foremost having to do what is necessary for achieving communion in the faith across the ages. In such a perspective, infallible teachings of the ordinary universal magisterium appear to be less rare than sometimes imagined. Five chapters, written in the style of *quaestio disputata*, take up this subject. The last chapter in this section, coauthored with Guy Mansini, O.S.B., addresses the much-discussed passage from *Lumen Gentium*, number 8, which teaches that the one Church of Christ subsists in the Catholic Church. It has been included because it is connected in an important way to the theme of this project: the sacramental presence of Christ to the Church. To speak of Christ's presence to the Church is to speak of all the gifts and instruments of salvation that Christ gave to the one Church as having a continued, concrete existence in some agent. And that is in the Catholic Church, because she alone has all the gifts with which Christ endowed the one Church. The one Church of Christ subsists in the Catholic Church.

Two chapters explore the ordained priesthood as first and foremost the sacramental representation of Christ the Head, who teaches, sanctifies, and pastors his Church. The ordained priest is the sacramental continuation of Christ acting for the Church. The sacramental conformation to Christ the Head, Shepherd, and Spouse of the Church is the key for understanding not only how the priest can be said to speak *in nomine ecclesiae* but also the kind of spiritual paternity the priest is called to live. This second section of the book concludes with an essay coauthored with Guy Mansini, O.S.B., about the sort of affective and spiritual conformation to Christ that priestly mission and life calls for.

Four chapters concerning matters of theological anthropology comprise the last section of this book. The first chapter investigates the thought of Augustine of Hippo as a resource for a theology of the body. Augustine understood the sexual differentiation of the first couple in a sacramental sense. The creation of man, male and female, was not simply for the purpose of procreation but was part of God's creative plan, meant to foreshadow the spousally ordered unity between Christ and the Church. God who created human persons as male and female redeems them as male and female. The next chapter, foundational for the two that follow, traces Pope John Paul II's development of the theological anthropology of *Gaudium et Spes* in his encyclical *Veritatis Splendor*. At the center of this development is a profound integration of Christology, freedom, and communion with the image of God in the human person. The third chapter in this section investigates how the state of consecrated virginity witnesses to the truth of the human body created for and redeemed by Christ. The last chapter, again coauthored with Guy Mansini, O.S.B., takes up a matter of theological anthropology: how Christ, the Word made flesh, provides the content of the moral law relative to sexuality and marriage.

I want to thank Professor Matthew Levering, who asked me to assemble these essays for the Faith and Reason series of Sapientia Press, for all his help and constant encouragement with this project. No small measure of gratitude is owed to a number of colleagues who aided me in their comments and criticisms of my writings: Guy Mansini, O.S.B., John Grabowski, Christopher Thompson, Damien Dougherty, O.F.M., James Swift, C.M., and Edward Richard, M.S. I especially give thanks to my wife, Shawn McCauley Welch, for her unswerving support and patience, and many hours of fruitful theological conversation.

Abbreviations

AAS	*Acta Apostilicae Sedis*
CCC	*Catechism of the Catholic Church*
CCL	*Corpus Christianorum Series Latina*
CDF	Congregation of the Doctrine of the Faith
CSEL	Corpus Scriptorum Ecclesiasticorum Lantinorum
DM	*Dives in misericordia*
DS	Denzinger Sch?nmetzer
DV	*Dei Verbum*
ERD	Ethical and Religious Directives
EV	*Evangelium vitae*
FC	*Familiaris consortio*
GS	*Gaudium et spes*
HG	*Humani generis*
HV	*Humane vitae*
LG	*Lumen gentium*
MD	*Mulieris dignitatem*
NCCB	National Conference of Catholic Bishops
NPNF	A Select Library of the Nicene and Post-Nicene Fathers
PDV	*Pastores Dabo Vobis*
PG	J. P. Migne, ed., Patrologia Graeca
PL	J. P. Migne, ed., Patrologia Latina
PO	*Presbyterorum progressio*
RH	*Redemptor hominis*
ST	*Summa theologiae*
TOB	*Theology of the Body*
UR	*Unitatis redintegratio*

USCC	United States Conference
USCCB	United States Conference of Catholic Bishops
VS	*Veritatis Splendor*
WSA	*Works of Saint Augustine*

CHAPTER 1

The Infallibility of the Ordinary Universal Magisterium*

THE SECOND Vatican Council's Dogmatic Constitution on the Church, *Lumen Gentium* (*LG*), number 25, teaches:

> Although the individual bishops do not enjoy the prerogative of infallibility, they do nevertheless proclaim Christ's doctrine infallibly even when dispersed around the world, provided that while maintaining the bond of communion among themselves and with Peter's successor, and teaching authoritatively on a matter of faith or morals, they are in agreement that a particular judgment is to be held definitively.[1]

This teaching of Vatican II raises the problem of how to know when the ordinary universal magisterium has proposed some doctrine as definitive. The distinguished theologian Francis A. Sullivan, S.J., has attempted to address this problem at some length.[2] Recalling a passage in Pius IX's letter *Tuas Libenter* (*TL*), he claims that the universal and constant consensus of Catholic theologians is a sign by which we can recognize that a doctrine has been taught as definitive. The Latin term used by Pius IX,

---

* A version of this essay appeared in *Heythrop Journal* 39 (January 1998): 18–36.

1 I follow Father Francis A. Sullivan's translation given in his book *Creative Fidelity* (New York: Paulist Press, 1996), 102.

2 Sullivan, *Creative Fidelity*, 93–108. See also Francis A. Sullivan, "The Doctrinal Weight of *Evangelium Vitae*," *Theological Studies* 56 (1995): 560–65; idem, "Reply to Germain Grisez," *Theological Studies* 55 (1994): 732–37; idem, "The Secondary Object of Infallibility," *Theological Studies* 54 (1993): 536–50; idem, *Magisterium* (New York: Paulist Press, 1983), 119–52.

constans, means "unchanging and immovable." This indicates, according to Father Sullivan, that the consensus about a doctrine as definitively taught must be of the kind that is irreversible and changeless.[3] On the other hand, Sullivan says, "it follows that in the absence of such a consensus among Catholic theologians, it would be difficult to maintain that a doctrine had been taught by the ordinary universal magisterium as definitively to be held."[4] It also follows, according to Sullivan, that if there is a breakdown in consensus on a point of doctrine about which formerly there was a consensus, then "it would seem necessary to conclude that this was not the kind of *constant* consensus that points to infallible teaching."[5] Sullivan points to the problem of monogenism and polygenism as an example from the history of theology that illustrates this conclusion.[6]

Sullivan also gives another principle important for interpreting whether a doctrine has been taught definitively. He proposes that canon 749.3, which applies to defined dogmas, be extended to apply to the infallible but undefined dogmas of the ordinary universal magisterium as well.[7] Canon 749.3 says that "no doctrine is to be understood to be infallibly defined unless this fact is clearly established." Applying this canon to definitive but undefined dogmas, Sullivan claims that no doctrine is to be understood as having been definitively and infallibly taught unless this fact is clearly established. He argues that this kind of fact could not really be said to be established unless there was a consensus among theologians that a doctrine had been definitively and infallibly taught.

Now, it is evident that in both principles the consensus of theologians weighs very heavily. Both principles must be applied when judging whether the ordinary universal magisterium has actually taught a particular doctrine definitively. On the one hand, it could not be claimed that a doctrine had been so taught unless there was a consensus among theologians to that effect. On the other, this consensus must prove itself over the long haul; it must be constant and universal.

In what follows I will carefully examine Sullivan's interpretation and application of these principles and argue against them. I will claim that while it may be true that the constant consensus of theologians is a sign

---

[3] Sullivan, *Creative Fidelity*, 100–101, 103, 107; idem, "Reply to Germain Grisez," 736; idem, "Guideposts from the Catholic Tradition," *America* (December 9, 1995): 6.

[4] Sullivan, "Reply to Germain Grisez," 736.

[5] Sullivan, *Creative Fidelity*, 104.

[6] Ibid., 104–5.

[7] Ibid., 106; see also idem, "The Secondary Object of Infallibility," 549.

that the ordinary magisterium has taught a doctrine definitively, nevertheless, the absence of consensus does not necessarily warrant the conclusion that a doctrine has not been taught definitively. The consensus among theologians can be a sign of, but is not a necessary condition for, the definitive teachings of the ordinary universal magisterium. Lastly, I will urge that the discussion about these definitive teachings would be greatly aided if it took place in the context of what some theologians have called "catholicity in time."[8] Key to the concept of catholicity in time is the *communio* structure of the Church. The communion of the Church must extend not only synchronically but diachronically as well, so that the Church of the present age shares in the faith and identity of the Church of the past, right to the Church of the very beginning. I want to suggest that the quest for identifying definitive doctrines should be understood as closely connected with the task of achieving catholicity in time and communion across time.

I will develop this presentation in four parts. In the first part, I will scrutinize and criticize Sullivan's contention that canon 749.3 should apply to undefined dogmas taught by the ordinary universal magisterium. The second part will examine Sullivan's contention that the debate over monogenism and polygenism illustrates the principle that a breakdown in the consensus among theologians is sufficient to nullify a claim that a doctrine had already been definitively taught. In the third part, I will critique Sullivan's interpretation of *TL*. The claim that Sullivan makes about the importance of the consensus of theologians is grounded upon his understanding of this papal letter. It is in this section that I will advance my claim that the consensus of theologians may be a sign of definitive teachings but is not a necessary condition for such teachings. In the fourth and final part, I will lay out my suggestion for a new context for the current discussion about the ordinary universal magisterium and definitive teachings.

It is hoped that these conclusions and reflections will contribute to the discussion about undefined dogmas and the problem of the infallibility of the ordinary universal magisterium. At the same time this presentation does not purport to identify, let alone address, all the important questions with regard to this problem.

---

8 For example, Avery Dulles, *Catholicity of the Church* (Oxford: Oxford/Clarendon, 1985).

Canon 749.3 and the Infallible Teaching of the Ordinary Universal Magisterium

> No doctrine is to be understood to be infallibly defined unless this fact is clearly established as such. (Can. 749.3)[9]

Sullivan asserts that this canon, which explicitly is applicable to defined dogmas, ought also to be applied to undefined dogmas taught by the ordinary universal magisterium. He reasons that this extension is justified because the obligations and consequences for the faith are identical regardless of whether a doctrine has been infallibly taught by a solemn definition or by the ordinary universal magisterium.[10] Vatican I and canon 750 of the 1983 *Code of Canon Law* stipulate that the faithful must believe with "divine and catholic faith" those doctrines proposed as divinely revealed.[11] This response is called for whether such doctrines are taught as solemnly defined or infallibly taught by the ordinary universal magisterium. The new formula of the profession of faith says essentially the same thing.[12] Canon 751 of the 1983 Code says that a person is guilty of heresy if that person obstinately denies a doctrine that must be believed with divine and Catholic faith, and it makes no distinction between solemnly defined dogmas and doctrines taught definitively and infallibly by the ordinary universal magisterium. Given this, Sullivan comes to the conclusion that just as defined dogmas ought not be considered infallible unless that fact is clearly established, so too for undefined dogmas that the ordinary universal magisterium teaches.

Sullivan submits that careful attention should be given to the final phrase of canon 749.3, which in Latin reads *nisi id manifeste constiterit* and is translated by the Canon Law Society of America as "clearly established." He points out further that *Harper's Latin Dictionary* translates *constat* to mean settled, established, undisputed, certain, or well known. Sullivan argues that while the *Code of Canon Law* does not give specific criteria by which a fact can be known as "settled" or "established," it does insinuate or suggest that there will be a general consensus about such a fact. Moreover, the canon says that in addition to being settled and undisputed, a defined

---

[9] I follow the English translation of this canon given in Canon Law Society of America, trans., *Code of Canon Law, Latin-English Edition* (Washington, DC: Canon Law Society of America, 1983), 283.

[10] Sullivan, *Creative Fidelity*, 106–7; idem, "Reply to Germain Grisez," 734; idem, "The Secondary Object of Infallibility," 549.

[11] Sullivan cites DS 3011 in *Creative Fidelity*, 106n49.

[12] Congregation for the Doctrine of the Faith (CDF), *Origins* 18 (March 16, 1989): 663; cf. *AAS* 81 (1989): 104–6.

doctrine must be manifestly such. But to whom should this fact be so manifest? Sullivan says that it must be manifest to Catholic theologians who are charged with the responsibility of assessing the dogmatic weight of the teachings of the Magisterium.[13] Therefore he comes to the conclusion that "one could hardly claim that a doctrine had been infallibly defined and was *manifestly* 'settled, established, undisputed,' if there was a serious disagreement among Catholic theologians about this alleged fact."[14]

Significantly, Sullivan rejects the interpretation made by some theologians that the canon refers to the context and formulation of an infallible doctrinal definition. In other words, one ought not to conclude that a teaching of the Magisterium is a solemn definition unless the very formulation of the doctrine itself together with its context makes this clear. Sullivan rejects this interpretation in an exchange with Germain Grisez.[15] Grisez criticized what he called Sullivan's translation of *nisi id manifeste constiterit* as questionable. He argued that "while something can be manifestly the case without having been shown by anyone to be so, 'established' suggests that cogent arguments have been given and accepted as such."[16] The Latin text of the canon, according to Grisez, is open to another interpretation, namely, "one should not judge that this or that magisterial statement is a solemn definition unless the very formulation and its context makes this clear."[17] It follows then that the canon is not applicable to undefined dogmas taught by the ordinary universal magisterium because "a teaching of the latter sort is not expressed in a single statement, whose formulation and context could make clear that the doctrine is being proposed infallibly."[18]

Sullivan responds to this criticism by pointing out that he simply follows the English translation of *constat* accepted by the Canon Law Society of America and given in *Harper's Latin Dictionary.* He concludes that there is no basis for objecting to this translation and thus, no basis for Grisez's opinion "that the canonical directive must refer to the formulation and context of an infallible definition, and therefore cannot be applied by analogy to the infallible teaching of the ordinary magisterium."[19]

Now it seems to me that Sullivan has probably shown that the translation of the Latin text of the canon he follows is sound. But he has still not

---

13 Sullivan, "Reply to Germain Grisez," 733–34; cf. idem, *Creative Fidelity*, 43–44.

14 Sullivan, *Creative Fidelity*, 44.

15 Sullivan, "The Secondary Object of Infallibility"; Germain Grisez, "The Ordinary Magisterium's Infallibility," *Theological Studies* 55 (1994): 721–32.

16 Ibid., 731.

17 Ibid.

18 Ibid.

19 Sullivan, "Reply to Germain Grisez," 734.

shown that the canon, even in his preferred translation, does not refer in some sense to the formulation and context of the infallible definition itself. I submit that there are good reasons for holding that the formulation and context of the teaching of the Magisterium is important for determining whether that teaching involves a solemn definition.

In chapter three of his monograph *Creative Fidelity*, Sullivan says that it is not easy at the present time to determine whether theologians are agreed that a doctrine has been defined. In former times one could judge whether there was a consensus among theologians that a doctrine was defined because they assigned theological notes to doctrines. Since theologians no longer do this today, "there is no simple way to ascertain the fact of such a consensus." Sullivan maintains that "[i]t is up to the theologian to show, by other criteria, that it is manifestly the case that a doctrine has been defined.[20] He identifies several criteria: the history of a council known from its *Acta*, the literary genre of council documents, and the distinction between chapters and canons, which can be either doctrinal or disciplinary.[21] Thus the *Acta* and the historical records of a council can supply valuable evidence of a council's intention to define a doctrine. The history of the controversy that provoked the calling together of a council can also be of capital importance for identifying the exact point of doctrine that it intended to define. Likewise, the literary genre of council documents can be important for assessing the dogmatic weight that a council wanted to give to its teaching. Doctrinal canons, for example, can explicitly refer to the specific point of doctrine that a council intended to define in the corresponding chapter. For example, Sullivan writes with regard to the canons of *Pastor Aeternus*:

> These canons pronounce the sentence of "anathema" against those who presume to contradict certain elements of the doctrine contained in the corresponding chapter. The gravity of such a sentence expressed the intention to define a positive statement whose contradiction is condemned in the canon even though in the chapter the council does not use the term: "we define." One can therefore identify only those precise statements whose contradiction is condemned in the corresponding canons.[22]

It is clear that in all of the criteria Sullivan gives, the formulation and the context of a doctrinal decree of the Magisterium is of paramount

[20] Sullivan, *Creative Fidelity*, 44.
[21] Ibid., 44–55.
[22] Ibid., 48.

importance for ascertaining whether a doctrine has been defined. However, it does not seem that Sullivan has integrated these observations into the question of whether canon 749.3 should be applied to the recognition of undefined dogmas. It is very hard to see how these important observations can be reconciled with his claim that this canon does not mean to assert that the criterion for identifying defined doctrine is based on formulation and context. It is difficult to see how Sullivan can maintain this argument when he skillfully shows how the formulation and context of doctrinal decrees are critical, even indispensable, for determining whether a doctrine has been defined.

If this is all true, then surely canon 749.3 cannot be applied in a straightforward way to undefined dogmas, because they do not have the same precise formulation as defined dogmas and the same kind of identifiable context. The criteria that Sullivan proposes seem to admit as much. The doctrinal decrees, for example, at Nicea, Trent, or Vatican I, all call for very careful interpretation, as Sullivan rightly insists; nevertheless, they clearly express in a single doctrinal statement a teaching that is proposed as defined. Undefined dogmas are different. Because they are not the subject of solemn definition, undefined dogmas are not expressed in precise formulations. To understand this, one has only to compare chapter 4 and the corresponding canons of *Pastor Aeternus*, which define papal infallibility to the doctrine of the communion of the saints as taught by the ancient creeds but never the subject of a solemn definition. On the other hand, when it is a question of recognizing defined dogmas, one looks for evidence that there was a clear intention to define a particular point of doctrine. This cannot be implicit; it must be indicated in the doctrinal decree itself in some way that makes it clear that doctrine is being proposed as solemnly defined. I do not mean to suggest that Sullivan would deny this. The point here is that his discussion must be connected to the question of whether canon 749.3 can be applied to undefined dogmas.

There are good reasons for thinking, as Sullivan's own criteria suggest, that the final phrase of the canon 749.3, *nisi id manifeste constiterit*, must refer in some way to the formulation and context of the proposed doctrinal definition itself; otherwise, the canon itself would ignore sound criteria for interpreting defined doctrines. In other words, the requirement that defined dogmas must be clearly or manifestly established means that there must be a clear intent to define a doctrine in the doctrinal definition itself.[23] If this is

[23] The Holy See's official response to the Final Report of the Anglican–Roman Catholic International Commission made a similar point: "For the Catholic Church, the certain knowledge of any defined truth is not guaranteed by the reception of the faithful that such is in conformity with Scripture and tradition,

the case, then it becomes apparent why canon 749.3 cannot be applied in an analogous fashion to undefined dogmas that are not taught with the same kind of precise formulation and context that is proper to solemn doctrinal definitions.[24] It remains true, of course, that when theologians try to identify undefined dogmas they must painstakingly inquire as to whether the pope and the bishops have been in agreement that a particular doctrine must be held definitively. I conclude then that canon 749.3 is of little help to theologians in their quest to recognize undefined dogmas taught by the ordinary universal magisterium. Whether and to what extent the consensus of theologians is a sign or condition for recognizing an undefined dogma is an issue that will be addressed in the next section.

Pius IX and the Universal and Constant Consensus of Catholic Theologians

In a number of his writings Sullivan claims that Pius IX in *TL* attached great importance to the constant and universal consensus of theologians for ascertaining whether the ordinary magisterium has taught a particular doctrine definitively as a matter of faith.[25] In *TL* Pius IX wrote, among other things, against the idea that theologians were obligated to hold only

---

but by the authoritative definition itself on the part of authentic teachers" (emphasis mine). See *Origins* 21 (1991): 444.

[24] Mention should be made here of the fact that there appears to be something of an exception to this. *Evangelium Vitae* (*EV*), for example, explicitly invokes the teaching authority of the ordinary universal magisterium with regard to direct killing of the innocent, abortion, and euthanasia. See *EV* 57, 62, and 65. Here we have an instance of the papal magisterium confirming the teaching of the ordinary universal magisterium in such a way as to make the definitive nature of that teaching clear and relatively easy to identify as such. Sullivan admits, rightly, that there are good reasons to think that Pope John Paul intended to invoke the infallibility of the ordinary universal magisterium as set out in *LG* 25. Indeed, the Pope explicitly says that he is teaching in communion with the bishops of the Catholic Church and refers in a note to *LG* 25 in each of the three doctrinal formulations. The Pope's language in each of the formulas makes it clear that he is confirming a teaching that he and the bishops want all Catholics to hold definitively. Nevertheless, Sullivan holds that "it is too soon to know whether there will be the consensus of theologians that would show that it is 'clearly established' that the immorality of murder, abortion and euthanasia are infallibly taught." See Sullivan, *Creative Fidelity*, 160. Against this I would argue that when *EV* clearly confirms the infallibility of the ordinary universal magisterium for three of its teachings, then our knowledge of this rests upon the authority of the teaching that the Pope confirms and the papal confirmation itself rather than a future consensus of theologians.

[25] See note 3.

defined dogmas of the Church. This notion was voiced during a meeting of Catholic theologians at Munich in 1863. The Pontiff declared:

> For even if it is a matter of that subjection which must be given in the act of divine faith, it must not be limited to those things which have been defined by the express decrees of Councils or the Roman pontiffs and of this apostolic see, but must also be extended to those things which are handed on by the ordinary magisterium of the whole church dispersed throughout the world as divinely revealed, *and therefore are held by the universal and constant consensus of Catholic theologians to pertain to the faith.*[26]

Sullivan reasons that it is safe to conclude that Pius IX recognized the consensus of theologians as a "clear sign" that the ordinary magisterium had definitively taught a doctrine *de fide.*[27] In a 1995 essay published in *America* he also goes so far as to say that the words of Pius IX about the consensus of theologians in *TL* were "another criterion" for demonstrating this kind of teaching.[28] Sullivan draws the conclusion from all this that if it becomes apparent at some point that there is no longer a consensus among theologians that a doctrine has been taught definitively, then we should conclude that there is no longer the constant consensus that denotes an infallible, definitive teaching.[29] We should recall that the absence of this kind of consensus is important according to Sullivan because without it, it is difficult to claim that the ordinary universal magisterium has definitively taught a particular doctrine.[30]

In what follows I will test Sullivan's contention that the problem of polygenism and monogenism is an example and an illustration of these conclusions that he draws from *TL*. I will then briefly examine his interpretation of the nature and the significance of Pius IX's assertions in *TL*. This method of procedure seems justified given the emphasis that Sullivan's book *Creative Fidelity* attaches to the problem of polygenism and monogenism, as a test for his claim about the importance of the universal and constant consensus of Catholic theologians.

Sullivan claims that the case of polygenism and monogenism shows how there can be a consensus about a doctrine as definitive that breaks down, thus failing to fulfill a necessary condition for saying that a doctrine

---

26 I follow John Boyle's translation in his essay "The Ordinary Magisterium: Towards a History of the Concept," *Heythrop Journal* 20 (1979): 97. The italics are Boyle's.

27 Sullivan, "Reply to Germain Grisez," 36.

28 Sullivan, "Guideposts from the Catholic Tradition," 6.

29 Sullivan, *Creative Fidelity*, 104.

30 See quote cited in note 4 above.

has been proposed definitively. It seems appropriate to quote Sullivan on this point.

> Here we have an instance of a consensus that seemed strong enough in 1870 to justify defining a doctrine as a dogma of faith, but which has not remained constant and is no longer universal. It would hardly seem reasonable to argue that since the former consensus had fulfilled the conditions required for the infallible exercise of [the] ordinary universal magisterium, the subsequent lack of consensus could not nullify the claim that the doctrine had already been infallibly taught.[31]

At Vatican I there was a conciliar draft in favor of defining monogenism as a dogma of faith. Sullivan argues that although the draft was never discussed or acted upon, it was noted several times in the *Acta* that there was no opposition to such a definition. This lack of opposition, coupled with the unanimity of the commission that prepared the draft, suggests to Sullivan that prior to Vatican I there was a consensus among bishops and theologians that monogenism was a definable doctrine and that polygenism was contrary to the Council of Trent's teaching that the sin of Adam was one in origin and communicated by propagation.

But is it not risky to draw such conclusions based simply upon the consensus of a conciliar commission and a draft that was never discussed and that the Magisterium never acted upon? Thanks to the interruption of the Council we will never know what a discussion on the unapproved schema would have revealed about precisely why and on what basis it was thought that monogenism was a definable doctrine. Moreover, the question of polygenism as it had been posed by the science of the day was a new one. It was certainly not a question that had crossed the mind of the Fathers at the Council of Trent. Rahner, among others, reminds us that prior to *Humani Generis* (*HG*) the declarations of the Magisterium do not take up an explicit position on monogenism.[32] The descent of all humanity from historical Adam was something taken for granted prior to the advent of modern theories of evolution. But if polygenism was a new question and a new challenge, then can we really speak of a consensus prior to Vatican I that the descent of all human persons from Adam was definable doctrine and that polygenism was contrary to Trent? Even if we were to assume there was a consensus in 1870 at Vatican I on mono-

31 Sullivan, *Creative Fidelity*, 105.

32 Karl Rahner, *Sacramentum Mundi*, vol. 4 (New York: Herder, 1968), s.v. "monogenism," 105.

genism the most that could be claimed would be that there was a consensus about a new question that prior Church teaching did not envisage and that Vatican I itself did not elevate to the status of doctrine.

Sullivan, on the other hand, claims that Pius XII some eighty years after Vatican I in his encyclical *HG* continued to uphold this "consensus." There Pius XII proclaimed that Catholic theologians could not hold the theory of polygenism because it was not apparent how such a view could be reconciled with the sources of revelation and with what the Church teaches with regard to original sin as originating from sin committed by an individual, Adam, and through generation, passed on to all.[33] For Sullivan, *HG* shows that in the time since Vatican I the former "consensus" had begun to break down. He cites Karl Rahner to the effect that a suggestion has developed in Catholic theology, some twenty years after the encyclicals, that polygenism is compatible with the doctrine of original sin—a suggestion tolerated by the Magisterium. But both *HG*'s and Rahner's positions require careful interpretation. If we pay careful attention to *HG* it is clear that the Pope did not present his teaching as declaring absolutely and definitively that polygenism is irreconcilable with the doctrine of original sin.

We must recall that Pius XII said that it was "in no way apparent how" (*nequaquam appareat quomodo*) such an opinion as polygenism could be reconciled with the doctrine of original sin. The words that the Pope chose to use are important. It seems correct to say that Pius XII taught that there was an apparent impossibility of upholding original sin together with the hypothesis of polygenism, but he did not say that it would always be impossible, and the fact that he did not is very significant. Theologians are generally agreed that the primary concern of Pius XII in *HG* with regard to polygenism was to defend the doctrine of original sin. Karl Rahner must be counted as one of these theologians. He also observed with regard to *HG*:

> Polygenism is rejected because and insofar as it is not clear how it can be reconciled (*componi queat*) with the ecclesiastical doctrine of original sin. This statement bars the way to a polygenist view of the origin of mankind, as long as its compatibility with the dogma of original sin is not established. . . . Hence in spite of *Humani Generis*, some form of polygenism may be prudently maintained.[34]

---

[33] *HG* 37. I give the English translation as it appears in Claudia Carlin, I.H.M., *The Papal Encyclicals 1939–1958* (Wilmington, NC: McGrath, 1981).

[34] Rahner, *Sacramentum Mundi*, s.v. "monogenism," 4:106.

Several other theologians reached similar conclusions about *HG*. One of the most telling is that of Henri Rondet:

> Indeed official commentators did not fail to observe that the theological "note" attaching to the doctrine of monogenism had changed. Formerly the contrary thesis had been labeled "close to heresy" if not worse; henceforth it would only be temerarious; later still, in the measure that theologians made it their own, the most that could be said against it is that it could not be safely taught (*tuto doceri non potest*). In a noteworthy lecture given in Paris the following year, an exegete explained this qualification by recalling the dictum of an anonymous wit: "The pope has locked the door and put the key in his own pocket."[35]

The conclusion seems inescapable. In *HG* the Pope only issued a carefully qualified rejection of polygenism. In that encyclical we do not have, as Sullivan seems to allege, a repetition of the unqualified rejection of polygenism that we find in the unapproved schema of Vatican I. The subtleties of that encyclical also tell us that in 1950 the Bishop of Rome, the head of the apostolic college, did not judge the prior teaching of the ordinary universal magisterium on original sin as completely, definitively, and forever rejecting polygenism. Were it otherwise, the teaching of *HG* would not have been so meticulously qualified.

What is the import of all this? I think it makes clear that the case of polygenism does not serve to illustrate Sullivan's thesis that a breakdown in the consensus among theologians about the definitive status of a doctrine is sufficient to nullify the claim that the doctrine had already been definitively taught by the ordinary universal magisterium. The Church's most authoritative teaching on polygenism was recent; we have seen that it did not completely shut the door on this hypothesis and evidently did not judge prior Church teaching to have done so. In the end, all we have in the case of polygenism is a conciliar draft from Vatican I that took up a new question but was never acted upon or promulgated and a papal encyclical that at

---

[35] Henri Rondet, *Original Sin: The Patristic and Theological Background*, trans. Cajetan Finegan, O.P. (Staten Island, NY: Alba House, 1969), 243. See also J. O'Rourke, "Some Considerations about Polygenism," *Theological Studies* 26 (1965): 411. O'Rourke, who argued in favor of monogenism, nevertheless wrote: "It seems correct to say that the words of Pius XII are not to be understood as declaring absolutely that polygenism is irreconcilable with the Catholic doctrine of original sin. The words do state that in no way does it appear how polygenism could be reconciled with Catholic doctrine. Thus if one wanted to embrace a polygenistic hypothesis, the burden of proof would be upon the person proposing the hypothesis; he would have to show how polygenism could be reconciled with the Catholic doctrine of original sin."

bottom amounts only to a conditional rejection of polygenism. It is truly hard to see then how polygenism can serve as an example to instance how a doctrine that once seemed to qualify as taught infallibly by the ordinary universal magisterium could later be rendered null due to subsequent breakdown in consensus among theologians. The case of polygenism does not seem able to bear the weight that Sullivan would assign to it.

The Consensus of Theologians: A Sign Not a Condition

Still, having said this, the question remains as to whether Sullivan's principle about the consensus of theologians is a valid one. The answer to this question depends largely on the accuracy of his interpretation of Pius IX's *TL*. The claim that he makes is based on a conclusion that he draws from this papal letter. I contend that Pius IX may well have asserted that the constant and universal consensus of theologians is a sign and is evidence that a teaching is definitive, but I submit that there is little reason to think that Pius IX meant to say that the absence of that sign warranted the conclusion that the ordinary universal magisterium had not taught a particular doctrine definitively. Furthermore, I claim that there is no evidence for thinking that in *TL* Pius IX ever meant to suggest the idea that if at some point there is no longer a consensus among theologians that a doctrine has been taught definitively, then this lack of consensus is enough to nullify the claim that the doctrine was a definitive teaching of the ordinary universal magisterium. I think that this is all apparent if we pay close attention to the historical context of this papal letter and to the entire contents of the letter itself.

It is helpful to recall some of the historical circumstances that form the background of *TL*. The letter was occasioned by a congress of German theologians at Munich in 1863. Ignaz Döllinger, a leader of what came to be called the German Catholic historical school of thought, and two of his colleagues had issued invitations for Catholic scholars to meet in Munich in September 1863 as a part of a series of proposed theological congresses. German theologians at the time were divided between the historically minded scholars like Döllinger and neo-Scholastic scholars. Döllinger hoped that the Munich meeting would accomplish some kind of reconciliation between the two groups so that they might present a united front against attacks from secular academics. As the study by John Boyle has shown, Pius IX was initially displeased with the plans for a meeting of German scholars in Munich, independent from an explicit initiative from Church authorities.[36] He also feared that the meeting would involve public attacks and criticism

[36] Boyle, "The Ordinary Magisterium," 14–29.

of the Roman Curia. Nevertheless, the meeting was held on September 28, 1863, and Pius IX's fear about a stinging public criticism of the Curia did not materialize. After the meeting ended, the Pope's first reaction was rather favorable until he received reports from his nuncio. The papal nuncio detailed the events of the meeting, including a resolution that limited matters of faith only to those doctrines that had been explicitly defined, as well a speech given by Döllinger in which the German professor denounced the effect Roman censures had on theology and claimed a certain German pre-eminence for the theological sciences. In the meantime, Archbishop von Scheer of Munich gave the Pope an essentially positive report about the meeting. *Tuas Libenter* is a reply to the Archbishop of Munich by the Pope. As John Boyle has noted, the letter really addressed the concerns raised by the papal nuncio.

Tuas Libenter, dated December 21, 1863, must be seen in this context and interpreted as a whole. Boyle's study of this papal letter is especially helpful in this regard. Pius IX insisted on a number of points that are worth recalling because they reveal the tone and intent of this letter. They are of capital importance for understanding his affirmation about the constant and universal consensus of theologians. While *TL* recognized the good intentions of the gathered scholars, the Pope objected to the fact that they had even come together apart from the initiative of magisterial authority. Pius IX wrote:

> [W]e could only marvel at seeing the invitation to the congress prepared and sent in the name of private persons, without any intervention of the initiative, authority or mission of the ecclesiastical authority to which alone pertains by proper and native right to watch over and direct especially the teaching of theological matters. As you well know, such a thing is new and wholly without precedent in the Church.[37]

Pius IX went on to voice his fear that a meeting of theologians like that at Munich might "give example of the gradual usurpation of the right of ecclesiastical rule and of the authentic magisterium."[38] The Pope continued on to say, in a now famous passage, that the act of faith is owed not only to defined dogmas but to those things "handed on by the ordinary magisterium of the Church scattered throughout the world as divinely revealed and therefore are held by the universal and constant consent of Catholic theologians to pertain to the faith."[39] But he was also anxious to

[37] I follow Boyle's translation in "The Ordinary Magisterium," 395.
[38] Ibid., 396.
[39] Ibid., 397.

assert that theologians also owed obedience to the Roman Curia with regard to doctrinal matters that are not *de fide*:

> [T]he members of the congress should realize that it is hardly enough for Catholic scholars to receive and reverence the dogmas of the Church mentioned above; it is also necessary that they subject themselves both to the decisions pertaining to doctrine which are issued by the Roman Congregations and those matters of doctrine which are held by the common and constant consent of Catholics as theological truths and conclusions so certain, that even if opinions contrary to those matters of doctrine cannot be called heretical, they would still merit some other theological censure.[40]

Boyle also points out that after *TL* further correspondence from Rome proposed such strict regulations for congresses of theologians that for all practical purposes it thwarted the planned series of such meetings.[41] One thing is clear: *TL* is not a papal letter that is written to contribute to a discussion about criteria for recognizing the definitive teachings of the ordinary magisterium. It was a clear and unambiguous warning to theologians about their duty to submit to the hierarchical authority of the Church in matters of doctrine, and it served as a notification to theologians that they were not even to meet together on their own initiative without the approval of the competent magisterial authorities. Clearly, this papal letter was written at a time when theologians operated under vastly different conditions than they do now!

Let us return to Sullivan's interpretation of this letter and the conclusions he draws from it. Given what we have noted about *TL*, it does not seem possible to believe, as Sullivan seems to believe, that Pius IX ever intended to suggest that a breakdown in the consensus of theologians with regard to whether a doctrine taught by the ordinary magisterium would somehow nullify a claim that a doctrine had already been definitively taught. It is true that Pius IX spoke of the constant and universal consensus of theologians. But are we really justified in thinking that he meant to say or to imply that a breakdown in consensus means that *an essential condition* for recognizing a definitive teaching of the ordinary universal magisterium has not been met? Surely, this was not the claim of a Pope who did not even want theologians to gather together except at the invitation of the Magisterium, and only then under its watchful eye. It remains true of course that Pius IX affirmed that the constant and universal consensus of Catholic

---

40 Ibid.

41 Ibid., 395n40. Also see Hubert Jedin and John Dolan, eds., *History of the Church*, vol. 8, *The Church between Revolution and Restoration*, trans. Peter Becker (New York: Crossroad, 1981), 246.

theologians was evidence of the definitive teachings of the ordinary magisterium. But there is no reason to believe that this Pope, who insisted that theologians must subject themselves to the doctrinal decisions of the Roman Congregations, understood this to be not only a sign of, *but also a condition for, definitive teachings whose absence would throw into doubt that the ordinary magisterium had taught a doctrine definitively.* A sign is one thing, a condition is another. Sullivan seems to assume that sign and condition mean the same thing in this instance.[42]

My point here is not to belittle the importance that Pius IX undoubtedly attributed to the "constant and universal consensus of theologians." Rather, the point is that we should not assume too much from this affirmation. While the question of how and by what criteria we can recognize a definitive teaching is an important one, we must resist the temptation to make that question a central one for Pius IX in *TL*. The most that we should conclude is that Pius IX asserted that the consensus of theologians is evidence and a sign, but not necessarily a condition, of the definitive teaching of the ordinary universal magisterium. Therefore it seems justified to conclude that while the constant universal consensus of theologians can be an important sign of this kind of teaching, the absence of the sign does not necessarily mean that the ordinary universal magisterium has not taught a doctrine definitively.

Concluding Reflections and a Suggestion for a New Context

It seems to me that the current discussion about the definitive teachings of the ordinary universal magisterium could be helped if it were conducted within the context of catholicity in time and if it firmly kept in mind the nature of the Church as a communion. If the Church is the visible sign of that grace that draws human creatures into communion with one another and into communion with the Trinity, through Christ, by the power of

---

[42] This leads to another difficulty with Sullivan's position. It appears that it is caught in a logical fallacy. We have seen that he wishes to affirm that the consensus of theologians is a sign that the ordinary magisterium has taught definitively. But Sullivan, going beyond Pius IX, claims that it follows that if there is no consensus among theologians then there has not been a definitive teaching of the ordinary magisterium. This argument appears to be guilty of the logical fallacy of denying the antecedent. It seems to be saying the same thing as someone who says: "Where there is smoke there is fire, and therefore it follows from this that where there is no smoke there is no fire." But it does not follow that where there is no smoke there is no fire because there are smokeless fires. There are also times when there is a definitive act of the ordinary universal magisterium without the consensus of theologians.

the Spirit, then we must remember that our communion with one another stretches through time and is not limited to this present age. In other words, the question about definitive teachings should be explored in the context of the communion of the Church that must extend diachronically across time, so that the Church in the present age shares fully in the faith of previous generations.

Avery Dulles, for example, maintains that in Catholic ecclesiology the Church is understood as participating in a definitive, albeit imperfect, manner in the fullness of God's gift in Christ.[43] He reminds us that it is this definitive but imperfect participation that effects a real communion between the numerous and different generations of Christians in the Church. But catholicity in the Church, as Dulles constantly insists, is a heterogeneous unity, not a homogeneous one. Therefore this communion between different generations of the Church is marked by a real "communion in difference" as each generation has its own distinctive character that complements what earlier generations have initiated. In other words, the catholicity of the Church in time is analogous to her catholicity in space or in geographical extension. Dulles writes:

> Just as the Church's geographical catholicity requires a variety of cultural forms, so her temporal catholicity calls for responsiveness to the times and seasons. The present form of the apostolic mission, writes Wolfhart Pannenberg, "has the task of bringing to new expression in each age the catholic fullness of the church."[44]

The challenge to each generation of Catholics is to adapt and retrieve the Catholic faith according to the needs of the times and in terms understandable to present-day believers. Mere rote repetition will not do if the fullness of Christ is to be communicated to new generations and if doctrines of the faith are to make real differences in the lives of believers in the world. Mere repetition of the truths of the faith would simply conceal rather than radiate the light of the gospel.[45] On the other hand, Dulles, recalling a point

---

43 Dulles, *Catholicity of the Church*, 92.

44 Ibid. Dulles cites Wolfhart Pannenberg, *The Church*, trans. Keith Crim (Philadelphia: Westminster Press, 1983), 68.

45 Recently, Christopher Walsh has called attention to the fact that Henri de Lubac made this point brilliantly by understanding Christian doctrine according to the Trinitarian missions. Christian doctrine according to de Lubac has an irreversible and definitive character because it is given to us in the Son, the unique and definitive Word of the Father. At the same time, thanks to the impulse and motivation of the creative Spirit breathed upon us by Christ, Christian doctrine develops in time. The truths of Christian doctrines are for all times and thus have a living and dynamic

made by Yves Congar, warns that the process of adaptation and retrieval involves the danger of theologians becoming zealous innovators rather than retrievers, thereby doing violence to the heritage of the Church's faith.[46]

Dulles claims that the four principles Congar proposed to help avoid this danger are still valid today.[47] One of those principles was a concern for a communion with the whole.

The entire truth of revelation has been entrusted to the whole Church, and thus it lies beyond the isolated grasp of an individual or group in space or time. It remains true, of course, that the identification of definitive doctrines taught by the ordinary universal magisterium requires careful research and analysis. Clearly, it is not sound to claim that a doctrine is a definitive one simply because it has been taught in general without interruption or contradiction over a long period of time.[48] It is necessary to show that a particular point of doctrine has been taught by the bishops in union with the pope as undoubted and certain[49] and that the doctrine is something that has been revealed or is necessary to hold in

form. The Spirit leads the Church to plumb the infinite depth of the mystery of Christ again and again. De Lubac urges us to avoid an immobile conservatism that is afraid of the future and unfaithful to the truth that the creative Spirit is "a perpetual principle of progress and fulfillment in the Church." On the other hand, Walsh observes that de Lubac is equally insistent upon avoiding an extreme progressivism that wants to go beyond the historical Christ and his Church. See Christopher J. Walsh, "Henri de Lubac in Connecticut: Unpublished Conferences on Renewal in the Postconciliar Period," *Communio* 23 (1996): 786–805. Cf. Henri de Lubac, *Christian Faith*, trans. Brother Richard Arnandez, F.S.C. (San Francisco: Ignatius Press, 1986), 245–50.

46 Ibid., 105.

47 Yves Congar, *Vraie et fausse Réforme dans l'Église*, rev. 2nd ed. (Paris: Cerf, 1968), 211–17. Baldly summarized, the four principles of authentic reform that Congar proposed were (1) a charity and pastoral sensitivity that accepted the given reality of the Church and a commitment to labor with that given; (2) the concern for communion with the whole Church, as mentioned above; (3) a willingness to be patient with delays; (4) an awareness of the fact that genuine Catholic Christian reform is not innovation but renewal. It must be founded upon principles given in the gospel and tradition.

48 A number of theologians have argued against this mistake. See, for example, Karl Rahner, "Magisterium," *Sacramentum Mundi*, vol. 3 (New York: Herder, 1968), 356; Germain Grisez, "Infallibility and Specific Moral Norms," *Thomist* 49 (1985): 277–78; and Sullivan, *Magisterium*, 126–27.

49 J. Kleutgen pointed this out long ago in his commentary on the second schema on the Church submitted at Vatican I. He explained these doctrines of the ordinary and universal magisterium as doctrine of faith or morals that have been transmitted as undoubted. See Giovanni Domenico Mansi, *Collectio Conciliorum Recentiorum*, vol. 53 (Arnhem: Holland, 1927), p. 313. Kleutgen's commentary is cited by *LG* 25 in footnote 40.

order to defend the deposit of revelation.[50] I want to suggest that a clear sense and awareness of communion across time and catholicity in time has to guide the effort to identify these teachings. J. A. DiNoia has rightly observed that the teaching activity of the Church is always directed toward fostering communion.[51] Catholicity in time and communion across time is not only gift; it is also a task to be accomplished. It involves, as mentioned above, not mere repetition of doctrine but a genuine retrieval that makes it intelligible for the present age. This may mean, for instance, that it is necessary for a doctrine to be reinterpreted in the light of other doctrines, the way, say, Vatican II reconsidered the ordained priesthood in view of the Church understood as a communion. Or it may mean that the biblical sources for the doctrine may require reevaluation in order that doctrine might be reinvigorated or "ressourced" for the present age.

An example of this that can be instructive is the controversy over the virginal conception of Jesus in the 1960s and 1970s. Scholars such as Raymond Brown and others steered a middle course between the considerable number of scholars at the time who concluded that the virginal conception was merely a theologoumenon[52] and those theologians who accepted the doctrine but claimed it was not a definitive teaching of the ordinary universal

---

50 Here it is important to recall what *LG* 25 taught about the object of infallibility: "This infallibility, with which the divine Redeemer willed His Church to be endowed in defining a doctrine of faith and morals extends as far as extends the deposit of divine revelation which must be religiously guarded and faithfully expounded" (Walter Abbot, ed., *Documents of Vatican II* [Baltimore: America Press, 1966], 48). See also the Theological Commission's explanation of the text, which clarifies the meaning of this passage: "The object of the infallibility of the Church thus explained, has the same extension as the revealed deposit; hence it extends to all those things, and only to those, which either directly pertain to the revealed deposit itself, or are required in order that the same deposit may be religiously safeguarded and faithfully expounded." Sullivan observes, rightly, that *LG* 25 and this explanation have in mind the distinction between the primary and secondary objects of infallibility. I follow Sullivan's translation of the Commission's explanation in his *Magisterium*, 132. For the Latin text, see *Acta synodalia sacrosancti Concilii Oecumenici Vaticani* II 3/1 (Typis Polyglottis Vaticanis, 1973), 251.

51 See J. A. DiNoia's essay, "Communion and Magisterium: Teaching Authority and the Culture of Grace," *Modern Theology* 9 (1993): 403–15.

52 It is important to remember here that a "theologoumenon" is not something that expresses an official doctrine of the Church or a matter of faith. Rahner defines it this way: "A theologoumenon is a proposition expressing a theological statement which cannot be directly regarded as official teaching of the Church, as a dogma binding inFaith, but which is the outcome and expression of an endeavor to understand the faith by establishing connections between binding doctrines of faith and by confronting dogmatic teachings with the whole of secular experience and all a man—or an age—knows." See Rahner, *Sacramentum Mundi*, vol. 6 (New York:

magisterium or that it was not clearly so.[53] Brown and other scholars such as Frederick Jelly showed that belief in the virginal conception was early and constant and that the ordinary magisterium consistently and universally taught the virginal conception of Jesus.[54] Therefore, they concluded that the doctrine should be categorized as an undefined dogma of faith. At the same time, against those with fideist tendencies, Brown and other scholars were equally insistent that a modern evaluation and reappropriation of the doctrine was still necessary even though the doctrine was already taught definitively.[55] Brown, in particular, argued for a serious examination of the doctrine and a critical approach to the biblical evidence in order that its credibility might be enhanced for the Church today. He concluded that while the historicity of the virginal conception could not be completely resolved by historical criticism alone, nevertheless the biblical evidence favored it and defin-

Herder, 1968), s.v. "theologoumenon," 172. Joseph Fitzmyer, S.J. pointed out that a theologoumenon may prescind from factuality. See his *To Advance the Gospel* (New York: Crossroad, 1981), 41–78.

53 Theologians who regard the virginal conception as a theologoumenon or do not think it belongs to the content of Christian faith include Rosemary Ruether, "The Collision of History and Doctrine: The Brothers of Jesus and the Virginity of Mary," *Continuum* 7 (1969): 93–105; Piet Schoonenberg, "Die Nieuwe Katechismus und die Dogmen," in *Dokumentation des Holländischen Katechismus* (Freiburg, 1967), xiv–xxxix, esp. xxxvii–xxxviii; idem, "Event and Happening: Hermeneutical Reflections on Some Contemporary Disputed Questions," *Theology Digest* 17 (Autumn 1969): 196–202, esp. 201; Otto Knoch, "Die Botschaft des atthäusevangeliums über Empfängis and Geburt Jesu vor dem Hintergrund der Christusverkündigung des Neuen Testaments," in *Zum Thema Jungfrauengeburt* (Stuttgart: KBW, 1970), 37–59; Gisela Lattke, "Lukas 1 und die Jungfrauengeburt," in *Zum Thema Jungfrauengeburt,* 61–89; Louis Evely, *L'Évangile sans mythes* (Paris: Editions universitaires, 1970); Gerhard Lofink, "Gehört die Jungfrauenburt zur biblischen Heilbotschaft?" *Theologische Quartalschrift* 159 (1979): 304–6; John McKenzie, "The Mother of Jesus in the New Testament," *Concilium* 168 (1980): 3–11; Rudolf Pesch, "Gegen eine doppelte Wahrheit. Karl Rahner und die Biblewissenschaft," *Vor dem Geheimnis Gottes den Menschen verstehen. Karl Rahner zum 80. Geburtstag,* ed. Karl Lehman (Freiburg: Katholische Akademie/Munich: Schnell & Steiner, 1984), 10–36. See also Richard P. McBrien, *Catholicism,* 3rd ed. (San Francisco: Harper, 1994), 542.

54 Raymond Brown, *The Virginal Conception and the Bodily Resurrection of Jesus* (New York: Paulist Press, 1970), 31–35; Frederick Jelly, "Mary's Virginity in the Symbols and the Councils," *Marian Studies* 20 (1970): 69–93, esp. 63–84, 89; Austin Vaughn, "Magisterium on Mary's Virginity," *Marian Studies* 21 (1971): 75–90.

55 Brown, *The Virginal Conception,* 37–38; Vaughn, "Magisterium on Mary's Virginity," 83f.

itive Church teaching resolved the remaining ambiguity.[56] Walter Kasper came to a similar conclusion.[57]

Sullivan himself cites the doctrine of the virginal conception as an example of a doctrine infallibly taught by the ordinary universal magisterium and numbers himself among the majority of Catholic theologians who hold this to be the case.[58] But what if, for example, a majority of Catholic theologians had ended up denying the virginal conception, claiming that it was a theologoumenon—which Brown, writing in 1972, observed as an example of a "trend that was making headway."[59]

The controversy over the virginal conception can remind theologians that it can be necessary sometimes for them to work for the retrieval and re-reception of a consensus about the definitive status of a doctrine that in the present age has weakened or is in danger of disappearing, lest the Church's catholicity in time be weakened. A chief concern of any judgment about definitive teachings must be for communion with the previous generations of Christians that have gone before us as well as a concern for the retrieval of the wholeness of the Catholic faith for our time. Otherwise, theologians risk making definitive doctrines appear to have more to do with a juridical cognitive uniformity than with fostering the unity of the communion in faith.[60] It also seems true that to the extent that a

56 Brown, *The Virginal Conception*, 66–68. Also see idem, *Biblical Exegesis and Church Doctrine* (New York: Paulist Press, 1985), 37n11.

57 Walter Kasper, "Letter on the 'Virgin Birth,'" *Communio* 15 (1988): 262–66.

58 Sullivan, *Creative Fidelity*, 138. On the other hand, I cannot agree with Richard Gaillardetz, who argues that "this example suggests that in the face of controversy the determination of authoritative studies of any teaching not solemnly defined can be pursued only tentatively." See his *Witnesses to the Faith: Community, Infallibility, and the Ordinary Magisterium of Bishops* (New York: Paulist Press, 1992), 174. Gaillardetz claims that the attribution of definitive status to "controversial" doctrines is subject to "legitimate disagreement." This viewpoint is problematic on several levels and a complete reply to it is not possible here. I would point out one problem: Suppose, for instance, that some time in the future the resurrection of the body became a controversial doctrine as it was in the early centuries. Would we really be justified in saying that its definitive and infallible status would only be tentative because it had become controversial? I maintain that controversy or the lack of it is not really helpful in determining the definitive status of a doctrine taught by the ordinary universal magisterium.

59 Brown, *The Virginal Conception*, 24. Brown also observed that there had been an unquestionable unanimity with regard to the historicity of the virginal conception. "But after Vatican II the solid front is cracking in many places." See ibid., 22.

60 If theologians forget that the teaching activity of the Church is primarily directed toward fostering communion, then the Magisterium and the Church herself lie open to an essentially sociological interpretation. As J. A. DiNoia has pointed out, the Church then tends to be reduced to a social construct, and the Magisterium is

definitive teaching of the ordinary universal magisterium is not received as such by the present age or a future one, then this non-reception works against the Church in her task of achieving catholicity in time and communion across time. Any judgment about what has been taught definitively will have to be concerned with showing how it does not undermine but rather contributes to this task.

To sum up and conclude: while consensus among theologians can be an important sign of definitive teaching of ordinary universal magisterium, it should not be regarded as an essential condition that must be met before it can be said that a particular doctrine has been definitively taught. It has also been argued that the current discussion about definitive teachings might be better grounded if it was re-situated in the context of the task of achieving catholicity in time and communion across time between the different generations of Christians in the Church. Questions about what the ordinary universal magisterium has taught definitively are questions about what is required for full communion with our fathers and mothers, and what is required for the present age to allow the wholeness of the Catholic faith to come to a new expression.

---

seen as an aspect of community management. In this scheme DiNoia observes that "[t]he ascendancy of one set of viewpoints over others in contention can come to be viewed chiefly as a function of bureaucratic power struggles in which self-interest and self-preservation are chief objectives." See "Communion and Magisterium," 405.

CHAPTER 2

On the Ordinary Universal Magisterium: Reply to Criticism*

IN AN ARTICLE on the ordinary universal magisterium,[1] Richard Gaillardetz took issue with some of my observations and criticisms that I wrote on the same subject.[2] I suggested the discussion about the definitive teachings of the ordinary universal magisterium could be helped if it were conducted within the context of catholicity in time and the *communio* structure of the Church. Our communion with one another in Christ and the Spirit stretches through time and is not limited to the present age. I stated that questions about what the ordinary universal magisterium has taught definitively have to do with the task of achieving catholicity in time and communion across time between different generations of members of the Church. Obviously, theologians have an important role to play in this process. My article examined and criticized some principles that Francis Sullivan proposed as important for determining whether a doctrine had been definitively taught by the ordinary universal magisterium. I presented arguments against some of his principles because I believed that, despite his good intentions, they were of limited value or worked against the task of identifying definitive doctrines of the ordinary universal magisterium. My primary interest was, and remains, what is

* A version of this essay appeared in *Theological Studies* 64 (September 2003): 598–609.

1 Richard Gaillardetz, "The Ordinary Universal Magisterium: Unresolved Questions," *Theological Studies* 63 (2002): 447–71.

2 See chap. 1 above. Originally published as "The Infallibility of the Ordinary Universal Magisterium: A Critique of Some Recent Observations," *Heythrop Journal* 39 (1998): 18–36. Also, of related interest, see chap. 4 below, originally published as "Christ, the Moral Law, and the Teaching Authority of the Magisterium," *Irish Theological Quarterly* 64 (Spring 1999): 17–28.

helpful to the Church in bringing the wholeness of the Catholic faith to a new expression and therefore to accomplish catholicity in time and communion in time.

Here I reply to Gaillardetz's criticisms and, in doing so, offer some further reflections on the ordinary universal magisterium.

An Accurate Reading of Sullivan

Gaillardetz takes exception to my criticism of Sullivan. After describing what he believes is the difficulty of directly discerning episcopal consensus today, Gaillardetz observes that Sullivan has proposed the constant and universal consensus of theologians and the common adherence of the faithful as criteria for determining whether the ordinary universal magisterium has taught a doctrine definitively. He points out that Sullivan derives the criteria of the consensus of theologians from Pius IX's letter *Tuas Libenter* (*TL*). Gaillardetz goes on to note my criticism of Sullivan's argument about the importance of the consensus of theologians. I made the point that Sullivan's argument depends largely on the accuracy of his interpretation of *TL*. I examined the historical context of that papal letter and argued for modesty as to what it could contribute today to the discussion about criteria for discerning definitive teachings of the ordinary universal magisterium. I contended that the most we should conclude was that Pius IX asserted that the constant and universal consensus of theologians is a sign that the ordinary universal magisterium has taught a doctrine definitively. I claimed that it does not follow that Pius IX meant that the consensus of theologians is not only a sign but also a condition for definitive teachings, the absence of which would throw into doubt that the ordinary universal magisterium had taught a doctrine definitively. I went on to criticize Sullivan for not making what I think is an important distinction between a sign and condition. Gaillardetz, ignoring the context of my argument, quotes my conclusion to this effect. He then alleges that I misread Sullivan's argument about the criteria of universal and constant consensus of theologians. He writes:

> As best as I can ascertain, however, Welch has misread Sullivan's argument, for nowhere does Sullivan assert that either criteria are necessary conditions for the exercise of the ordinary universal magisterium. Rather, he recognizes that there is an important distinction between a factual instance of universal episcopal teaching to be held as definitive by the faithful and the verification that such a teaching has been so proposed.[3]

[3] Gaillardetz, "The Ordinary Universal Magisterium," 464–65. Gaillardetz speaks of "either criteria" (meaning the constant and universal consensus of theologians

In fact, this is exactly what Sullivan wrote about the consensus of theologians, and in many of these very words. In my *Heythrop Journal* article I cited a passage from Sullivan's book *Creative Fidelity*, where he refers to an unapproved proposal to define monogenism at Vatican I.

> Here we have an instance of a consensus that seemed strong enough in 1870 to justify defining a doctrine as a dogma of faith, but which has not remained constant and is no longer universal. It would hardly seem reasonable to argue that *since the former consensus had fulfilled the conditions required for the infallible exercise of ordinary universal magisterium*, the subsequent lack of consensus could nullify the claim that the doctrine had already been infallibly taught.[4]

There is another text in *Creative Fidelity*, which I did not cite in the *Heythrop* article, where Sullivan speaks in a similar manner:

> It is true of course, that if something is indeed taught infallibly, subsequent dissent cannot negate it. But, *to fulfill the conditions required for the infallible teaching of the ordinary universal magisterium*, the consensus must not only be universal; it must also be constant.[5]

I should also point out that in my article I chose to use the terms "sign" and "condition" because they are the terms Sullivan uses in his writings.[6] Sometimes Sullivan speaks about the consensus as a sign; sometimes he refers to it as a condition, as in the passages above. I called attention to the fact that there is an important distinction between the two.

An Excessive Claim about the Consensus of Theologians

What about Gaillardetz's objection that I somehow overlook Sullivan's recognition that there is a critical distinction between a factual instance of a definitive universal episcopal teaching and a verification of such a teaching? Again, I am afraid Gaillardetz has missed the point of my critique of Sullivan. Nothing I wrote denied the fact that there has to be some way(s) of recognizing definitive teachings of the ordinary universal magisterium. I did not deny that the constant and universal consensus of theologians could be a way to

---

and the common adherence of the faithful), but he clearly refers to the consensus of theologians with regard to me since I make no argument about the latter.

4 See page 10 above, note 31, citing Sullivan, *Creative Fidelity*, 105. Emphasis mine.

5 Sullivan, *Creative Fidelity*, 106.

6 See ibid., 103, 105, 106; idem, "Reply to Germain Grisez," 736.

recognize them. My main point was that while the consensus of theologians can be an important sign that the ordinary universal magisterium has taught a doctrine definitively, the absence of this sign does not necessarily mean that a doctrine has not been taught definitively. Sullivan quite clearly argues that the consensus of theologians is necessary for us to know whether the ordinary universal magisterium has taught a doctrine definitively. Besides the one quoted above, a very clear and important instance of this argument appears in Sullivan's *Creative Fidelity* with regard to the teaching in *Evangelium Vitae* (*EV*) against direct killing of the innocent, direct abortion, and euthanasia. Sullivan admits there are good reasons to think that Pope John Paul intended to invoke the infallibility of the ordinary universal magisterium as set out in *Lumen Gentium* (*LG*), number 25; nevertheless, he writes, "[i]t is too soon to know whether there will be the consensus of theologians that would show that it is 'clearly established' that the immorality of murder, abortion and euthanasia are infallibly taught. What this would mean is that the Church has taken an irreversible stand on these issues."[7]

According to Sullivan, despite the fact that the Pope, the head of the apostolic college, has made the confirmation that the ordinary universal magisterium has taught these doctrines definitively, it is still not clearly established that the ordinary universal magisterium has done so. Clear establishment awaits a consensus of theologians.

It might be that objected that Sullivan, at least in the passage cited above, does not represent the consensus of theologians as a formal or constitutive condition of the infallible doctrines taught by the ordinary universal magisterium. On the other hand, he seems to say that the consensus of theologians is something like a logical condition of our ability to claim there has been such an exercise of the teaching authority of the ordinary universal magisterium. In other words, while Sullivan does not make the exercise of the ordinary universal magisterium when it teaches a doctrine infallibly subject to the consensus of theologians, he does seem to make the *claim* to such a doctrine subject to this consensus.

I must confess I am at a loss as to why anyone should believe that the consensus among theologians should hold so much weight. What reason is there to believe this when there is nothing in *TL* that requires us to think that Pius IX meant to teach that without the constant consensus of theologians, the definitive teachings of the ordinary universal magisterium cannot be recognized or verified? After reviewing the evidence again, I am even more certain of the correctness of my conclusion that Pius IX, who has the reputation, rightly or wrongly, of being one of the more authoritarian popes

---

[7] Sullivan, *Creative Fidelity*, 160. See pages 7–8 above, note 24.

in papal history, did not mean any such a thing about the consensus of theologians. Nothing in what Gaillardetz writes offers any evidence against this conclusion. Unfortunately, Gaillardetz passes over my entire treatment of Pius IX and *TL*, and simply assumes that Sullivan's interpretation of that papal letter is correct. If Sullivan and Gaillardetz want to argue that the lack of consensus of theologians or a breakdown in consensus means that we cannot then verify that the ordinary universal magisterium has taught a doctrine definitively, then they will have to do so on some other basis than an appeal to Pius IX and *TL*. Some other argument must be made.

The three confirmations in *EV* of the definitive teachings of the ordinary universal magisterium against direct killing of the innocent, direct abortion, and euthanasia illustrate the point I wish to make about the consensus of theologians. Let us assume for the sake of argument that Sullivan is correct about the lack of consensus of theologians "that would show that it is 'clearly established' that the immorality of murder, abortion and euthanasia are infallibly taught."[8] My argument is that there are other ways to recognize that these teachings are definitively and, hence, infallibly taught by the ordinary universal magisterium. First, it would not be difficult to show, as *EV* 54 points out, the common adherence of the faithful to the Church's doctrine about the inviolability of innocent human life. Second, there is the fact that, according to the encyclical (*EV* 62), the Pope consulted the bishops, and they showed unanimous agreement about this teaching. Thirdly, there is the confirmation of the Pope, the head of the apostolic college of bishops, that this teaching is definitive, "unchanged and unchangeable." All these things are more than enough for us to recognize the fact that the immorality of direct murder, direct abortion, and euthanasia have been

8 Gaillardetz and Sullivan do not seem to agree on this point. Gaillardetz thinks that, because these teachings in *EV* have received the least criticism from theologians, there would appear to be a long-standing consensus on the "general tenor of all three moral condemnations." On the other hand, it can also be pointed out that the Pope, in his confirmation of these moral condemnations, has also illustrated that the Magisterium can teach particular moral norms definitively and infallibly. Prior to *EV* there were some theologians who disputed this possibility even with regard to abortion. Some eleven years prior to *EV*, Richard McCormick, arguing against Grisez, wrote: "They [theologians] simply disagree—as most would and should—with Grisez that the immorality of direct abortion is infallibly taught by the ordinary magisterium. More generally, they deny that such particular norms are the proper object of infallibility." See McCormick, "Medicaid and Abortion," *Theological Studies* 45 (December 1984): 715–21, at 720. In another telling passage McCormick also claimed, "Rahner's analysis would deny the very possibility of infallible teaching where direct abortion is concerned. *And it is safe to say that this is the common conviction of theologians*" (ibid., emphasis mine).

taught definitively and infallibly by the ordinary universal magisterium. While the consensus of theologians with regard to this fact would be a further sign, we do not need it to recognize the fact that these doctrines have been infallibly taught.

Two Different Ways of Manifesting

In my *Heythrop Journal* article, I also criticized Sullivan for asserting that canon 749.3 ("No doctrine is to be understood to be infallibly defined unless this fact is clearly established as such"), which is applicable to defined dogmas, should also be applied to undefined dogmas and definitive teachings of the ordinary universal magisterium.[9] The point I tried to make was that canon 749.3 and its requirement of "clearly established" cannot be applied in a univocal way to the latter. I think it is better not to use this term from canon 749.3 for the undefined dogmas and definitive teachings of the ordinary universal magisterium because it is a juridical term that refers to the formulation of defined doctrine. To use the term univocally introduces confusion about how definitive teachings of the ordinary universal magisterium are known and recognized. There is a distinction between "teaching something" (ordinary universal magisterium) and "teaching by way of defining" (extraordinary magisterium). The *manifeste constiterit* of canon 749.3 bears on the latter, as is clear from the context. The question is whether something is defined, and the answer is, so to speak, "not unless it is clear from the very formulation of the words, or the context."[10] For these reasons I argued canon 749.3 could not be applied in a straightforward way to the undefined dogmas and definitive teachings of

---

[9] Defined dogmas refer to those doctrines that are taught as divinely revealed truth proclaimed by a solemn judgment of the Magisterium. They are proclaimed either by an ecumenical council or, more rarely, by the pope *ex cathedra*. An undefined dogma is a truth taught by the ordinary universal magisterium dispersed throughout the world as divinely revealed, although not in a solemn judgment or definition. Dogmas, both defined and undefined, touch directly on the deposit of faith and call for the response of divine faith. On this point see the discussion in Sullivan, *Creative Fidelity*, 41–44, 93–108. Cf. *Code of Canon Law*, can. 750.1; John Paul II, *Ad Tuendam Fidem*, no. 2: Pius IX, *TL*. Definitive teachings are those doctrines that are connected to the deposit of faith and therefore call for firm acceptance in order to protect the faith. On this see *Code of Canon Law*, can. 750.2 and *Ad Tuendam Fidem*, no. 3.

[10] I also contended that the knowledge of defined dogmas is something that rests and depends on the definition itself rather than on the consensus of theologians as Sullivan believes. "I claim it would be absurd to claim that the fact that a doctrine had been infallibly defined was manifestly 'settled, established, undisputed,' if there

the ordinary universal magisterium. They do not have the same precise formula and identifiable context as defined dogmas. By its very nature, the ordinary universal magisterium does not say it is defining. There cannot be, in the very form and context of the many discrete acts in which the ordinary universal magisterium is to be located, anything to alert us, as there is for a conciliar or papal definition. I assert that it remains the case that when theologians try to identify undefined dogmas they must painstakingly inquire as to whether the pope and the bishops have been in agreement that a particular doctrine must be held definitively.

Gaillardetz asks me how this is not equivalent to inquiring into the intention of a pope or council to define a doctrine. For one thing, it is not equivalent because one has to look for something different in the case of the definitive teachings of the ordinary universal magisterium. Now, it is certainly true to say that these teachings must be recognizable in some sense. But this recognition will be different from when the extraordinary magisterium defines a dogma. We can think of recognition in several ways. Certainly, there is a difference between "manifesting by defining" (extraordinary magisterium) and "manifesting by leaving clues" (ordinary magisterium).

An analogy may help to make my point. The manifesting of the infallible teachings of the ordinary universal magisterium might be compared to a lover's manifestations of love that show an intent to marry. One could observe an intention from the lover's exclusive relationship with the beloved—the flowers, the dinners, the long heart-to-heart conversations, the talk about children with the beloved, and so on. No one of these things by itself "manifests" the intention to marry, but taken all together, they do. "See, he must mean to marry her, for look what he said to her and did for her in the past five months." This sort of manifesting the intention to marry is different from the proposal, which is formal and explicit and "defining" (akin to the extraordinary magisterium carefully defining a doctrine). So the infallible teachings of the ordinary universal magisterium are like the lover's pre-proposal actions and words. They do not say "this is an infallible and irreversible doctrine" in a formal, explicit definition. They do say "this is Christian truth."[11] The question of recognizing doctrines infallibly taught

---

were no consensus among Catholic theologians about this alleged fact" (Sullivan, "Reply to Germain Grisez," 734).

11 I think a strong argument can be made that it was on the basis of this kind "manifesting" that it was just to charge Arius with heresy before the Council of Nicea in 325. Another example is the judgment of a Roman synod in 377 that the Christological doctrine of Apollinarius was heretical before the Council of Constantinople in 381. Of course a number of Fathers reached the same conclusion about Apollinarius before 381 as well.

by the ordinary universal magisterium is usually a matter of thoughtful review and gathering of many ordinary magisterial acts, to see whether there is uninterrupted universality.

Papal Confirmation

This brings me to another issue that Gaillardetz raises. It certainly is the proper business of theologians to tackle the question of whether a doctrine has been taught infallibly by the ordinary universal magisterium. But it is not only the business of theologians. There are times when it is also the proper business of the pope, who is head of the whole body of Catholic bishops, to determine when the whole episcopate has taught a doctrine infallibly. There can be a papal confirmation of this fact. Gaillardetz admits that there can be such a papal confirmation but thinks it can only function as a kind of notary public, whereby the pope sets his seal on what has clearly emerged in the consciousness of the Church. A papal confirmation would be akin to a notary who affirms he has witnessed the proper signature. In the face of doubts or uncertainty about a doctrine the pope, like a notary confronted with doubts about a proper signature, would transcend his authority if he attempted a confirmation in such a situation. If there is a serious question among theologians as to whether a teaching has been definitively proposed by the ordinary universal magisterium, Gaillardetz contends that a papal confirmation would be inappropriate. A confirmation, according to Gaillardetz, cannot substitute for lack of evidence. There are several significant problems with this argument. The role attributed to theologians is exaggerated, and my criticism mentioned earlier about the consensus of theologians applies here. There is no reason to think that theologians can so limit the exercise of the teaching authority of the head of the apostolic college. Second, the decision about what counts as evidence and what does not count as evidence is built into the nature of the teaching office, whether it is an exercise of the pope's ordinary magisterium or the extraordinary magisterium. The pope is not like a notary, because in an act of confirmation he makes a judgment about what has been taught down through the ages by the apostolic college. Third, historically the pope's role of confirming what belongs, or what does not belong, to the deposit of faith as handed on by the ordinary universal magisterium has never been limited as Gaillardetz has envisioned. When the papacy functioned as a court of appeal in the first millennium, the bishop of Rome did not limit himself as a notary who simply confirmed the end result of a process. The popes understood themselves as making a judgment about matters that were disputed at the time.

If there can be no act of the college of bishops without the pope who is its head (*LG* 23), if the pope is the visible principle and foundation of unity of the bishops (*LG* 23), and if the participation of the pope is required for the ordinary magisterium to be universal, then it seems sound to think that another criterion for identifying the definitive teaching of the ordinary universal magisterium is whether there has been a papal confirmation of it even in matters that are controversial. This criterion is at least as important as the universal and constant consensus of theologians. To be sure, the absence of papal confirmation would not mean that we could not recognize a definitive teaching of the ordinary universal magisterium, but its presence could greatly aid theologians in their quest to identify the definitive teachings of the ordinary universal magisterium.

In one of his many articles on the Magisterium, Sullivan points out how papal definitions (extraordinary magisterium) can sometimes be "needed to overcome a threat to the Church's unity in the faith and bring about a consensus, or restore one that had been lost."[12] Is the extraordinary magisterium the only way a pope could meet such threats or restore a consensus about a doctrine that has been lost? Why should we not think that the pope can also address a threat to the faith and seek to restore a lost consensus about some point of faith by confirming and identifying definitive teachings of the ordinary universal magisterium? Is not this form of papal teaching activity an older way of addressing threats to the Church's unity in faith than the extraordinary way of papal definitions? Rather than seeing Pope John Paul's confirmations as a novel or inappropriate way of exercising his teaching office, an argument can be made that he returned to an older way of exercising the papal magisterium. The Pope in this way is very conscious of teaching as the head of the apostolic college, together with his brother bishops, continuing to pass down or defend what they have received.[13]

---

[12] In *Dictionary of Fundamental Theology*, ed. René Latourelle and Rino Fisichella (New York: Crossroad, 1994), s.v. "magisterium," 619.

[13] This is not the place to make this argument in detail. I am thinking of the popes in the first millennium, sometimes in the midst of controversy, who made certain judgments about doctrine, and these judgments were not understood as defined dogmas. One is reminded of Leo the Great's judgment that the Robber Synod at Ephesus in its statement of faith parted from the authentic Catholic tradition. Other times the popes received decisions of local councils as true expressions of the Catholic faith. In *EV* the language the Pope uses in his confirmation of definitive Church teaching shows that he is conscious of teaching as head of the college and together with the bishops. Unfortunately, this is camouflaged in the English translation, which has the Pope speaking in the first person singular ("I declare," "I confirm"). The official Latin in *EV* 57, 62, and 65 uses the first person plural: *confirmamus, declaramus, confirmamus*, respectively.

In a critique of the work of Sullivan, Livio Melina has made an important observation:

> How could we see a strong relationship in a son who said to his father or a young man who said to his bride-to-be: "I will only believe you when you solemnly swear to me on the Bible that you are not lying to me"? Analytical distinctions are valuable only within a greater context, otherwise the concentration on them destroys the vital synthesis (losing the forest for the trees). Authority is that charism that makes life grow in truth. It is realized as a complete and ordinary phenomena, before distinctions and formal and solemn expressions. The loss of this basic and fundamental dimension runs the risk of reducing the discussions on the Magisterium to a dry and minimalistic juridical formalism. Its recovery allows us to focus on the ordinary exercise of the universal magisterium as the normal dimension of the charism of infallibility, and welcomes also the ordinary Magisterium of the Pope as the authoritative witness of the head of the college of the same Magisterium.[14]

It is important, I think, that we not look at the definitive teachings of the ordinary universal magisterium through the spectacles of how the extraordinary magisterium teaches.[15] Otherwise we will not be clear about what we should be looking for and may in fact overlook the definitive teachings of the ordinary universal magisterium and their relation to the deposit of faith. Given the long history of ecumenical councils and their doctrinal definitions, and given the more recent history of the first Vatican Council with its emphasis on the capability of the pope to issue doctrinal definitions, it is easy to think of doctrine primarily in terms of defined dogmas. There is a real danger today of regarding what is most important about a doctrine to be whether it has been defined. But what is really important about a doctrine is its significance and relationship to the deposit of faith. Some of the most significant doctrines of the faith, such

---

[14] Livio Melina, "The Role of the Ordinary Universal Magisterium: On Francis Sullivan's *Creative Fidelity*," *The Thomist* 61 (1997): 605–15, at 615.

[15] Ironically, Sullivan criticizes Gaillardetz precisely on this point. See Sullivan, "The Ordinary Universal Magisterium," *The Jurist* 56 (1998): 338–60, at 346–47, where he takes issue with Gaillardetz's claim in *Witnesses to the Faith*, 167, that "the 1983 Code of Canon Law required for the exercise of the ordinary universal magisterium a formal papal approbation modeled on that given to conciliar decrees." Gaillardetz does not given a reference to this in the Code. I cannot find that it says this anywhere. Sullivan points out that Gaillardetz seems to refer to canon 341.2, which has to do with extra-conciliar decrees issued by the college of bishops, not with the ordinary universal magisterium. At any rate, this example shows how easy it is to think of the ordinary magisterium in terms of the extraordinary magisterium.

as the hope for the resurrection of the body, have never been defined. In fact, some defined doctrines depend on undefined ones. The bodily Assumption of the Blessed Virgin Mary is a case in point; it depends on the undefined dogma of the bodily resurrection.

The Status of an Article of Faith Cannot Become Tentative

This touches, too, on a question I posed with regard to Gaillardetz's work and his response to me. I disagreed with Gaillardetz's argument that "in the face of controversy, the determination of the authoritative status of any teaching not solemnly defined can only be pursued tentatively."[16] I objected that if at some time in the future the resurrection of the body became controversial, would we really be justified in saying that its definitive and infallible status would be only tentative because it had become controversial? Gaillardetz answers, provocatively, "Yes," arguing that there would need to be a demonstration of the diachronic and synchronic unity of the episcopate; a public consultation of bishops; or even an exercise of the extraordinary magisterium, conciliar or papal, in a solemn definition.

My response: all of these things would be unnecessary. It should be perfectly legitimate for a bishop or pope who faced such a heresy to simply appeal to what is confessed in the creed. The point I tried to make was that Gaillardetz's argument leads to rather unsound conclusions and massive problems. It would become legitimate, in the face of controversy, to doubt the infallible status of a doctrine that is utterly fundamental to the deposit of faith at least until there was a head count of bishops or a solemn definition. I chose the resurrection of the body to illustrate my point because it is an article of faith found in the creed. As such, I agreed with Sullivan that the articles of faith in the creed are the first place to go to see examples of undefined dogmas and hence infallible teachings of the ordinary universal magisterium.[17] It should be rather clear that the Church has taught the doctrine of the resurrection of the body as central to her faith and that the response owed to it is one of divine faith. It also seems rather clear that to suspend assent to it or to withhold assent altogether puts one outside the Catholic faith communion, whatever the controversy may be. Gaillardetz's argument removes a fundamental tool needed by bishop or pope for the defense of the faith: the ability to appeal to the creed.[18]

---

[16] Gaillardetz, "The Ordinary Universal Magisterium," 465.

[17] Sullivan, *Creative Fidelity*, 96.

[18] There is also an additional problem: for one thing, there is nothing to suggest that when the Fathers at Vatican II (*LG* 25) reaffirmed the ability of the ordinary universal

There are also other problems. In the face of controversy or "serious questions," the assent owed to articles of faith in the creed would suddenly no longer be that of divine faith, as it has been for centuries, but of something less than that. Presumably, even the withholding of assent could be justified at least until there was a definition or a formal consultation of all bishops. The problem here is that the Church has consistently maintained that the articles of faith are altogether certain and has consistently reminded the faithful that they are obligated to "firmly believe" them.[19] This obligation would really be empty and vacuous if it were contingent on some controversy that might arise in the future.

In conclusion, I repeat the point I made in my *Heythrop Journal* article: the question about the definitive, infallible teachings of the ordinary universal magisterium must be approached from the standpoint of working for communion with the previous generations of Christians that have gone before us, as well as from a concern for the retrieval of the wholeness of the Catholic faith for our time. Catholic theology must scan the tradition for doctrines taught by the ordinary universal magisterium that should be brought forward to be received by the current generation because of the clear, uninterrupted, and definitive way those doctrines have been taught and lived down through the centuries. This task is about finding forgotten riches of the Catholic tradition. If theologians are to assist the Church in bringing the wholeness of the Catholic faith to a new expression, and therefore achieving catholicity in time and communion in time, then they will avoid a rigid restricting of the binding character of doctrines to those that have been dogmatically defined.

---

magisterium to teach doctrines definitively they meant to limit an appeal to this form of teaching to non-controversial matters. I can find nothing in the documents of the Vatican or the Acta that would support this idea.

19 Avery Dulles has pointed this out in *The Assurance of Things Hoped For* (New York: Oxford University Press, 1994). After citing numerous professions of faith Dulles writes: "The Church has asserted that its own faith is altogether certain and has required the faithful to confess that they 'firmly believe' the articles of faith. Negatively, the magisterium rejects the idea that mere probability, let alone merely hypothetical assent, suffices" (p. 230).

CHAPTER 3

On Recognizing Infallible Teachings of the Ordinary Universal Magisterium*

ACCORDING TO *Lumen Gentium* (*LG*), number 25, the college of bishops, in communion among themselves and with the pope, can proclaim doctrine infallibly outside of an ecumenical council when they are in agreement that a particular doctrine is to be held definitively. *LG* refers here to what Catholic theology knows to be the ordinary universal magisterium. How do we know when the ordinary universal magisterium has taught a doctrine infallibly? This question has been addressed by the distinguished Jesuit ecclesiologist Francis A. Sullivan in some articles and in his book *Creative Fidelity*.[1] I have had occasion to examine and criticize Sullivan's treatment of the question.[2] Another scholar, Richard Gaillardetz, offered his own criticism of my views and my critique of Sullivan.[3] In a short article in *Theological Studies* Sullivan replied to my criticisms of his work.[4] In his reply to me, Sullivan explained more clearly than he did in his book *Creative Fidelity* about what he holds

* A version of this essay appeared in *New Blackfriars* 86 (November 2005) 591–97.

1 See also Sullivan, "The Doctrinal Weight of *Evangelium Vitae*," 560–65; idem, "The Secondary Object of Infallibility," 536–50; idem, "Reply to Germain Grisez," 732–37; idem, *Magisterium*, 119–52.

2 See chap. 1 above, "The Infallibility of the Ordinary Universal Magisterium: A Critique of Some Recent Observations." In response to Richard Gaillardetz's reading of Sullivan, see chap. 2 above, originally published as "Reply to Richard Gaillardetz and Francis Sullivan on the Ordinary Universal Magisterium," *Theological Studies* 64 (September 2003): 598–609. Also, of related interest, see chap. 4 below, "Christ, the Moral Law, and the Teaching Authority of the Magisterium."

3 Gaillardetz, "The Ordinary Universal Magisterium," 447–71.

4 Sullivan, "Reply to Lawrence J. Welch," 610–15.

concerning the conditions for and criteria of the infallible teaching of the ordinary universal magisterium. The chief point of disagreement between Sullivan and me turns on the weight of importance that should be given to the consensus of theologians for recognizing when the ordinary universal magisterium has taught a doctrine infallibly. In addition, it is unclear whether Sullivan thinks that a judgment by the pope that a particular doctrine has been taught infallibly by the ordinary universal magisterium is enough for such a doctrine to be "manifestly established" and recognizable. Let me explain.

Sullivan now states he agrees that the absence of a consensus among theologians does not mean there has not been a definitive teaching of the ordinary universal magisterium. At the same time, Sullivan says, "What I do hold is that without such a consensus it would be difficult *to be certain* that the conditions for infallible teaching had been fulfilled."[5] He reasons "that because Catholic theologians are professionally qualified to make informed judgments about the degree of authority with which doctrines have been taught by the magisterium, a lack of consensus among them as to whether a doctrine had been taught infallibly would make it questionable whether that fact was 'manifestly established.' "[6]

But does this not hold the recognition or knowability of the infallible teachings of the ordinary universal magisterium hostage to the present or future consensus of theologians? Sullivan's position seems to me to still attribute too much to the importance of the consensus of theologians because it downplays the fact that there are other ways for us to recognize the infallible teachings of the ordinary universal magisterium. This problem surfaces in Sullivan's interpretation of the status of the teaching in *Evangelium Vitae* (*EV*) against direct murder, direct abortion, and euthanasia. I believe that the Pope identifies these teachings as infallibly taught by the ordinary universal magisterium. A confirmation by the head of the apostolic college, together with the common adherence of the faithful down through the ages to these doctrines, is more than enough to "clearly establish" that here is a case of infallible teaching. But Sullivan argues that there is uncertainty about the Pope's intentions and concludes:

> It is too soon to know whether there will be the consensus of theologians that would show that it is "clearly established" that the immorality of murder, abortion and euthanasia are infallibly taught. What this would mean is that the Church has taken an irreversible

5 Ibid., 615.

6 Ibid.

stand on these issues.[7]

The question in my mind is whether Sullivan still really wants to hold that we await the "clear establishment" that the Catholic Church has taught irreversibly on the immorality of murder, abortion, and euthanasia because there is not yet a consensus of theologians that would show it. What if it could be shown that the Pope really did mean to identify these teachings as infallibly taught by the ordinary universal magisterium? Would not this be enough for us to recognize that the Church in her ordinary universal magisterium has taught infallibly the immorality of murder, abortion, and euthanasia? On the other hand, if a papal confirmation were not enough and if we would still need to await a consensus of theologians to be certain that the conditions for infallible teaching had been fulfilled, would not the consensus be more important than the judgment by the Pope about *what is* an infallible teaching of the ordinary universal magisterium?

In his book *Creative Fidelity*, Sullivan admits that there are good reasons for thinking that the Pope meant to invoke the infallibility of the ordinary universal magisterium in *EV*, but contends that "questions remain" about the Pope's intentions. These intentions were thrown into doubt according to Sullivan because of remarks reported to have been made by then Joseph Cardinal Ratzinger at a press conference held when the encyclical was released to the public.[8] These comments of Cardinal Ratzinger were known to Sullivan from a partial report of the press conference that was published in *Origins*.[9] Sullivan admits "that it is a bit risky to draw firm conclusions from a partial report of what was said at a press conference."[10] Nonetheless, Sullivan argues, "If it really was the intention of the pope to invoke the teaching of Vatican II about the infallibility of a consensus of the universal episcopate in proposing a doctrine as definitively to be held, one would expect the cardinal to have said so."[11] Sullivan reaches this conclusion even though he identifies some good reasons for thinking that the Pope intended to invoke the infallibility attributed to the teaching of the ordinary universal magisterium.[12]

I do not believe Sullivan's argument will hold. It is weak not only because it requires us to believe that there is uncertainty about the Pope's intentions based on what did *not* happen to be mentioned in an incomplete report of a press conference, but more importantly because there are strong

7 Sullivan, *Creative Fidelity*, 160.
8 Ibid., 159.
9 *Origins* 42 (April 6, 1995): 728.
10 Sullivan, *Creative Fidelity*, 158.
11 Ibid.
12 See ibid., 159.

indications within the encyclical itself—some of which Sullivan even admits—of the Pope's intentions.[13]

Before I examine *EV* let the words of *LG* 25 be recalled, which lay down the conditions for the infallible teaching of the ordinary universal magisterium.

> Although the individual bishops do not enjoy the prerogative of infallibility, they nevertheless proclaim Christ's doctrine infallibly whenever, even though dispersed through the world, but still maintaining the bond of communion among themselves and with the successor of Peter, and authentically teaching matters of faith and morals, they are

[13] In fact, comments attributed to Cardinal Ratzinger in an interview with George Weigel on September 20, 1997, point in the exact opposite direction. On the subject of the formulation of the teaching in *EV* on murder, direct abortion, and euthanasia, Cardinal Ratzinger made remarks that indicated that the Pope did intend to invoke the infallibility of the ordinary universal magisterium. "Ratzinger, who once laughed aloud at the 'good Ratzinger/bad Ratzinger characterization,' had a different recollection of his discussions with John Paul II about how certain things should be done. It was widely reported, for example, that John Paul had wanted to invoke his papal authority to define infallibly the three principal teachings of the 1995 encyclical, *Evangelium Vitae* [The Gospel of Life]—'that the direct and voluntary killing of the innocent, direct abortion, and euthanasia are always gravely immoral'—and Ratzinger somehow prevented this. The prefect denied that this is what had happened, and described the kind of consultations that had in fact taken place. During the preliminary discussions leading up to the preparation of the encyclical, John Paul was 'interested to have the suggestions of our congregation about what [was] possible,' Ratzinger said. While *Evangelium Vitae* was being drafted, 'the Holy Father was waiting for our response as to what was the [best] way to think about these problems; there was never an opposition, because the Holy Father wanted to be informed about precise possibilities.' Ratzinger understood that the Pope 'wanted to give a very strong formulation' to the three teachings in question; the Pope 'was always open to the CDF's suggestions [about] how this should be done.' Through the process of consultation, it was decided that the best way to underscore the seriousness of what was being taught would be to footnote each declaration of grave immorality in *Evangelium Vitae* with a reference to paragraph 25 of *Lumen Gentium*, Vatican II's Dogmatic Constitution on the Church—where the Council had confirmed the infallibility of the 'ordinary, universal magisterium' of the world's bishops in communion with the bishop of Rome. The universality of the Church's teaching on these three questions, in other words, was the guarantee that these teachings were true, certain, and unchangeable. John Paul and Ratzinger had agreed that this was the way of formulating *Evangelium Vitae* that was 'most corresponding to the tradition of the Church'" (George Weigel, *God's Choice: Pope Benedict XVI and the Future of the Catholic Church* [New York: HarperCollins, 2005], 182–83). While these remarks are interesting and significant, the most important reasons for thinking that the Pope thought the Church's teaching on murder, abortion, and euthanasia are infallibly taught are to be found in *EV* itself.

in agreement on one position as definitively to be held.[14]

What is the evidence for thinking that in *EV* the Pope intended to identify the teachings against murder, abortion, and euthanasia as infallibly taught by the ordinary universal magisterium? What reasons are there to think that the Pope understood himself as confirming the infallible teaching of the whole apostolic college of bishops dispersed throughout the world? In a word there are numerous reasons why we should draw these conclusions.

The passage from *LG* 25, quoted above, is footnoted in each of the three paragraphs in *EV* 57, 62, and 67 that judge murder, abortion, and euthanasia to be gravely immoral. This kind of footnoting in *LG* 25 is unprecedented in a papal encyclical. There is something in addition to the ordinary papal magisterium here. It is clear from the beginning of the encyclical that the Pope intended the teachings of *EV* to be an expression not only of the ordinary papal magisterium but also of episcopal collegiality, as the official "Vatican Summary" of the encyclical points out.[15] In this way, there is something unique about *EV* as an encyclical. In *EV* 5 the Pope describes his consultation with the cardinals in an extraordinary consistory that met in the spring of 1991. The Pope says that in that consistory the cardinals unanimously asked him "to reaffirm with the authority of the Successor of Peter the value of human life and its inviolability, in the light of present circumstances and attacks threatening it today." Next, Pope John Paul relates how in response to this request of the cardinals he wrote a letter to each and every one of his brother bishops asking for their help and cooperation. The Pope states that the encyclical, which is meant to be "a rigorous reaffirmation of the value of human life and its inviolability," is "the fruit of the cooperation of the Episcopate of every country of the world."

Second, as Sullivan notices, the Pope presents the taking of innocent human life as a matter of faith and morals based on the natural law and the written word of God. This is important because the Pope makes clear that the Magisterium is teaching on a point that is capable of being infallibly taught. It teaches about something that pertains to the deposit of faith, which the Magisterium must guard and defend. This point is important because one of the conditions for the infallible teaching of the ordinary universal magisterium according to *LG* 25 is that the whole episcopate must teach on a matter of faith and morals.

Third, the Pope explicitly says that he is teaching in communion with

---

14 This quotation of *LG* is from the English translation found at the Vatican website, www.vatican.va/archive/hist_councils/ii_vatican_council/documents/vat-ii_const_19641121_lumen-gentium_en.html.

15 *Origins* 14 (April 6, 1995): 728.

bishops of the Catholic Church with regard to murder, direct abortion, and euthanasia (*EV* 57, 62, 67). Significantly, in the case of direct abortion (*EV* 62) the Pope mentions that he is teaching "in communion with the Bishops—who on various occasions have condemned abortion and who in the aforementioned consultation, albeit dispersed throughout the world, have shown unanimous agreement concerning this doctrine." The reference here to *LG* 25 could not be any more obvious. For it speaks of the bishops, even though dispersed in the world, as proclaiming Christ's doctrine infallibly, provided that they maintain the bond of communion between themselves and the pope, and are in agreement about a matter of faith and morals that is to be definitively held. Thus the Pope is saying, in effect, that the Church's teaching meets an important condition for an infallible teaching of the ordinary universal magisterium. One cannot help but notice, too, the clear expression of episcopal collegiality being made in the encyclical.

Fourth, the Pope says in each of the paragraphs that these doctrines are taught by the ordinary universal magisterium, which "by the authority which Christ conferred upon Peter and his Successors" confirms (or in the case of abortion, declares) what is taught by the whole episcopate. In the official Latin text of the encyclical, the Pope uses the first person plural *confirmamus* (*EV* 57, 65), "we confirm," and *declaramus* (*EV* 62), "we declare," in the judgments against murder, direct abortion, and euthanasia (mistakenly transposed and translated into the first person singular in the English translation). The language the Pope uses in each of the three paragraphs is highly significant because it manifests that in confirming the teachings of the ordinary universal magisterium, the Pope understands himself as speaking together with the bishops as head of the episcopal college with the authority Christ gave to Peter. Again, there is a plain expression of episcopal collegiality. The Pope is saying that he and the bishops are clearly in agreement about an important matter of faith and morals.

Fifth, the Pope says that murder, direct abortion, and euthanasia are acts that are always morally evil without exception. In *EV* 57, the Holy Father states that "direct and voluntary killing of an innocent human being is always gravely immoral" and that "there are no privileges or exceptions for anyone." The Pope makes reference to the supernatural sense of faith of the people of God that shows universal agreement in matters of faith and morals. In *EV* 62, the Church's teaching on abortion is said to be "unchanged and unchangeable." The consultation of the bishops is described as having "shown unanimous agreement concerning this doctrine." *EV* 65 condemns euthanasia as "a grave violation of the law of God, since it is the deliberate and morally unacceptable killing of a human person." What is stated in *EV* 57 about the direct killing of an innocent person as always being immoral without exception obviously applies to euthanasia as well. That these teachings are unchangeable and that these evil acts against human life are condemned as admitting no exceptions shows that the Pope is confirming that the whole episcopate is in agreement that these teachings are to be held definitively. Such agreement among the Pope and the bishops that a doctrine is to be held definitively is also one of the conditions *LG* 25 laid down for the infallible teaching of the ordinary universal magisterium.

There are two things we should conclude from the foregoing. First, that in *EV* the Pope clearly indicates his intention to invoke the infallibility of the ordinary universal magisterium for the Church's teaching against murder, direct abortion, and euthanasia. Second, the Pope is claiming in *EV* that all the conditions specified by *LG* for the ordinary universal magisterium to teach something infallibly have been fulfilled. That is, the Pope, the head of the college of bishops, confirms and declares that he and the bishops are in agreement that these teachings, being a matter of faith and morals pertaining to the deposit of faith, are irreversible and are to be held definitively by the faithful. Sullivan's argument that there is uncertainty about whether the Pope intended to invoke the infallibility of the ordinary universal magisterium because of what Cardinal Ratzinger did not say about it in a press conference cannot stand up to a close reading of *EV*.

If there is a clear papal confirmation that the ordinary magisterium has infallibly taught a doctrine, I do not see how Sullivan or anyone can still hold that without the consensus of theologians it would be difficult to be certain that the conditions for infallible teaching had been fulfilled. If the pope is the visible principle and foundation of the unity of bishops (*LG* 23), if there can be no act of the college of bishops without the pope who is its head (*LG* 23), and if the participation of the pope is required for the ordinary magisterium to be universal, then it is reasonable to think the pope, who is head of the whole body of Catholic bishops, can determine when the whole episcopate has taught a doctrine infallibly. On the other hand, if we still awaited a consensus of theologians for the clear establishment of this kind of teaching, then the consensus of theologians would be more important for knowing that the ordinary magisterium has infallibly taught a doctrine than a confirmation by the head of the apostolic college. This is a conclusion that Sullivan may not want to hold, but the emphasis he places on the consensus of theologians moves in the direction of it and does not clearly exclude it.

The Importance of the Consensus of Bishops for Infallible Teachings of the Ordinary Universal Magisterium

Sullivan says in his reply to me in *Theological Studies* that he does "not believe that one can appeal to a past consensus of bishops as infallible if they are no longer agreed in teaching that doctrine."[16] As an example he cites the teaching that unbaptized infants would be deprived of the beatific vision if they died without baptism and the bishops at the Council of Florence who "taught that all pagans and Jews would go to Hell if they did not become Catholics before they died."[17] While I think these may be questionable as examples,[18] I would agree that it is possible that if one could

---

16 Sullivan, "Reply to Lawrence J. Welch," 611.

17 Ibid.

18 I do not think that the teaching on unbaptized infants being deprived of the beatific vision serves as an example because as the International Theological Commission observed, the doctrine "did not possess the certitude of a statement of faith or the same certitude as other affirmations whose rejections would entail the denial of a divinely revealed dogma or of a teaching proclaimed by a definitive act of the magisterium." See "The Hope of Salvation," *Origins* 36 (April 26, 2007): no. 34, p. 734. As for the teaching of the Council of Florence, Sullivan seems to have changed his views, at least to some extent, on how to interpret its teaching. In his book *The Church We Believe In*, Sullivan asks whether the Catholic Church changed its mind on the question of the necessity of being in the Church for salvation because there seems to be a contradiction between Florence and the Second Vatican Council, which affirmed the possibility of salvation for those who "through no fault of their own do not know the gospel of Christ or his Church" (*LG* 16, as cited in *The Church We Believe In* [New York: Paulist Press, 1988], 119). Sullivan asks: "Is there any way of reconciling these positions?" He gives this answer: "If I am not mistaken, the underlying dogma has always really been what Vatican II explicitly declared it to be: 'There is no salvation for those who are culpably outside the Church.' The difference between Florence and Vatican II is that Florence judged all those outside guilty, and Vatican II presumed them to be innocent. What has changed is a way of judging other people" (ibid., 120). So what has changed is not doctrinal. Some four years later Sullivan substantially repeated this point even more fulsomely as part of his very fine study of the doctrine *Extra Ecclesiam nulla Salus*, entitled *Salvation Outside the Church: Tracing the History of the Catholic Response* (New York: Paulist Press, 1992), 199–204. I believe Sullivan's earlier and careful interpretation of Florence is sound. There is something after all that both Florence and Vatican II teach: the necessity of the Church for salvation. The dogma that was really being taught at Florence was not the judgment that non-Christians were culpably outside the Church. It is true, the bishops no longer judge all non-Christians to be culpably outside the Church, but this judgment was really extrinsic to the underlying dogma that was taught. Was this judgment about the culpability of non-Christians a doctrine? It is hard to see how it was. Such a

show that there was an interruption in the consensus of bishops on a particular teaching, then it might be an indication that there is not the kind of episcopal consensus that would alert us to a definitive and infallible teaching. On the other hand, I do not believe that this is absolutely the case. In other words, it seems to me that there could be a breakdown in consensus among bishops about a particular point of doctrine that has in fact been taught infallibly prior to a later lack of consensus.[19]

A strong argument could be made, for example, that something like this occurred during the iconoclast controversy in the eighth century. The use and veneration of images that was common at least since the fifth century came to be rejected not only by numerous bishops but several patriarchs of Constantinople as well.[20] Prior to the solemn proclamation of the Church's faith regarding holy images at the Seventh Ecumenical Council in 787, the teaching of the Church on this point of doctrine was taught by what we would call the ordinary universal magisterium. This doctrine of the Church was taught most especially in and through the Church's liturgical tradition and practice as well as in the common teaching of bishops. The popes (Gregory I and Gregory II) and other bishops who defended the holy images taught quite clearly that the Church's teaching was permanent and irreversible. In other words, the popes and bishops appealed to a prior consensus. They did not think that because there was no longer the kind of consensus among bishops in their own time that it was not possible to appeal to the long-standing prior consensus of former times *and that such a consensus was binding on all bishops for all times.*

"judgment" seems to pertain more to the incomplete and imperfect formulation the Church can sometime express in her teachings. If anything, Florence demonstrates more the historicity of dogma than it does to serve as an example of how one should not appeal to the past consensus of bishops about a doctrine if the bishops are now no longer agreed in teaching that doctrine. Sullivan in *Salvation Outside the Church* observes: "These limits of the cultural, geographical, psychological horizons of medieval Christians are historical factors which profoundly conditioned their expression of the doctrine of the necessity of the church for salvation" (p. 201).

19 I mentioned in my article in *Theological Studies* that Sullivan himself seems to recognize there can be times that a prior consensus has been lost, but is still binding and needs to be restored and received again. In one of his articles on the Magisterium, Sullivan points out how papal definitions (extraordinary magisterium) can sometimes be "needed to overcome a threat to the Church's unity in the faith and bring about a consensus, or restore one that had been lost." See *Dictionary of Fundamental Theology*, s.v. "magisterium," 619.

20 For instance, Anastasius (730–754), Constantine II (754–766), Nicetas I (766–780), and Paul IV (780–784). The latter later recanted his iconoclasm.

It certainly seems sound to say that the Church's teaching on holy images prior to the Seventh Ecumenical Council was taught infallibly by the ordinary universal magisterium, despite the fact that there was not the consensus among bishops in the eighth century that had existed in former centuries.

In the *Heythrop Journal* I spoke of the task of the Church to achieve a communion across time so that the present age of the Church shares fully in the life, faith, and identity of the Church of the past. The Church of the present time is challenged to preserve and assimilate everything that is of the faith that she has received from the Church that has gone before her. My point is this: a lack of consensus of bishops about a particular point of doctrine about which there was a former consensus could be a sign of impaired communion. Something like this seems to me to have occurred during the iconoclast controversy and at other times in the Church's history, and something like it could occur again. Therefore I cannot agree with Sullivan, at least not absolutely and in every case, that one cannot appeal to a past consensus of bishops as infallible if they are no longer agreed in teaching that doctrine. Finally, Sullivan asks me in *Theological Studies* if it really would be just for a person to incur the penalty of excommunication if it were not "manifestly established" that a doctrine had been infallibly taught by the ordinary universal magisterium.[21] Obvi-

[21] Sullivan, "Reply to Lawrence J. Welch," 614. Sullivan refers here to the fact that I took issue with his claim that canon 749.3 ("No doctrine is to be understood to be infallibly defined unless this fact is clearly established as such"), which is applicable to defined dogmas, should also be applied to undefined dogmas and definitive teachings of the ordinary universal magisterium. I argued that it is better not to apply canon 749.3 and its requirement of *manifeste constiterit* to undefined dogmas and definitive teachings of the ordinary universal magisterium in a univocal way because it is a juridical term that refers to the formulation of defined doctrine. To use the term univocally introduces confusion about how definitive teachings of the ordinary universal magisterium are known and recognized. There is a distinction, I pointed out, between "teaching something" (ordinary universal magisterium) and "teaching by way of defining" (extraordinary magisterium). One has to look for something different in the effort to identify the infallible and definitive teachings of the ordinary universal magisterium. Sullivan in reply acknowledges that it is obvious that "the criteria by which one can know with certainty that a doctrine has been defined are different from those by which one can be certain that a doctrine has been taught infallibly by the ordinary universal magisterium." Still, Sullivan judges that "the difference between the criteria is irrelevant" (see "Reply to Lawrence J. Welch," 614). I admit that these teachings of the ordinary universal magisterium must be recognizable in some way. But there is a difference between "manifesting by defining" (extraordinary magisterium) and "manifesting by leaving clues" (ordinary magisterium). I am glad that Sullivan thinks this is obvious, but I do not believe it is obvious to every theologian. It is all too easy to think that the infallible teachings of the ordinary universal magisterium should

ously to be excommunicated for obstinately denying an infallible teaching of the ordinary universal magisterium it must be possible for that teaching to be reasonably recognized. The difference between Sullivan and myself seems to amount to whether one can still recognize, without difficulty, an infallible teaching of the ordinary universal magisterium even if there is not a consensus of theologians that the conditions for such a teaching have been fulfilled. Or, as Sullivan might put it, whether the lack of a consensus of theologians would make it questionable that it was "manifestly established" that a doctrine has been infallibly taught.

My short response is: not if the pope, who, as head of the college of bishops, alerts us that the ordinary universal magisterium has taught a doctrine infallibly. Thanks, in part, to what the Pope points out in *EV*, I think that the immorality of murder, abortion, and euthanasia are good examples of infallible teachings of the ordinary universal magisterium that can be recognized without great difficulty. Even though there may not have been a consensus of theologians about this fact,[22] the Pope's teaching about their status is now enough to "manifestly establish" them as the very kind of infallible teachings envisioned by *LG* 25.

---

look like the infallible teachings of the extraordinary magisterium, and thus to conclude that therefore there must be very few of them.

22 It is worth repeating a point here that I made in note 8 of my *Theological Studies* article: Prior to *EV* Richard McCormick claimed that most theologians disputed the idea that the Church even had the authority to teach about abortion infallibly, let alone that the Church had done so through the ordinary universal magisterium. Some eleven years prior to *EV* Richard McCormick, arguing against Grisez, wrote: "They [theologians] simply disagree—as most would and should—with Grisez that the immorality of direct abortion is infallibly taught by the ordinary magisterium. More generally, they deny that such particular norms are the proper object of infallibility." See his "Medicaid and Abortion," 720. In another telling passage McCormick also claimed "Rahner's analysis would deny the very possibility of infallible teaching where direct abortion is concerned. *And it is safe to say that this is the common conviction of theologians*" (ibid., emphasis mine). If McCormick was correct about the fact that many theologians believed that particular moral norms cannot be the proper object of infallibility, then what *EV* teaches about direct murder, direct abortion, and euthanasia as being taught infallibly by the ordinary universal magisterium has enormous consequences for contemporary Catholic moral theology.

CHAPTER 4

Christ, the Moral Law, and the Teaching Authority of the Magisterium*

IN AN IMPORTANT essay Francis A. Sullivan, S.J., takes up the question as to whether the ordinary and universal magisterium has infallibly taught some moral doctrines.[1] Sullivan explores this question in reference to the encyclicals *Veritatis Splendor* (*VS*) and *Evangelium Vitae* (*EV*). Do these recent encyclicals promote the claim that there are some moral doctrines that have been infallibly taught by the ordinary and universal magisterium? After a careful examination of the encyclicals Sullivan concludes that they do give support to this claim. Concerning *VS*, Sullivan shows there are good reasons to think that the encyclical means to teach "that all traditional Catholic moral doctrine is, in the final analysis, the Church's interpretation of the contents of the Ten Commandments as reaffirmed and further specified in the New Testament."[2] *Veritatis Splendor* teaches, Sullivan argues, that the whole moral law, including the natural moral law, is contained in revelation. Furthermore, *VS* teaches that it is through supernatural revelation that we can know the moral law in an integral way. Sullivan reasons that if this true, and if the Magisterium has been entrusted with revelation in order to give it authoritative and possibly infallible interpretation, then it follows that

* A version of this essay appeared in *Irish Theological Quarterly* 64 (Spring 1999): 17–28.

1 Francis A. Sullivan, "Infallible Teaching on Moral Issues? Reflections on *Veritatis Splendor* and *Evangelium Vitae*," in *Choosing Life: A Dialogue on* Evangelium Vitae, ed. Kevin Wm. Wildes, S.J., and Alan C. Mitchell (Washington, DC: Georgetown University, 1997), 77–89.

2 Ibid., 80.

the authority of the Magisterium to teach moral doctrine is identical to its authority to teach and interpret revealed truth.[3] Some important consequences follow from this, according to Sullivan. He writes:

> This would insert all moral issues into the primary object of infallibility and make it much easier to claim that many traditional Catholic moral doctrines have been infallibly taught by the ordinary universal magisterium. Among such traditional Catholic moral doctrines are those concerning murder, abortion, and euthanasia.[4]

EV condemned murder, abortion, and euthanasia as particularly grievous violations of the moral law. Sullivan goes on to claim that there are "good reasons" to think that "Pope John Paul intended to invoke not the infallibility that Vatican I attributed to papal definitions but the infallibility that Vatican II attributed to the teaching of the ordinary and universal magisterium."[5]

I think that Sullivan is on to something important in his interpretation of *VS* and *EV*. He is right to point out that both encyclicals suppose that the ordinary and universal magisterium can teach infallibly about moral matters. He is correct in arguing that the authority of the Magisterium to teach moral doctrine infallibly is coincident to teach and interpret revealed truth.

While it is true and it is very important to say that the entire moral law is better grasped and understood in the light of revelation, it does not seem that the Pope meant to affirm in *VS* or *EV* that all moral precepts of the natural moral law are revealed and fall within the primary object of

---

3 Ibid., 83.

4 Ibid.

5 Sullivan, "Infallible Teaching on Moral Issues?," 87. Sullivan goes on to invoke his thesis that a doctrine ought not to be understood as infallibly taught unless this fact is clearly established. For this fact to be clearly established there must a consensus of theologians about it. Sullivan concludes that at the present time it is too early to know whether there will be a consensus of theologians that shows that it is clearly established that the ordinary and universal magisterium has infallibly taught the immorality of murder, abortion, and euthanasia. Here, I disagree with Sullivan. The consensus of theologians is not necessary for knowing when the ordinary and universal magisterium has infallibly taught a doctrine. In the case of *EV*, I contend that when the encyclical clearly invokes the infallibility of the ordinary and universal magisterium for three of its teachings, then our knowledge of this rests upon the authority of the declaration itself rather than a future consensus of theologians. For a fuller discussion of my disagreement with Sullivan's thesis on the consensus of theologians see chapter 3 above, "On Recognizing Infallible Teachings of the Ordinary Universal Magisterium."

infallibility. To be fair, I think Sullivan might now acknowledge this point because of assertions made in the motu proprio *Ad Tuendam Fidem*, promulgated on June 30, 1998,[6] after Sullivan had written his article. It seems clear now in the light of *Ad Tuendam Fidem* that while the Pope in *VS* considered a great deal of the moral law to be contained in revelation (first object of infallibility) he also supposed that other precepts of the natural moral law pertain to revelation (secondary object of infallibility). *Ad Tuendam Fidem* affirmed, in effect, that there are certain moral doctrines that belong to the secondary object that are to be definitively held by the faithful.[7] The official commentary on the motu proprio gave Church teachings against prostitution, fornication, and euthanasia as examples of these truths that must be definitively held.[8] There can be some moral matters that are not, strictly speaking, divinely revealed but nevertheless have a logical connection to revelation. In such matters, which can be said to pertain to revelation rather than *to be contained* in revelation, the Magisterium has the authority to teach them, infallibly if necessary, in order to safeguard divine revelation. None of this changes the fact, which Sullivan has noticed, that if the Magisterium's authority in moral matters is identical with its authority to teach revealed truth, then it is easier to claim that numerous traditional moral doctrines have been infallibly taught by the ordinary and universal magisterium. It could be argued that because many traditional teachings on morality fall within the primary or secondary object of infallibility, and because these moral doctrines have been the common teachings of the bishops and popes down through the centuries, then these teachings have met the required conditions for the infallibility of the ordinary universal magisterium as stipulated by Vatican II.

Although it cannot be maintained that *VS* teaches that the entire moral law is contained in revelation, Sullivan's point that something important is being said in *VS* and *EV* with regard to how revelation enables us to grasp

---

6 For an English translation see *Origins* 28 (July 15, 1998).

7 The primary object of infallibility would be all those things contained in the deposit of faith, that is, those things that are divinely revealed. This is to be distinguished from the secondary object of infallibility which refers to those matters which although are not revealed are so connected with revelation that it is necessary for the Magisterium to teach them in order to safeguard and explain the deposit of revelation. The Magisterium can teach these matters infallibly too. Sullivan argues, rightly, that *Lumen Gentium* (*LG*), number 25, recognized the distinction between the primary and secondary objects of infallibility when it taught that infallibility "extends as far as extends the deposit of divine revelation, which must be religiously guarded and faithfully expounded."

8 *Origins* 28 (July 15, 1998).

the entire moral law in an integral way is correct. The argument I wish to make is that what *VS* teaches about the integral knowledge of the moral law and what it teaches about the entire moral law being contained in, or pertaining to, revelation and what it teaches about the competency of the Magisterium in moral matters, ultimately rests on a Christological foundation, the unity of creation and redemption in Christ. *Veritatis Splendor* teaches that the moral law finds its unity in Christ. The moral law is one in Christ. If the teaching of *VS* can be shown to have this Christological foundation, then it will properly situate what Sullivan has noticed in *VS*, namely, the argument that the Magisterium's authority to teach moral doctrine is coincident with its authority to interpret revelation. It will also serve to further clarify and strengthen the related argument that a number of traditional moral doctrines have been infallibly taught by the ordinary and universal magisterium. All of these claims rest upon a Christological foundation. What allows them to be made is the affirmation of the close relationship between Christ and the natural moral law. If the moral law, as it is known by reason and revelation, is not seen as one in Christ, then we will have misunderstood why *VS* claims what it does about the competency of the Magisterium in moral matters. Furthermore, we will have failed to grasp the truth that goodness and truth of the natural moral law and the revealed moral law are fully manifested in Christ, and that it is to this goodness and truth that we as human persons are called.

My presentation unfolds in two parts. In the first part I will review why Sullivan thinks that the authority of the Magisterium to teach moral doctrine is concurrent with its authority to teach revelation. In the second part I will show that *VS*'s teaching that the moral law is known in an integral way only by revelation and its claim that the authority of the Magisterium to teach on moral matters is identical to its authority to interpret revelation are doctrines that rest ultimately upon a Christological basis. Obviously there are many implications raised by this thesis, and they cannot all be treated here. The scope here is very limited. It is my hope, however, that these reflections and conclusions will call attention to *VS*'s teaching about the relationship between the whole moral law and Christ, as well as illuminate the theological basis for the claim in *VS* about the authority and competence of the Magisterium with regard to the moral law.

The Moral Law and Revelation

Sullivan cites several passages from *VS* that he argues show that the Pope identified the Magisterium's authority on moral matters as identical with its authority to interpret divine revelation.[9] I give below some of the most important passages cited by Sullivan:

> Consequently the decisive answer to every one of man's questions, his religious and moral questions in particular, is given by Jesus Christ, or rather is Jesus Christ himself. (*VS* 2)[10]
>
> Because the Church has been sent by Jesus to preach the Gospel and to "make disciples of all nations . . . teaching them to observe all" that he has commanded (cf. Mt 28:19–20), she today once more puts forward the Master's reply, a reply that possesses a light and a power capable of answering even the most controversial and complex questions. (*VS* 30)
>
> This good is established, as the eternal law, by Divine Wisdom which orders every being towards its end: this eternal law is known both by man's natural reason (hence it is "natural law"), and—in an integral and perfect way—by God's supernatural Revelation (hence it is called Divine law). (*VS* 72)
>
> These are the goods safeguarded by the commandments, which, according to St. Thomas, contain the whole natural law. (*VS* 79)[11]
>
> In teaching the existence of intrinsically evil acts, the Church accepts the teaching of Sacred Scripture . . . (1 Cor 6:9–10). (*VS* 81)

On the basis of these passages, as well as the others that I have not cited here, Sullivan concludes that "John Paul II is effectively basing the authority of the Magisterium in all moral issues on its authority to interpret divine revelation."[12]

This interpretation does seem sound. One of the most important claims is in *VS* 2, quoted above, in which Christ is said to give answer to man's religious and moral questions. This passage goes on to quote *Gaudium et Spes* (*GS*), number 22: "In fact, it is only in the mystery of the Word Incarnate that light is shed on the mystery of man. For Adam, the first Man, was a figure of the future man, namely, of Christ the Lord. It is Christ, the last Adam, who fully discloses man to himself and unfolds his noble calling by revealing the mystery of the Father and the Father's love." The Pope makes

---

9 Sullivan cites *VS* 2, 5, 28, 30, 72, 79, 81, 82, 116. He also asserts that these passages show that *VS* teaches the whole moral law to be contained in revelation. I have already dealt with the problem of this claim.

10 All quotations from *VS* and all other papal encyclicals quoted in this chapter are from official Vatican translations.

11 Citing St. Thomas Aquinas, *Summa theologiae* (*ST*), I–II, q. 100, a. 1.

12 Sullivan, "Infallible Teaching on Moral Issues?," 81–82. Sullivan also cites *VS* 5, 28, 82, 116.

this central anthropological affirmation of Vatican II constitutive of the anthropology of *VS*.[13] Pope John Paul II insists in *VS* that a Christological anthropology must inform moral theology. The answer to moral questions about the human person is Jesus Christ, "the light of the nations." Therefore the Pope urges that "[p]eople today need to turn to Christ once again in order to receive from him the answer to their questions about what is good and what is evil" (*VS* 8). Moreover, "Christ is the 'Beginning' who, having taken on human nature, definitively illumines it in its constitutive elements and in its dynamism of charity towards God and neighbor" (*VS* 53). Sullivan may know of some these passages and their important Christological-anthropological claims (he does not cite *VS* 8 or *VS* 58), but he does not discuss them in his essay or explain how important they are for understanding why *VS* claims what it does about the moral law and the Magisterium's competency to interpret the moral law.

The Moral Law: One in Christ

This fundamental claim of *VS* is clear: if Christ is the full revelation of the human person then there are no moral issues that somehow lie outside of him or apart from him. There are no great moral questions that Christ does not in some way answer. For Christ's reply to our questions "is a reply that possesses a light and a power capable of answering even the most controversial and complex questions" (*VS* 30). It certainly seems to follow that the Church's authority in moral matters rests upon her authority to interpret the revelation entrusted to her by Christ. This point is further underscored in *VS* 72, which claims that although the eternal law is knowable from natural reason it is only known in an integral and perfect way in the light of divine revelation. Thus the Church according to *VS* 82 accepts the teachings of the Scriptures when she teaches the existence of intrinsically evil acts. The citation from St. Thomas in *VS* 79 that the commandments contain the whole natural law is another important indication that the Pope means to teach that the whole moral law is contained in or pertains to divine revelation, and that therefore the authority of the Magisterium in moral matters is coincident with its authority to interpret divine revelation.

Sullivan also observes that *VS* strongly upholds "the binding force of the natural moral law" and maintains that there is a distinction between this natural moral law and moral law as revealed by God.[14] *Veritatis Splen-*

13 I have discussed this at greater length in chap. 10 below, "*Gaudium et Spes*, the Divine Image, and the Synthesis of *Veritatis Splendor*," originally published by the same name in *Communio* (Winter 1997): 793–814.

14 Sullivan, "Infallible Teaching on Moral Issues?," 80.

dor, number 74, acknowledges that "the moral order, as established by the natural law, is in principle accessible to human reason." However, revelation discloses to us that human reason is impaired in its knowledge of the moral law because of sin. Due to the Fall, the moral law itself cannot be known from reason as God intended. The encyclical insists that we must keep in mind that human reason is fallen, wounded by sin, and thus capable of only a partial and imperfect knowledge of the moral law. Thanks to divine revelation, we are given an integral and complete knowledge of the moral law. This insistence is apparent above in the quotation from *VS* 72. But Sullivan cites two other passages as well.

> Some people, however, disregarding the dependence of human reason on Divine Wisdom and the need, given the present state of fallen nature, for Divine Revelation as an effective means for knowing moral truths, even those of the natural order, have actually posited a complete sovereignty of reason in the domain of moral norms regarding the right ordering of life in this world. (*VS* 36)[15]

> Man is able to recognize good and evil thanks to that discernment of good from evil which he himself carries out by his reason, in particular by his reason enlightened by Divine Revelation and by faith, through the law which God gave to the Chosen People, beginning with the commandments on Sinai. (*VS* 44)

Sullivan observes, rightly, that the conclusion *VS* draws seems clear: if we need revelation to know the moral law in its integrity, and if the Church's Magisterium has been given the charism of authentically and infallibly interpreting revelation, then the authority of the Church's Magisterium in moral matters coincides with her authority to authentically interpret divine revelation.

There is another important passage in *VS* 45 that Sullivan does not cite and that I believe reveals the Christological basis for *VS*'s teaching that the moral law is contained in or pertains to revelation as well as its teaching about the competence of the Magisterium in moral matters.

> Even if moral-theological reflection usually distinguishes between the positive or revealed law of God and the natural law, and, within the economy of salvation, between the "old" and the "new" law, it must not be forgotten that these and other useful distinctions always refer

[15] This claim coheres with the teaching of St. Thomas. For example, St. Thomas teaches in *ST* I–II, q. 100, a. 5, ad 1, that sin obscures the natural law. For St. Thomas, sin impacts the efficacy of the natural law.

> to that law whose author is the one and the same God and which is always meant for man. The different ways in which God, acting in history, cares for the world and for mankind are not mutually exclusive; on the contrary, they support each other and intersect. They have their origin and goal in the eternal, wise and loving counsel whereby God predestines men and women "to be conformed to the image of his Son" (Rom 8:29). God's plan poses no threat to man's genuine freedom; on the contrary, the acceptance of God's plan is the only way to affirm that freedom. (*VS* 45)

We must remember that the natural moral law does not affirm or protect some good of the human person that is somehow unrelated to the human person's salvation and ultimate end.[16] *Veritatis Splendor* makes the point that the whole moral law finds its unity in Christ. Both natural law and revealed law have their goal and origin in the fact that the Father predestines us to be conformed to the image of the Son. This Christocentric emphasis, prominent especially in the Pope's Trinitarian encyclicals, is a theme that is present and consistently applied throughout *VS*. In what follows below I want to unpack how this emphasis forms the indispensable basis for the claim that the whole moral law is contained in or pertains to revelation. In other words, this claim about the moral law is something rooted in a Christological anthropology.

According to *VS* the natural law is knowledge of that truth and goodness about the human person that is known from reason or the light of understanding that God gave to us at creation. *Veritatis Splendor*, quoting St. Thomas, defines natural law as "nothing other than the light of understanding infused in us by God, whereby we understand what must be done and what must be avoided. God gave this light and this law to man at creation."[17] But the natural law also has to do with the truth about the human nature of the person. Thus, in *VS* 50 we read:

---

[16] It should be noted that this affirmation adheres perfectly to the moral teaching of St. Thomas who taught that all laws are ordered to the New Law or the evangelical law and are perfected by it. According to St. Thomas the end and goal of all law is to make the human person good, righteous, virtuous, and just (*ST* I–II, q. 92, a. 1). Only the New Law, the evangelical law, can accomplish this goal (*ST* I–II, q. 106, a. 2; *ST* I–II, q. 107, a. 2). It should be recalled that St. Thomas did not somehow define natural law without reference to theology. See also St. Thomas's Commentary on Romans 1, *Super epistolas S. Pauli lectura*, ed. Raphael Cai, O.P., 8th rev. ed. (Turin and Rome: Marietti, 1953).

[17] *VS* 12. The Pope cites St. Thomas Aquinas, *In Duo Praecepta Caritatis et in Cecem Legis Praecepta. Prologus: Opuscula Theologica*, 11, no. 1129, ed. Taurinen (1954), 245; cf. *ST* I–II, q. 91, a. 2; cf. *VS* 36, 40, 42.

> At this point the true meaning of the natural law can be understood: it refers to man's proper and primordial nature, the "nature of the human person," which is the person himself in the unity of soul and body, in the unity of his spiritual and biological inclinations and of all the other specific characteristics necessary for the pursuit of his end. "The natural moral law expresses and lays down the purposes, rights and duties which are based upon the bodily and spiritual nature of the human person."[18]

This natural law, this light of understanding given to us at creation is nothing less than a certain participation in the eternal law. Appealing to St. Thomas, the Pope writes that reason draws its own truth and authority from the eternal law, which is none other than divine wisdom itself. Similarly, in *VS* 42, the Pontiff cites the comments of St. Thomas on Psalm 4: "*The light of your face, Lord, is signed upon us, thereby implying that the light of natural reason whereby we discern good from evil*, which is the function of the natural law, is nothing else but an imprint on us of the divine light."[19] We ought to speak then of a participatory theonomy whereby our obedience to God's eternal law has to do with human reason and will sharing in the divine wisdom and providence.

In *VS* 43 the Pope defines the meaning of the eternal law: the wisdom, reason, and will of God that lovingly guides and arranges the whole created world. He recalls that the Second Vatican Council taught that "supreme rule of life is the divine law itself, the eternal, objective and universal law by which God out of his wisdom and love arranges, directs and governs the whole world and the paths of the human community. God has enabled man to share in this divine law, and hence man is able under the gentle guidance of God's providence increasingly to recognize the unchanging truth."[20] Augustine, we are reminded, explained that the eternal law is "the reason or the will of God, who commands us to respect the natural order and forbids us to disturb it."[21] St. Thomas equated the eternal law with "the type of the divine wisdom as moving all things to their due end." But God in his wisdom, according to the Angelic Doctor, cares for the human person not "from without" but "from within," that is, "through reason, which, by its natural knowledge of God's eternal law, is consequently able to show man the right direction to take in his free actions."[22] Thus the Pope concludes

---

18 The last sentence of this passage quotes *Donum Vitae* (February 22, 1987), *AAS* 80 (1988): 74.

19 *ST* I–II, q. 91, a. 2.

20 The Pope quotes *Dignitatis Humanae*, no. 3.

21 The Pope cites Augustine's *Contra Faustum*, bk. 22, chap. 27.

22 *ST* I–II, q. 93, a. 1.

that the human expression of the eternal law is the natural law, and he cites St. Thomas again:

> Among all others, the rational creature is subject to divine providence in the most excellent way, insofar as it partakes of a share of providence, being provident both for itself and for others. Thus it has a share of the Eternal Reason, whereby it has a natural inclination to its proper act and end. *This participation of the eternal law in the rational creature is called natural law.*[23]

At this point it is important to connect what the Pope has written here about the eternal law with what he has written about it in his encyclical *Dominum et Vivificantem*, number 33. Here the Pope appears to go beyond St. Thomas:[24]

> This Word is the same Word who was "in the beginning with God," who "was God," and without whom "nothing has been made of all that is," since "the world was made through him." He is the Word who is also the eternal law, the source of every law which regulates the world and especially human acts.

The eternal law is a "someone": the Son of the Father. The Pope takes the classical teaching on the eternal law and firmly connects it to Christology. If the eternal law refers to the wisdom and reason of God then we must think of it in reference to the eternal Logos who is the eternal Son. For Pope John Paul II the natural law, which is a participation in the eternal law, can-

---

23 Ibid. Emphasis mine.

24 Or is St. Thomas more precise than the Pope here? In *ST* I–II, q. 93, a. 1, ad 2, St. Thomas argues that the eternal law is appropriated to the Son because of the association between type and word. St. Thomas teaches: "With regard to any sort of word, two points may be considered: viz., the word itself, and that which is expressed by the word. For the spoken word is something uttered by the mouth of man, and expresses that which is signified by the human word. The same applies to the human mental word, which is nothing else than something conceived by the mind, by which man expresses his thought mentally. So then in God the Word conceived by the intellect of the Father is the name of a Person: but all things that are in the Father's knowledge, whether they refer to the Essence or to the Persons, or to the works of God, are expressed by this Word, as Augustine declares (*De Trin.* xv. 14). And among other things expressed by this Word, the eternal law itself is expressed thereby. Nor does it follow that the eternal law is a Personal name in God: yet it is appropriated to the Son, on account of the kinship between type and word." (I give the translation of the English Dominicans, *Summa Theologica*, vol.1 [Chicago: Benziger Bros., 1947]).

not be dissociated from the fact that human persons exist from the beginning, through the Son, the Word, the one Lord. To speak then of the light of natural reason as being nothing less than an imprint on us of the divine light is to really speak about our creation in the Son. Natural law, then, is not somehow autonomous from the fact that the Father has created us in and for his Son so that we might share in the very life of the Trinity. Pope John Paul II does not abstract the natural law in the order of creation from the Father's plan to elevate it in Christ. We are created with a radical orientation toward the Son, and we are called to be sons and daughters in the Son by the power of the Spirit. Thus *GS* 22: "It is Christ, the last Adam, who fully discloses man to himself and unfolds his noble calling by revealing the mystery of the Father and the Father's love." In many ways, *VS* involves a creative thinking out and application of this truth.[25]

By connecting the eternal law and the natural law to Christology, the Pope further integrates his emphasis upon the original centrality or primacy of Christ. This emphasis is evident in his first encyclical, *Redemptor Hominis* (*RH*) and continues throughout his later writings, including *VS*. It is the context for the claim that "[h]e is the Word who is also the eternal law." For example, in *RH* 7, the Pope contends that "we must con-

---

25 David Schindler has made the helpful observation that the Pope's thought involves an ontological Christocentricism as opposed to a moral Christocentricism. The latter certainly sees Christ as the center of human existence, but mainly by intention. Divine revelation in Christ gives us important elements to be added to the final, eschatological content of anthropology. Still, the revelation in Christ makes little or no impact upon the original or creational content of anthropology. In other words, a moral Christocentricism underestimates our creation in the Son. Christology tends to be seen as having implications for anthropology rather than informing it from the ground up. A moral Christocentricism, Schindler acknowledges, "may recognize the receptive and dialogical dimensions of human existence, the reality of sin and the need for liberation by God from the slavery of sin, but it leaves these elements more or less in a state of juxtaposition to the elements which constitute its original anthropology—and of course juxtaposition is precisely the problem, for it creates the appearance that the elements subsequently added are arbitrary, or of secondary importance." An ontological Christocentricism, which marks the Pope's thought, is different. "What I mean by an ontological Christocentricism then is one which insists that a (re)-centering in Jesus Christ makes a difference already in the original content of man's imaging of God. Such Christocentricism thus sees receptivity as anterior to creativity in the primitive structure of the creaturely act, relation as a constitutive element of the human person, sin as concretely affecting the human person from the beginning of its (infralapsarian) existence—sees all of these expressions of the primacy of God-in-Jesus-Christ *in the understanding precisely of man*" (David Schindler, "Christology and the *Imago Dei*: Interpreting *Gaudium et Spes*," *Communio* 23 (Spring 1996): 172.

stantly aim at Him 'who is the head,' 'through whom are all things and through whom we exist,' who is both 'the way, and the truth.'" Christ is presented in *RH* 7 as the Head, and the Pope cites numerous passages from the Scriptures that refer to the total primacy of Christ in creation and redemption. Furthermore, in *RH* 8 we read that Christ as Redeemer reveals the "fundamental truth concerning creation." In *Dives in Misericordia*, number 4, the Pope maintains that Christ, mercy incarnate, best manifests God's relationship of love with the human race that exists from the mystery of creation. *Redemptoris Mater* (*RM*) discusses at length in *RM* 7 and *RM* 8 our election in Christ from the beginning. And in his apostolic letter on the advent of the third millennium, *Tertio Millennio Adveniente*, number 4, the Pontiff contends that "Christ, the Son who is one in being of the Father, is therefore the one who reveals God's plan for all creation, and for man in particular."

The emphasis upon the primacy of Christ especially with regard to creation was not absent from the Holy Father's weekly catecheses. On the catechesis for March 5, 1986, "Creation is the Work of the Trinity," we read:

> St. Paul speaks of "one Lord, Jesus Christ, through whom are all things and through whom we exist" (1 Cor 8:6). In the Letter to the Colossians we read: "He [Christ] is the image of the invisible God, the firstborn of all creation; for in him all things were created, in heaven and on earth, visible and invisible . . . all things were created through him and for him. He is before all things, and in him all things hold together" (Col 1:15–17). The Apostle emphasizes the active presence of Christ both as cause of creation ("through him") and as its final cause ("for him"). . . . Creation is the work of the Triune God. The world "created" in the Word-Son, is "restored" together with the Son to the Father, through that Uncreated Gift, the Holy Spirit, consubstantial with both.[26]

And in his catecheses on the mystery of predestination in Christ, May 28, 1986, the Pope observes:

> In the Letter to the Colossians we find that the truth of "predestination" in Christ is closely connected with the truth of "creation in Christ" [Col 1:15–16]. Thus, the world created in Christ the eternal Son bears in itself from the beginning, as the first gift of Providence, the call, or pledge of predestination in Christ.[27]

---

[26] John Paul II, *God, Father, and Creator: A Catechesis on the Creed*, trans. *L'Osservatore Romano*, English ed. (Boston: Pauline Books and Media, 1996), 210–11.

[27] Ibid., 264.

The primacy of Christ that the Pope so strongly affirms in his Trinitarian encyclicals and catecheses is fully operative in *VS*. It must be kept in mind when in *VS* he proclaims that "Christ is the 'Beginning' who, having taken on human nature, definitively illumines it in its constitutive elements and in its dynamism of charity toward God and neighbor" (*VS* 53). Christ's primacy forms an important foundation for the proclamations in *VS* that Christ is the "decisive answer to man's questions" (*VS* 2). He is "[a]t the source and summit of the economy of salvation, as the Alpha and the Omega of human history" (cf. Rev 1:8; 21:6; 22:13). Moreover, citing *GS* 22, the Pope proclaims in *VS* 8: "Christ sheds light on man's condition and his integral vocation." This constant insistence upon the primacy of Christ is the context for understanding the claim that the Word is the eternal law, as well as the claim in *VS* 45 that there is a distinction but not a separation between the natural law and the positive revealed law (divine law) because both have their origin and goal in the Father's loving counsel, whereby the Father predestines us to be conformed to the image of the Son. What the Pope takes very seriously is Christ, the Head and the Alpha, by whom the human race is redeemed and in whom we are created.[28] The very close connection between the order of creation

[28] It is pertinent to recall here how Pope John Paul insists upon creation as Christocentric, reading Genesis in the light of the Epistle to the Ephesians. For example, in his audience of October 6, 1982, the Pope said: "When we compare the testimony of the 'beginning' reported in the first chapters of Genesis with the testimony of Ephesians, we must deduce that *the reality of the creation of man* was already *permeated* by the perennial election of man in Christ: *called to holiness through the grace of adoption as sons*, 'predestining us to be his adopted sons through Jesus Christ according to the good pleasure of his will, to the praise and glory of his grace, which he has given to us in his beloved Son' (Eph 1:5–6)."

Moreover, "[f]rom the 'beginning,' man, male and female, shared in this supernatural gift. This endowment was given in view of him, who from eternity was 'beloved' as Son, although—according to the dimensions of time and history—it preceded the incarnation of this 'beloved Son' and also the 'redemption' we have in him 'through his blood' (Eph 1:17)." And, "[r]edemption was to become the source of man's supernatural endowment after sin and, in a certain sense, despite sin. This supernatural endowment, which took place before original sin, that is, the grace of original justice and innocence—and endowment that was the fruit of man's election in Christ before the ages—was brought about precisely *out of regard for him, that one and only Beloved*, while chronologically anticipating his coming in the body. In the dimensions of the mystery of creation, election to the dignity of adoptive sonship was proper only to the 'first Adam,' that is, to man created in the image and likeness of God as male and female." Quotations from the translation by Michael Waldstein, *Man and Woman He Created Them: A Theology of the Body* (Boston: Paulist Press, 2006), 505, emphases in the original. Hereinafter cited as *TOB*. It might be added that just as we should not consider creation apart from Christ, so it would seem that we must not think of natural law apart from him either.

and the order of redemption must be integrated into our understanding of the distinction between the natural law and the positive or revealed law. Just as creation and redemption are distinct but find their unity in Christ, so the natural law and the positive law find their unity in Christ, the Word, who is the eternal law.

To sum up, we have seen that in *VS* the natural law is presented as nothing less than the light of understanding given to us by the Father at creation. This light of understanding infused in us by God is a certain participation in the Word and Son in whom we are created. Thanks to the natural law, we can come to know something about the truth and goodness of the human person, and we can come to knowledge of the moral law. On the other hand, because of sin we do not know this moral law in its integrity and in its completeness. Our reason, our light of understanding, is fallen, and therefore our knowledge of the moral law is partial and incomplete. Nevertheless, creation although fallen is still good, and the natural law, including the natural moral law, is still, according to *VS*, the human expression of the eternal law. The natural law involves a certain participation in the eternal law. This eternal law refers to the wisdom, reason, and will of God, whereby God lovingly directs the good creation. Rigorously upholding the primacy of Christ, the eternal Word of God, the Pope claims that the Word is the eternal law. In him we are created, in him we are called to divine adoption from the beginning, and in him we are redeemed. The same Word of the Father who is the eternal law reveals "the fundamental truth concerning creation," fully discloses the truth about the human person, and therefore fully reveals the moral law. To be sure, *VS* acknowledges and affirms a distinction between the natural moral law known by reason and the moral law that is known by divine revelation. The Law, however, is one. Christ, the eternal Word, the Lord of history, is the Beginning and the End in the one plan of creation and redemption. In this Christocentric understanding, the natural law and what *VS* calls the positive law (divine law) correspond to the distinction between creation and redemption that is one in Christ. The natural law and the positive law (divine law) are one because they have both their origin and goal in the fact that we are chosen by the Father to be conformed to the image of the Son. The natural law then cannot be conceived as autonomous from the positive, revealed law. To affirm otherwise is to make a Christological and hence anthropological mistake about our origin in and through the Word and Son of God.

Conclusion

It seems true to conclude, as Sullivan does, that according to *VS* the Church's authority in moral matters is equivalent to her authority to interpret revelation. As Sullivan rightly observes, this makes it much easier to argue that the ordinary and universal magisterium has infallibly taught many traditional Catholic moral doctrines. I have sought to clarify and strengthen these claims by showing that they rest ultimately upon a Christological foundation. *Veritatis Splendor* teaches what it does about the competence of the Magisterium with regard to the moral law because it understands the moral law, as known by reason and by revelation, as one in Christ and because it understands that "Christ fully discloses the truth about man and unfolds his noble calling" (*VS* 2). It is because *VS* teaches that Christ is the decisive answer to our moral questions that it can teach that the Magisterium's authority in moral matters is coincident with its authority to interpret revelation.

Questions about the ordinary and universal magisterium and its authority to interpret the moral law are questions about communion—communion with Christ. If we forget this then claims about the Magisterium's competence to teach infallibly with regard to the entire moral law will go beyond their theological supply lines and run the real risk of appearing as purely juridical claims having little to do with the good of the human person. When *VS* points out that we must avoid a heteronomy of morality, whereby there is an imposition of norms unrelated to the good of the person, this applies too for a theology of the Magisterium that explains how it can be that the Magisterium can teach infallibly in moral matters. A sound theology of the Magisterium must be fully informed by the truth that morality has to do with a participated theonomy, whereby obedience to "God's law effectively implies that human reason and human will are created to participate in God's wisdom and providence" (*VS* 41). Faith is the entrance into this participation and communion. The teaching activity of the Magisterium must be understood as directed toward serving this communion by cultivating the graced intellectual and moral virtues that bring our hearts and minds into the union with the life of the Triune God.[29] To conceive of a natural moral law as somehow autonomous or external to our vocation to this union is not only to underestimate the competence of the Magisterium in moral matters, it also is to underestimate the fullness of the goodness that the Father desires for every person. For the end of the human person is nothing less than divine life in Christ. In him alone the Word, the eternal law, is given the complete revelation of the truth about the human person.

---

[29] DiNoia has spelled this out very helpfully in "Communion and the Magisterium," 404–18.

CHAPTER 5

An Excessive Claim: Sterilization and Immediate Material Cooperation under Duress*

FATHER JAMES KEENAN, S.J., has written on the important issue of institutional cooperation and the 1994 Ethical and Religious Directives (ERD) of the National Catholic Conference of Bishops (NCCB).[1] He observes that the subject of institutional cooperation has been the cause of substantial discussion among ethicists, bishops, and administrators of Catholic healthcare facilities. In an article for the *Linacre Quarterly*, Keenan addresses a number of issues related to institutional cooperation and concludes his article with an examination of duress, and immediate material cooperation with regard to sterilization.[2] In a second and shorter essay in *Ethics and Medics*, Keenan, responding to one of his critics, again takes up the issue of duress, immediate material cooperation, and sterilization.[3] Keenan's analysis raises several important ecclesiological and magisterial issues, especially with regard to the interpretation of magisterial documents. I cannot treat them all them here. I will argue that Keenan's claim that Catholic healthcare institutions, by reason of immediate material cooperation under duress, may at times permit contracting physicians to perform some direct sterilizations[4] is based upon a faulty

* A version of this essay appeared in *Linacre Quarterly* 66 (Novembeer 1999): 4–25.

1 NCCB, Ethical and Religious Directives for Catholic Health Care Services (Washington, DC: USCCB, 1995). See the full text reproduced in *Origins* 24 (December 15, 1994): 450–61.

2 James Keenan, "Institutional Cooperation and the Ethical and Religious Directives," *Linacre Quarterly* 64 (August 1997): 53–76.

3 James Keenan, "Cooperation and Hard Cases," *Ethics and Medics* 23.8 (August 1998): 1–3.

4 Keenan, "Institutional Cooperation," 71–73. Cf. "Cooperation and Hard Cases," 1.

reading of relevant Church documents. To hold Keenan's position is not only a misinterpretation of the 1994 ERD but also, more seriously, a misinterpretation of the teaching of the responsum of March 15, 1975, from the Holy See to the bishops of the United States. It is also a misinterpretation of the United States Catholic Conference (USCC) commentary on the responsum issued on November 22, 1977, and the NCCB clarification on tubal ligation issued on July 9, 1980.[5] My argument is based not only on the content of these documents but on the nature of their doctrinal and magisterial authority. Lastly, I will argue that if Keenan's interpretation were to be adopted it would have the unfortunate consequence of working against the efforts of the local church—of which any Catholic healthcare institution is an important part—to live in full communion with the universal Church. I have no doubt that Keenan does not intend or desire this outcome, but, intended or not, it results from his position.

This presentation will unfold in three steps. First, I will review Keenan's position about direct sterilization and immediate material cooperation under duress. Second, I will review briefly some basic principles of interpretation necessary for the proper interpretation of magisterial documents. I will then carefully examine the responsum from Rome, the 1977 commentary, and the 1980 clarification issued by the USCC-NCCB and the 1994 ERD. In the third and last step, I will argue that questions of institutional cooperation should be situated in the context of the Church understood as a communion and will point out how Keenan's position, if adopted, would work against ecclesial communion.

Keenan on Sterilization and Immediate Material Cooperation under Duress

First, it is fitting to review the principles of cooperation as laid out in the appendix of the ERD because Keenan draws upon these principles in his

[5] For an unofficial translation of the responsum (*Quaecumque Sterilizatio*), see *Origins* 6 (June 10, 1976): 34–35; for the official Latin text, see *AAS* 68 (November 1976): 738–40. For the text of the commentary, see "Sterilization Policy for Catholic Hospitals," *Origins* 7 (December 8, 1977): 399–400; for the clarification see "NCCB Statement on Tubal Ligation," *Origins* 10 (August 28, 1980): 175. Perhaps it should be noted that the text of the responsum was not made public in the United States until a physician, who had somehow obtained a copy of it, read it during a discussion at an international meeting of Catholic physicians. *Origins* then published an unofficial translation. Up until that point Archbishop Joseph Bernardin, then president of the USCC-NCCB, had summarized the responsum in a letter to U.S. bishops. For the text of Archbishop Bernardin's letter see *Linacre Quarterly* 42 (November 1975): 220.

articles about institutional cooperation. I will quote in full the relevant section. The appendix distinguishes between formal and material cooperation this way:

> If the cooperator intends the object of the wrongdoer's activity, then the cooperation is formal and, therefore, morally wrong. Since intention is not simply an explicit act of the will, formal cooperation can also be implicit. Implicit formal cooperation is attributed when, even though the cooperator denies intending the wrongdoer's object, no other explanation can distinguish the cooperator's object from the wrongdoer's object. If the cooperator does not intend the object of the wrongdoer's activity, the cooperation is material and can be morally licit.
>
> The second distinction deals with the object of the action and is expressed by immediate and mediate material cooperation. Material cooperation is immediate when the object of the cooperator is the same as the object of the wrongdoer. Immediate material cooperation is wrong, except in some cases of duress. The matter of duress distinguishes immediate material cooperation from implicit formal cooperation. But immediate material cooperation—without duress—is equivalent to implicit formal cooperation and, therefore, is morally wrong. When the object of the cooperator's action remains distinguishable from that of the wrongdoer's, material cooperation is mediate and can be morally licit.

In his two articles Keenan has tried to stress what he calls the "limitedness" of the issue of immediate material cooperation and duress with a case that he believes is representative. I will quote the case he gives in his August 1997 article.

> In an American city of 100,000 inhabitants there are two hospitals, one community and the other Catholic. In the field of obstetrics, the former provides a full selection of services which the latter for ethical reasons does not. The latter, instead, tries to protect and promote the values of its tradition. In renegotiating their contract with the Catholic administration, the obstetrics team demands a new proviso: they want permission to do tubal ligations on those women who want ligations *while* having their infant delivered through cesarian section. The team estimates that the number of direct sterilizations would be very limited. Their reasons for the proviso are simply that they believe it is unethical and medically contraindicative to "open" the patient twice. The team is well respected by the administration and is well established in the community. They are prosperous enough that they could move out of the facility, if they were not to

> receive the proviso. In all other matters they have acceded to the hospital and have regularly observed ERD. If they were to leave the Catholic health care facility, the facility believes it would not be able to deliver any obstetric services and thus would provide no alternative to the community facility.[6]

Keenan argues that this is a case of material but not formal cooperation. Moreover, he judges the activity of the healthcare facility as immediate material cooperation under duress for grave proportionate reason. According to Keenan, "[d]uress means that one's options have been constrained, but to preserve something that is threatened, one may cooperate to protect that value."[7] He recognizes that some seem to believe that the cooperation would be mediate material cooperation because the healthcare facility would be only authorizing the cesarian section, while the physicians would be insisting upon the tubal ligation.[8] Keenan says that while this opinion could be probable, he is more inclined to describe the activity as immediate because it is hard to see how in this case the Catholic healthcare facility could claim not to be authorizing both the cesarian section and the tubal ligation.

Keenan reasons that because the physicians in this case ask only to do tubal ligations on women who are already having a cesarian section that there is not any kind of direct sterilization being authorized by the healthcare facility. He identifies the issue of duress as "the threatened loss of all obstetrics from the Catholic healthcare facility to the large urban area." Two further considerations are said to follow. First, it is necessary to consider how the loss of obstetric services would impact women. Where else would women find the kind of values that embody a Catholic healthcare facility if the physicians make good on their threat to leave? Second, how real is the threat of the physicians to take their services elsewhere? Is there any chance that obstetric services could be obtained from other physicians who would be faithful to the ERD? Keenan submits that if the threat of the physicians to withdraw their services is real and there is little possibility of offering a genuine alternative, then "many seem to believe that prudence guides both the facility's administrators and the bishop to approve the contract."[9] He

6 Keenan, "Institutional Cooperation," 71. Keenan sketches a very similar case in his "Cooperation and Hard Cases," 2.

7 Keenan, "Institutional Cooperation," 68.

8 Aside from citing a similar case in Gary Atkinson and Albert Moraczewski, *A Moral Evaluation of Contraception and Sterilization* (St. Louis: Pope John XXIII, 1979), 86–87, Keenan does not specify to whom he refers here.

9 Keenan, "Institutional Cooperation," 72. Keenan does not specify the "many" who seem to believe that the bishop should approve the contract.

goes on to explain that the way to avoid scandal in this case would be to explain the kind of duress that confronts the healthcare facility and to point out the fact that only a limited number of exceptions are provided because the physicians insist that it is "medically contraindicative to not do a requested sterilization on a woman undergoing a cesarian section."[10] Keenan concludes this way, and I think it is important to include here in his own words:

> By cooperation, the health care facility is still able to offer its services while promoting its Catholic values. It is not opening up the possibility of losing an otherwise reputable obstetric team. In fact, it is keeping the team faithful to ERD and the Catholic tradition notwithstanding the exceptional case of tubal ligations on women undergoing cesarian sections. Certainly the facility is not approving the exceptions; rather under the duress of losing their services and therefore being unable to offer any comparable services to their patients, the Catholic facility acknowledges that it has no other alternative.[11]

In same article, Keenan bases his position not only on his interpretation of the ERD on cooperation but also on his interpretation of two other documents: the 1975 responsum from the Congregation for the Doctrine of the Faith on sterilizations in Catholic hospitals, and the USCC-NCCB commentary on it. In part 6 of his article Keenan examines the views of Russell Smith about immediate material cooperation and duress. He applauds Smith for turning to these two documents in order to understand the meaning of duress in the ERD. Keenan claims that "[d]uress appears repeatedly in these documents and Smith uses these as a key for interpreting ERD."[12]

The claim that both the responsum and the commentary treat the issue of duress in connection with cooperation with sterilization is made in several other articles of Keenan's. In an essay in *Theological Studies*, he says, "[f]or instance, the Congregation for the Doctrine of the Faith and the United States Catholic Conference have offered strict guidelines governing when a Catholic health care facility, under duress, could materially cooperate in sterilization."[13] In an essay for *Health Progress* it is claimed that "[m]ore recently, the Congregation for the Doctrine of the Faith (CDF) and the United States Catholic Conference (USCC) invoked the

---

10 Ibid.

11 Ibid., 73.

12 Ibid., 69.

13 James F. Keenan and M. Cathleen Kaveny, "Ethical Issues in Health-Care Restructuring," *Theological Studies* 56 (March 1995): 146 [footnotes omitted].

principle of cooperation in considering when a Catholic healthcare facility, under duress, could cooperate in sterilization."[14]

The serious problem with these claims is that while the responsum refers to material cooperation, it never speaks about duress. It is incorrect to claim that the responsum invoked the principle of cooperation under duress. It is equally mistaken to say that the responsum is one of two documents where "duress appears repeatedly." It is only half correct to represent the responsum and the commentary as offering "strict guidelines" because the responsum does not simply offer guidelines—it is a judgment about the meaning of the doctrine of the Church on sterilization. The commentary offers guidelines, and the responsum primarily expresses a doctrinal judgment by the Pope. These are two different things, and they ought to be distinguished from one another, if only because they do not have the same level of magisterial authority behind them. It is important to determine the nature and the authority of these documents if we are to make judgments about why and what kind of cooperation is justified or not justified by Catholic healthcare facilities.

Interpreting and Evaluating Magisterial Documents

When theologians interpret and apply the teaching documents of the Magisterium, it is crucial for them to take great care in assessing and evaluating these documents. The theologian should be sure to identify the magisterial source of the document. It is important to know whether a document emanates from the pope, an ecumenical council, a national conference of bishops, an administrative board of an episcopal conference, a regional council of bishops, or an individual bishop. Each and every one of these sources has its own specific authoritative weight and importance. The decrees of an ecumenical council, for instance, possess a greater level of authority than the statements of an episcopal conference. The judgment of the pope on what the Church teaches about some aspect of faith or morals enjoys a greater authority than a commentary on the papal judgment issued by a committee of a national conference of bishops. The theologian should also discern the level or degree to which the authoritative teachers in the Church intend to engage their authority. Thus the "Instruction on the Ecclesial Vocation of the Theologian," issued by the Congregation for the Doctrine of the Faith (CDF), reminds theologians that they "must take into account the proper character of every exercise of the Magisterium, considering the extent to

[14] James Keenan and Thomas Kopfensteiner, "The Principle of Material Cooperation," *Health Progress* 76 (April 1995): 24.

which its authority is engaged."[15] Furthermore, theologians are said to be charged with the job "to assess accurately the authoritativeness of the interventions which becomes clear from the nature of the documents, the insistence with which a teaching is repeated, and the very way in which it is expressed."[16] In addition to these points, Father Francis Sullivan has observed, rightly, that the theologian must also ascertain the historical context of a magisterial document and within that context determine the meaning of what is taught in the document.[17] With these principles in mind let us turn to the responsum of March 13, 1975, from the Holy See and the commentary of November 22, 1977, issued by the administrative board of the USCC-NCCB, and the clarification published on July 9, 1980.

In 1974 Archbishop John R. Quinn, in the name of the American bishops, asked Pope Paul VI for an authoritative clarification with regard to the Church's teaching on sterilization. At the time many questions were raised in the United States as to whether it was morally permissible, in some cases, for Catholic healthcare facilities to permit direct sterilization. What was being questioned at the time was directive 20 of the 1971 Ethical and Religious Directives for Catholic Health Facilities. Some theologians argued that direct sterilizations in some cases might be permitted on the grounds of the principle of totality. Archbishop Quinn asked in his query to the Pope: "Can we accept the general prohibition of direct sterilization in Catholic hospitals and still make a number of exceptions in particular cases to solve pastoral problems?"[18]

The responsum, *Quaecumque Sterilizatio* (*QS*), was the way the Pope answered this query of the American bishops. Although the document was issued though the CDF, it has the authority of the Pope's teaching office behind it. It should be recalled that Vatican II taught, in *Christus Dominus*, number 9, that the various offices of the Roman Curia act in the name of the pope and by his authority. Strictly speaking then, the Pope, the head of the apostolic college, is the source from which *QS* was issued. What level of papal authority was engaged in this document? The responsum is an exercise of the authority of the ordinary papal magisterium and as such expresses authentic doctrine of the Church. In the responsum, the Pope as head of the college of bishops gives his judgment (ordinary papal magisterium) as to what the entire college of bishops teaches and has taught (ordinary universal

---

15 CDF, "Instruction on the Ecclesial Vocation of the Theologian," no. 17, see *Origins* 20 (July 5, 1990): 118–26.

16 Ibid., no. 24.

17 Sullivan, *Creative Fidelity*, 4–5.

18 As quoted in William B. Smith, "Catholic Hospitals and Sterilizations," *Linacre Quarterly* 44 (May 1977): 109.

magisterium) about sterilization. When the Pope exercises his ordinary magisterium as he does in the responsum, he seeks to serve his brother bishops with their task of seeing that their particular churches live in full and complete communion with the universal Church (see *Lumen Gentium* [*LG*], *numbers* 25, 27; cf. *LG* 23). The Pope issued *QS* not only to answer the query put to him by the American bishops, but also to assist them in their efforts to make sure that each of their particular churches are faithful to fundamental moral principles in all of their activities, so that the universal Church might be completely present and recognizable in every diocese in the United States.

What does the responsum teach? First of all, it defines direct sterilization in the following way:

> Any sterilization which of itself, that is of its own nature and condition, has the sole immediate effect of rendering the generative faculty incapable of procreation is to be considered direct sterilization. . . . Therefore, notwithstanding any subjectively right intention of those whose actions are prompted by the care or prevention of physical or mental illness which is foreseen or feared as a result of pregnancy, such sterilization remains absolutely forbidden according to the doctrine of the church.[19]

Quaecumque Sterilizatio rejects the idea that the principle of totality might be applied to justify some sterilizations on the grounds that it is sometimes necessary to surgically interfere with the reproductive organs for the greater good of the person. It teaches that direct sterilization harms the dignity and ethical good of the human person because it removes an essential element of "foreseen and freely chosen sexual activity." Direct sterilization is said to be intrinsically evil (*intrinsece mala*).

Careful attention must be paid to article 3a of the responsum, which deals with cooperation and "management of the Catholic hospitals." This section begins: "Quaevis eorum cooperatio institutionaliter adprobata vel admissa ad actiones ex seipsis. . . . " Attention must be paid to the verbs used here, *adprobata vel admissa*. This is not a parallelism. Two distinct things are being affirmed in the use of these verbs. A translation:

> Any cooperation of the hospitals which involves approving [*adprobata*] or allowing [*admissa*] actions which are in themselves, that is, by their nature and condition, directed to a contraceptive end, namely, so that the natural effects of sexual actions deliberately performed by the sterilized subject be impeded, is absolutely forbidden.

[19] Here I follow the translation in *Origins* (June 10, 1976): 34. For the Latin text, see *AAS* 68 (November 1976): 738.

> For the official approbation of direct sterilization and, *a fortiori*, its management and execution in accord with hospital regulations, is a matter which, in the objective order, is by its very nature, or intrinsically, evil [*intrinsece mala*]. The Catholic hospital cannot cooperate with this for any reason. Any cooperation so supplied stains the mission entrusted to this type of institution and would be contrary to the necessary proclamation and defense of the moral order.[20]

The Latin text, with the verbs that it uses, clearly says that a Catholic hospital in its management and policies can neither actively approve nor passively permit direct sterilizations because they are intrinsically evil actions that always harm the person who is sterilized. The verb *admissa* can be translated as "allow," "permit," or "allow access to" or "permit access to." The Latin is stronger than the English translation that appeared in *Origins*, which translated *admissa* as "consent."[21] The cooperation that is forbidden is not simply a matter of a Catholic healthcare facility simply stating its "non-approval" of direct sterilization. Forbidden are hospital regulations that not only approve but allow or permit direct sterilization. Were the regulations of a Catholic healthcare facility to approve or allow such actions they would amount to the "official approbation" (*officialis approbatio*) of intrinsically evil actions. Formal cooperation, whether by regulations that approve or allow direct sterilizations, is absolutely ruled out for a Catholic healthcare facility.

Moreover, the responsum teaches that cooperation in direct sterilization "stains" or "besmirches" (*dedeceret*) the mission entrusted to the institution. It clearly affirms that approving or permitting sterilizations harms the mission of a Catholic hospital. The *Origins* translation renders the verb *dedeceret* as "unbecoming." While this is a possible translation, a strong case can be made for translating the verb as "stain" or "besmirch." Such a translation fits well with the context of the whole paragraph, which speaks of the official approbation of direct sterilization as matter that, in the objective order, is an intrinsic evil.

The next section of *QS* (3b) states that "[t]he traditional doctrine regarding material cooperation, with the proper distinctions between necessary and free, proximate and remote, remains valid, to be applied with

---

20 I have reworked this part of the translation that appeared in *Origins* (ibid.). Again, the translation that appears there is not an official translation. In any case the Latin text remains normative. For another translation see "Dialogue about Catholic Sexual Teaching," in *Readings in Moral Theology*, vol. 8 (New York: Paulist Press, 1993), 172–74. The latter translation renders *adprobata vel admissa* as "approved or admitted." This translation of these verbs is closer to my translation given above.

21 This is not correct according to *The Oxford Latin Dictionary*. "Consent" usually translates *consentire, assentire*.

the utmost prudence, if the case warrants."[22] There are a couple of important points about this paragraph that call for very careful interpretation. First, what is meant by "traditional doctrine," and where do we find it?

The phrase "traditional doctrine" (*traditionalis doctrina*) refers to something very specific. In this context traditional doctrine refers not so much to the teaching of the Magisterium but to the theological opinions of approved authors concerning some aspect related to faith and morals. By use of the term "traditional doctrine" the responsum refers to the nomenclature, reasoning, and explanation with regard to some subject—in this case material cooperation—about which there is some consensus in the writings of "approved authors."[23] In other words, we can expect to find the "traditional doctrine" in the consensus of those theologians whose writings have been published under ecclesiastical approbation. While there may be certain points of difference in the approved authors, the traditional doctrine about material cooperation has to do with those matters about which there is some consensus. The *consensus* of approved authors is important here. Traditional doctrine is not something simply collected from a consultation of theological writers of one's choosing.

More important, it is evident that what the papal document allows for in this paragraph is mediate material cooperation, not immediate material cooperation. The responsum alerts us to this fact as soon it as speaks of the distinction between proximate and remote as "remaining valid." These distinctions have to do with mediate material cooperation, not immediate material cooperation. Proximate or remote (mediate cooperation) refers to how closely the cooperation is associated with the sinful act. No one, to my knowledge, argues that these distinctions apply to immediate material cooperation because the object of the cooperator and the wrongdoer coincide in immediate material cooperation. The responsum also mentions the distinctions between necessary and free (contingent) cooperation.[24] But this gives us no reason to think that it is somehow referring us to immediate material cooperation.

Moreover, since *QS* reaffirms that sterilization is an intrinsic evil it should be abundantly clear why it does not and cannot allow immediate

[22] I follow the *Origins* translation here.

[23] It should be recalled that the Theological Commission at Vatican II had occasion to refer to queries to the approved theological writings. For an example see *Acta Synodalia Concilii Vaticani Secundi*, III/8, 88, n. 159. One moral theologian who has recognized this meaning of "traditional doctrine" is Smith, "Catholic Hospitals and Sterilization," 112.

[24] *Necessary cooperation* denotes a kind of cooperation without which a sinful act could not be performed. Example: Giving a cyberthief the computer password needed for electronically accessing and stealing from another person's bank account. *Free or*

material cooperation where, in the words of the 1994 ERD, "the object of the cooperator is the same as the object of the wrongdoer." For this would be the very kind of cooperation that is said to be "absolutely forbidden." The responsum, contrary to what Keenan claims, never mentions duress or immediate material cooperation, and it certainly does not mention duress in connection with immediate material cooperation. The responsum does not teach, even implicitly, that duress somehow turns implicit formal cooperation into a permissible form of immediate material cooperation. Nor does the responsum refer, even implicitly, to immediate material cooperation under duress in the case of direct sterilization.

It remains true that the responsum recognizes that there might be times when the principle of material (mediate) cooperation in direct sterilization might apply. On the other hand, the responsum only mentions this after it has rejected "[a]ny cooperation of the hospitals which involves approving or allowing actions which are in themselves, that is, by their nature and condition, directed to a contraceptive end." The use of these very restrictive terms shows that *QS* understands the possibility of mediate material cooperation to be rather rare and an uncommon occurrence.

Whenever material cooperation is applicable, the responsum cautions (in article 3c) that "great care must be taken against scandal and the danger of any misunderstanding by an appropriate explanation of what is really being done." Scandal should be understood in the theological sense, for example, behavior or attitudes that involve deeds or omissions that lead others to do or be tempted to do evil.[25] The responsum certainly leaves open the possibility that in some cases the chance of scandal might be so great that material cooperation should be avoided even though it otherwise might be supplied.

This brings me to the statements of the USCC (1977) and of the NCCB (1980). Again, in evaluating these documents we must ask: (1) what is the source of the document, (2) what is the weight of authority that is being exercised, and (3) what is the meaning of what is taught or affirmed in the document?

The 1977 document is a commentary on *QS* issued by the administrative board of the USCC-NCCB. The commentary, it should be noted, is not a statement of the entire conference of bishops and was not represented as such. Strictly speaking, the administrative board is not and did not purport

contingent cooperation is the kind of cooperation without which the sinful act could still be performed. Example: Turning on the computer for a cyberthief who already possesses the computer password necessary to electronically access and steal from a bank account.

25 For an example see the *Catechism of the Catholic Church* (*CCC*), no. 2284.

to be a doctrinal authority. What is the weight of the authority of the commentary? It is simply an interpretative guide designed to help bishops interpret and apply the doctrine that is reaffirmed by the papal magisterium in the responsum. What is normative for the commentary is the doctrine as taught by the responsum. This is important to remember when determining the meaning of what the commentary says. As an interpretative guide the commentary in no way replaces the responsibility of the local bishops, who remain the sole authorities responsible for seeing that the doctrine of the Church is correctly interpreted and applied in their dioceses. It should be borne in mind there can be no question here of a "doctrinal contradiction" where the commentary is at odds with papal teaching or where the commentary would legitimate a partial or incomplete interpretation and application of the responsum. Whatever the ambiguities of the commentary, and I believe there are some, the administrative board certainly intended it to be faithful to the meaning of what is taught by the Pope in *QS*.

What does this commentary affirm? First of all, the commentary repeats the teaching contained in the responsum that " 'any sterilization which of itself, that is, of its own nature and condition, has the sole immediate effect of rendering the generative faculty incapable of procreation' is completely forbidden."[26] On the one hand, the commentary repeats the responsum's insistence that direct sterilization "[m]ay not be used as a means of contraception nor may it be used as a means for the care or prevention of physical or mental illness which is feared and foreseen as a result of pregnancy." On the other hand, the commentary does not reproduce the responsum's assertion that this holds true even if on the face of things, those whose actions are prompted by such health concerns have subjectively right intentions. This is an unfortunate omission. The commentary does go on to acknowledge that the responsum teaches that "no mandate of public authority can justify direct sterilization nor can the principle of totality be invoked."[27]

Next, the commentary notes that not all procedures that bring about sterility are always prohibited. The responsum did judge article 20 of the 1971 ERD to be a faithful expression of Church teaching. Article 20 states that procedures that cause sterility may be permitted when they are directed to the cure or prevention of a serious pathological condition and are not directly contraceptive and when a simpler treatment is not possible or "reasonably available."[28] The commentary goes on to reproduce the three principles given in article 3a–c of the responsum.

---

[26] All quotations from the commentary are taken from the text that appears in "Sterilization Policy for Catholic Hospitals," 399–400.

[27] Ibid., 399.

[28] ERD 6.

The commentary then suggests six guidelines for hospital policy. Guidelines 2, 4, and 6 are of particular interest here. Guideline 2 speaks specifically about duress: "Material cooperation will be justified only in situations where the hospital because of some kind of duress or pressure cannot reasonably exercise the autonomy it has (i.e., when it will do more harm than good)." Guideline 4 cautions that "[i]n judging the morality of cooperation a clear distinction should be made between the reason for sterilization and the reasons for cooperation. If the hospital cooperates because of the reason for the sterilization, e.g., because it is done for medical reasons, the cooperation can hardly be considered material. In other words the hospital can hardly maintain under these circumstances that it does not approve sterilizations done for medical reasons, and this would make cooperation formal." The commentary says that in order for cooperation to be material "the reason for cooperation must be something over and above the reason for sterilization itself." In other words, the reason for cooperation must not be for medical reasons but for some other external reason. This becomes clear in guideline 4, which says, "Direct sterilization is a grave evil. The allowance of material cooperation in extraordinary cases is based on the danger of an even more serious evil, e.g., the closing of the hospital could be under some circumstances a more serious evil."

Unlike *QS*, the commentary explicitly mentions duress and material cooperation. How is this to be understood?

The commentary certainly does not intend to go beyond or conflict with the doctrine of the Church as stated in the responsum. To interpret the commentary as arguing that duress justifies immediate material cooperation would be to put the commentary in direct conflict with the responsum. Therefore when the commentary speaks of duress and material cooperation, it must be understood as referring to mediate material cooperation. This holds too for distinctions made in guideline 4 between the reason for sterilization and the reason for cooperation. Again, the form of cooperation here has to do with infrequent mediate material cooperation.

There are some ambiguities in the commentary that make it open to misinterpretation especially when a reader reads it out of context, forgetting that the responsum norms the commentary. Two ambiguities might lead such a reader to misinterpret both the commentary and the responsum. First of all, only when the commentary directly quotes the responsum does it reproduce the responsum's clear assertion that direct sterilization is a matter that in the objective order is intrinsically evil. The commentary certainly does not deny this assertion and does say: "Direct sterilization is a grave evil." The reader can be left to wonder whether this is the same thing as an intrinsic evil. This can lead to a further misunderstanding when coupled with the omission of the responsum's point that direct sterilization is "absolutely forbidden" even when there are subjectively good intentions prompted by illness "which is foreseen or feared as a result of pregnancy." A clear affirmation that direct sterilization is an intrinsic evil, as stated in *QS*, is absolutely critical for understanding that direct sterilization always harms the ethical good of the human person, and that it is for this reason that immediate material cooperation (implicit formal cooperation) cannot be licit even under duress.

Secondly, although the commentary quotes the responsum's reference to material cooperation and the distinctions between proximate and remote, and necessary and free, it does not mention these distinctions in the guidelines that it offers. Again, when the responsum mentions these distinctions it alerts the careful reader to and emphasizes the fact that the material cooperation that it recognizes as valid is mediate material cooperation. The fact that the commentary fails to reproduce these important distinctions may lead some readers to think that what is permitted in some cases is immediate material cooperation under duress for grave proportionate reason.

None of this is to gainsay the fact that the administrative board of the USCC had every intention for the commentary to be a faithful interpretation of *QS*. The only purpose for pointing out these ambiguities is to show how the commentary could be misunderstood. It is important to remember, however, that any ambiguities in the commentary must be resolved in favor of the doctrine as taught in the responsum.

Therefore, I submit: to invoke the USCC commentary as a justification of immediate material cooperation under duress is to misunderstand both the commentary and the responsum, or worse, it involves thinking, however implicitly, that the commentary contradicts the responsum. To repeat: material cooperation with direct sterilization as mentioned in the commentary can only refer to mediate material cooperation.

The fact that the 1977 commentary on the responsum contained ambiguities that led to certain misinterpretations is shown by the fact that the NCCB thought it necessary to issue in July 1980 a clarification due to "a certain confusion with regard to the morality of tubal ligation as means of contraceptive sterilization."[29] The statement was drafted by the NCCB Committee on Doctrine and was approved by the bishops by mail. To my knowledge the margin of approval was not publically disclosed. The clarification, unlike the commentary, is issued as a statement not simply of the administrative board but in the name of the entire NCCB.

What is the weight of the authority of the clarification? It is an interpretative guide issued in the name of the bishops' conference and approved by

29 "NCCB Statement on Tubal Ligation," 175.

the bishops. The clarification in several of its statements and directives does repeat and express the doctrine of the Church as taught by the ordinary universal magisterium. The purpose of the clarification is to help bishops dispel the confusion surrounding the teaching of the Church. The clarification in no way usurps the responsibility and authority of the local ordinary for assuring that the moral teachings of the Church are correctly interpreted, taught, and followed in his diocese. The clarification itself in fact mentions this responsibility of the local bishop. It is also important to remember here that the doctrine as taught by the responsum is normative for the clarification.

Apart from giving a stricter interpretation of material cooperation, the clarification repeats the traditional teaching on sterilization. It states that (1) direct sterilization is objectively immoral even if performed for medical reasons; (2) the principle of totality cannot be invoked to justify sterilization; and (3) formal cooperation in contraceptive sterilization whether by approval or toleration for medical reasons, is forbidden and totally alien to the mission entrusted to Catholic healthcare facilities. In its fourth point the clarification explains that the reason given for justifying material cooperation in the commentary on the responsum

> refers not to the medical reasons given for the sterilization but to grave reasons extrinsic to the case. Catholic healthcare facilities in the United States complying with "Ethical and Religious Directives" are protected by the First Amendment from pressures intended to require material cooperation in contraceptive sterilization. In the unlikely and extraordinary situation in which the principle of material cooperation seems to be justified, consultation with the bishop or his delegate is required.[30]

This seems to be a stricter interpretation of material cooperation than the one given in the commentary because it says that such cooperation involves only grave reasons extrinsic to the case that are said to be "unlikely" and an "extraordinary situation." It is not possible to argue that the clarification somehow permits immediate material cooperation under duress for a proportionately grave reason in the case of direct sterilization. Again, we must recall that when the clarification speaks of material cooperation it means mediate material cooperation. Any other interpretation would put the clarification in direct conflict with the doctrine of the Church as taught by the responsum.

What about the 1994 ERD of the NCCB and what they say about immediate material cooperation under duress? First, it should be recalled

---

[30] Ibid.

that the ERD were issued with unanimous approval by the bishops of the United States in the name of the NCCB. The ERD state:

> The purpose of these ethical and religious directives then is twofold: first, to reaffirm the ethical standards of behavior in health care which flow from the church's teaching about the dignity of the human person; second, to provide authoritative guidance on certain moral issues which face Catholic health care today.[31]

An explanatory note that accompanied the 1994 ERD says that "at the annual meeting of the National Conference of Catholic Bishops the directives were approved as the national code, recommended for implementation by the diocesan bishop."

The ERD are authoritative because they express the Church's universal moral teaching (ordinary universal magisterium) in communion with the entire apostolic college together with its head, the pope, and because they offer guidelines that seek to apply this teaching according to the judgment of the NCCB.

The ERD give authoritative guidance on moral issues that confront Catholic healthcare in the United States at a time when there are dramatic changes in healthcare ministry. On the other hand, doctrinally the ERD teach nothing new. They do not represent an advance in the development of the moral doctrine of the Church. It should also be pointed out that not all parts of the ERD have the same weight of authority. For instance, the guidelines on cooperation contained in the appendix of the ERD does not have the same weight of authority behind it as the ERD's reaffirmation of the Church's teachings on direct sterilization, direct abortion, or its reaffirmation that healthcare facilities must treat their employees respectfully and justly. The latter expresses the moral teachings of the ordinary universal magisterium (the common teaching of the bishops and the pope), while the appendix's guidelines on cooperation do not. To be sure, the appendix is authoritative since it is part of the ERD approved by the bishops. But it cannot be equated with the authority of the moral doctrine of the Church as expressed elsewhere in the ERD. The appendix does not mark a doctrinal advance in the Magisterium's moral teaching. It is certainly subject to revision in the way that the Church's teachings on direct abortion and justice in the workplace are not.

It should also be observed that the ERD in no way supplants or substitutes for the local bishop's responsibility for insuring that healthcare ministry is practiced according to the moral teachings of the Church. The

---

[31] See the text in ERD 45.

ERD are "recommended for implementation by the diocesan bishop." The bishop, of course, remains the authoritative teacher of the Church's moral teaching in his diocese and the authoritative interpreter and implementer of the ERD.[32]

Having noted the level of the authority of the ERD, what should be concluded as to what they say about immediate material cooperation in the case of duress?

Even as an authentic magisterium of the NCCB, the ERD could not be (and were not) intended to be interpreted in such a way as to be in conflict with the teaching of the ordinary papal magisterium. Again, we must keep in mind that what is normative for the ERD in the case of the Church's teaching on sterilization is the responsum. When the appendix speaks of immediate material cooperation in some instances of duress, it cannot mean this with regard to acts that are intrinsically evil such as sterilization. This would put the ERD in conflict with the responsum that teaches, as we have seen, that sterilization is an intrinsically evil act and that only mediate material cooperation is permissible in some cases. Another reason why it is mistaken to interpret what the appendix of the ERD says about immediate material cooperation and duress as applicable to intrinsically evil acts is that such an interpretation would put the ERD in contradiction with what *VS* teaches about intrinsic evil. In number 81 of that encyclical we read:

> If acts are intrinsically evil, a good intention or particular circumstances can diminish their evil, but they cannot remove it. They remain "irremediably" evil acts; per se and in themselves they are not capable of being ordered to God and to the good of the person. . . . Consequently, circumstances or intentions can never transform an act intrinsically evil by virtue of its object into an act "subjectively" good or defensible as a choice.

Understood in this way, duress is nothing more than a circumstance of the moral object and as such can never transform the intrinsically evil act into something "capable of being ordered to God and the good of the

---

32 The 1998 apostolic letter from Pope John Paul II, *Apostolos Suos* (which adds new canons to the *Code of Canon Law*), has affirmed: "Bishops, whether individually or united in Conference, cannot autonomously limit their own sacred power in favor of the Episcopal Conference, and even less can they do so in favor of one of its parts, whether the permanent council or a commission or the president." See *Apostolos Suos*, no. 20. The logic of this teaching and law of the Church follows from an understanding of Church as a communion. For the full text of this apostolic letter, see *Origins* 28 (July 30, 1998): 152–58.

person." It follows therefore that immediate material cooperation in intrinsically evil acts is impermissible even in the presence of duress.[33] I conclude then that the appendix of the ERD cannot be invoked to justify immediate material cooperation under duress for grave proportionate reason with regard to direct sterilization.

Let us return to the representative case proposed by Keenan. In that case, the Catholic healthcare facilities by its approval of the contract with the obstetrics team would give permission for a limited number of direct sterilizations. But this means that the Catholic healthcare facility would be permitting immoral actions that are intrinsically evil. It means that these healthcare facilities would be giving what the responsum says cannot be given: an official approbation of direct sterilization in its management and execution in accord with its regulations. No matter how much a Catholic healthcare facility says that it does not "approve" of direct sterilization, no matter how few direct sterilizations are permitted, the fact remains that the Catholic healthcare facility contractually permits acts that can never be ordered to God or the good of the person to take place on its campus. The opinion that under the duress of losing its services a Catholic healthcare facility can contractually permit direct sterilization cannot be reconciled with the moral doctrine of the Church, as a careful reading of the responsum shows.

Conclusion: A Question of Communion

The proper interpretation of the teaching of the Church is important for a local church whose bishop is charged with the responsibility of seeing that his church lives fully in union with the life of the universal Church. Obviously the work of a Catholic healthcare facility takes place within a local church and makes an indispensable contribution to its life and mission. If Keenan's claim about immediate material cooperation under the presence of duress with regard to direct sterilization was adopted by a Catholic healthcare facility—such as the one Keenan describes in his scenario—it would be acting contrary to Church teaching, and thus would be harming the efforts of the local church to live in communion with the universal Church.

Questions of institutional cooperation that confront Catholic healthcare facilities have an ecclesial context, and that context ought to be seen as the Church understood as a communion. Recent theological works and documents of the Magisterium have, rightly, drawn attention to the fact

---

[33] Father Kevin O'Rourke has criticized the views of Keenan precisely on this point. See "A Brief Response to Father Keenan," *Ethics and Medics* 23 (September 1998): 3–4.

that Vatican II's understanding of the Church as a communion is a, if not *the*, central idea of the Council's documents.[34]

In an ecclesiology of communion the universal Church is the communion of particular churches. In and through the particular churches the universal Church is present and concrete in the world. On the other hand, each particular church only exists fully as Church in the universal Church. This or that local church is not complete or self-sufficient by itself.[35] A local church is only fully ecclesial to the extent that it lives according to the universal bonds of ecclesial unity, that is, in the common faith, life, and worship of the Church, and including of course the principle of apostolic succession. Only in this way can the universal Church with all her essential elements be present and be recognized in any given local church. If any one of these elements is partially absent or absent altogether then what results is a state of impaired communion with the universal Church. Communion is not only a gift but an unfinished task that a local church will constantly be striving and struggling to achieve. As the visible principles of unity in their churches, bishops are agents of communion who seek to insure that their churches are living in communion with the universal Church. Understood in this way a bishop—who is in communion with all the other bishops of

34 For example see Jean-Marie R. Tillard, *Church of Churches: The Ecclesiology of Communion* (Collegeville, MN: Liturgical Press, 1992) [French original, *Église d'Églises: l'ecclesiologie de communion* (Paris: Cerf, 1987)]; Walter Kasper, "The Church as Communion: Reflections on the Guiding Ecclesiology Idea of the Second Vatican Council" in *Church and Theology* (New York: Crossroad, 1992); Miguel Garijo-Guembe, *Communion of the Saints* (Collegeville, MN: Liturgical Press, 1994) [German original, *Gemeinschaft die Heiligen: Grund, Wesen und Structur der Kirche* (Patmos Verlag, 1988)]; Joseph Ratzinger, *Called to Communion*, trans. Adrian Walker (San Francisco: Ignatius Press, 1996); Jerome Hamer, *The Church Is a Communion*, trans. Ronald Matthews (New York: Sheed and Ward, 1964) [French original, *L'Église est une communion* (Paris: Les Éditions du Cerf, 1962)]. The final report of the 1985 extraordinary synod of bishops observed: "The ecclesiology of communion is the central and fundamental idea of the council's documents." See "The Final Report," *Origins* 15 (December 19, 1986): 448. More recently see CDF, in its Letter to the Bishops of the Catholic Church on Some Aspects of the Church Understood as a Communion, *Origins* 22 (June 25, 1992): 108–12.

35 This is what some theologians call the mutual interiority of the Church. See for example Henri de Lubac, *The Motherhood of the Church*, trans. Sister Sergia Englund, O.C.D. (San Francisco: Ignatius Press, 1982), 201; de Lubac cites Yves Congar, "La collégialité de l'épiscopat et la primaute de l'évêque de Rome dans l'Histoire," *Angelicum* 47 (1970): 403–27. On the mutual interiority of the Church see CDF, "Some Aspects of the Church Understood as a Communion," which points out the formula of the Second Vatican Council: "The Church in and formed out of the Churches is inseparable from another formula: The Churches in and formed out of the Church" (109).

the world and with the pope—is the visible sign that a local church lives in communion with the universal Church.

If we understand the Church in this way, we can see that when a Catholic healthcare facility is faced with questions of licit and illicit cooperation it is also faced with the question of whether it will contribute to the efforts of a local or particular church to live in communion with the whole Church. What a Catholic healthcare facility decides about cooperation can advance or harm the work of a local church to insure that the universal Church is recognizable and fully present in all of the activities of the local church. When theologians, ethicists, and ethics boards help Catholic healthcare facilities determine whether and how much cooperation should be supplied, they should be careful to present such a question in its ecclesial context. In other words, they will situate questions of cooperation in the broader context of the Catholic healthcare facility as part of the local church engaged in the task of achieving communion with the universal Church. It is against this background that we can fully appreciate why consultation with the bishop—the visible principle of unity and communion—is so emphasized in recent Church documents. The danger is very real and great that if questions of licit and illicit cooperation—particularly in cases that involve actions that the Church has judged to be intrinsically evil—are not seen in the context of an ecclesiology of communion, then certain moral norms are more apt to be seen as mere legal rules extrinsically imposed from the outside, instead of norms proclaimed by the universal Church that promote the following of Christ and the dignity of the human person.

Postscript

After the publication of my criticism of his position Father James Keenan, S.J., wrote a reply to it.[36] Keenan objected that I had interpreted the responsum too strictly and that he saw no warrant for an *a priori* prohibition of immediate material cooperation under duress regardless of an institution's survival. I replied to Keenan,[37] arguing that the application of this form of cooperation was ruled out by the responsum's teaching that direct sterilization is an intrinsic evil and that as such, it always without exception harms a person. In my response I also drew attention to the correspondence between Joseph Cardinal Ratzinger, then prefect of the CDF,

[36] James Keenan, "Not an Excessive Claim, Nor a Divisive One, But a Traditional One: A Response to Lawrence Welch on Immediate Material Cooperation," *Linacre Quarterly* 67 (November 2000): 83–88.

[37] Lawrence J. Welch, "Direct Sterilization: An Intrinsically Evil Act: A Rejoinder to Fr. Keenan," *Linacre Quarterly* 68 (May 2001): 124–30.

and then NCCB's president Bishop Joseph Fiorenza. In that correspondence the CDF indicated its concern that the appendix to the ERD explaining the principles of cooperation could be used to conclude that intrinsically evil acts could be considered permissible if duress were present. The CDF cautioned that such a position was irreconcilable with the teaching of the Church. Thus, I concluded that my interpretation of *QS* was not too restrictive as Keenan had alleged.

Events in 2001, after the publication of my articles, further vindicated my interpretation of the 1976 responsum of the CDF. In 2001, with encouragement of the Holy See, the NCCB (now called the USCCB [United Catholic Conference of Bishops]) revised the 1994 ERD.[38] The bishops stated that the revisions were offered to assist Catholic healthcare organizations in analyzing the moral soundness of cooperative ventures and partnership with non-Catholic entities. Among the revisions was the following (directive 70): "Catholic health care organizations are not permitted to engage in immediate material cooperation in actions that are intrinsically immoral, such as abortion, euthanasia, assisted suicide, and direct sterilization." The appendix of the 1994 ERD, which tried to explain and articulate the principles of cooperation, was deleted because according to the bishops, experience showed that they "did not sufficiently forestall certain possible misinterpretations and in practice gave rise to problems in concrete applications of the principles."

Directive 70 of the revised ERD prohibits immediate material cooperation in actions that are intrinsically immoral. But this is something nearly everyone agrees on. I know of no ethicist or theologian who holds that Catholic healthcare organizations can engage in immediate material cooperation (implicit formal cooperation) in intrinsically evil actions. Moralists such as Father Keenan appealed to immediate material cooperation under duress. It was precisely this appeal to duress that was used to justify Catholic healthcare organizations allowing sterilizations in their facilities. At the press conference explaining the revised ERD, Archbishop Pilarcyzk stated that Catholic healthcare organizations cannot engage in immediate material cooperation even for reasons of duress. The Archbishop's remarks clarify the intention of the bishops in directive 70, but nevertheless the language of the directive says nothing about duress and gives no guidance on the issue. It does not contain specific and explicit language that makes it clear that the presence of duress does not justify immediate material cooperation. The bishops certainly saw the need for clarifying the ERD so that they cannot be interpreted in such as way as to permit direct sterilizations

---

38 *Origins* 31(July 19, 2001); www.usccb.org/bishops/directives.shtml.

in Catholic healthcare facilities or healthcare facilities managed by Catholic institutions. In the end, the revisions do not seem to give enough clarification or guidance to accomplish this goal.

Another way in which the revised ERD do not offer enough clarification is the absence of any written guidance concerning the principles of cooperation. The bishops decided to drop the appendix to the ERD explaining the principles of cooperation because it was open to unforeseen misinterpretations and misapplications. But in its place the bishops simply counseled that "[r]eliable theological experts should be consulted in interpreting and applying the principles of cooperation." The problem here is that if there is confusion about the correct interpretation of the principles of cooperation then what is needed from the bishops is more, not less guidance. One theologian, Father Kevin McMahon, has observed that leaving the proper interpretation of the principles to theologians is liable to result in more differing and erroneous interpretations that the revised ERD are meant to prevent.[39] Why should the bishops turn to others for an explanation of the principles of cooperation if they want to forestall misinterpretations? As Father McMahon points out supplying an explanation of the principles that the bishops invoke in the ERD is essential for the proper formation of consciences.[40] By choosing to omit an explanation of the principles of cooperation in the revised ERD, the bishops missed a teaching opportunity.

In my judgment, the revised ERD are still too easy to misinterpret and are not sufficient for preventing the unjustifiable cooperation of Catholic healthcare institutions in direct sterilizations. Some events after the revisions of the ERD appear to confirm this judgment. For example, in 2008, bishops in ten dioceses within the state of Texas found it necessary to begin a process of verifying whether some local hospitals were faithfully adhering to the ERD with regard to direct sterilization and other prohibited procedures. The bishops took this action after some researchers released a report—based on data available to the public—that appeared to show that direct sterilizations were still taking place in some Catholic hospitals.[41] On November 21, 2008, Bishop Alvaro Corrado, S.J., bishop of Tyler, Texas, released a statement on the matter of direct sterilizations in Catholic hospitals in the diocese. Bishop Corrado said that there had been a serious misinterpretation of the ERD in both Catholic hospitals in his diocese and

[39] Kevin T. McMahon, "Revising the ERDs '94: Goals, Opposition and Resolution," *Linacre Quarterly* 68 (May 2001): 116.

[40] Ibid.

[41] See "Texas Bishops Examine Reports of Ethical Lapses at Catholic Hospitals" and "Ongoing Confusion," *Our Sunday Visitor* (July 13, 2008): 3 and 12, respectively. The last story reports: "Trinity Mother Frances spokesman John Moore said their

that many direct sterilizations had been done. The bishop expressed his sadness that the sterilizations had taken place and stated that "I have to admit my failure to provide adequate oversight of the Catholic Hospitals as regards their protection of the sacred dignity of each human person."[42]

On February 15, 2010, Robert Vasa, bishop of the diocese of Baker, Oregon announced that he was ending formal Catholic sponsorship of St. Charles Medical Center-Bend. Bishop Vasa stated that the reason for his action was because the healthcare facility refused to adhere to Catholic teaching on direct sterilization. St. Charles Medical Center-Bend provides tubal ligations for patients and stated its disagreement with Bishop Vasa on the meaning of the ERDs. In a statement released to the media Bishop Vasa explained, "It would be misleading for me to allow St. Charles Bend to be acknowledged as Catholic in name while I am certain that some important tenets of the Ethical and Religious Directives are no longer being observed."[43]

---

hospital observes the ERD and provides only 'medically necessary sterilization' . . . which he said are necessitated by conditions such as cancer, heart disease and obesity." These reasons, of course, are not exceptions permitted in the ERDs or in Catholic morality.

42 *Catholic East Texas* newspaper (November 21, 2008).

43 See www.ktvz.com/Global/story.asp?S=11987340.

CHAPTER 6

Lumen Gentium, Number 8, and *Subsistit in*, Again*

IN LIGHT OF recent documents from the Congregation of the Doctrine of the Faith (CDF), Francis A. Sullivan has expounded his view again on the interpretation of *Lumen Gentium* (*LG*), number 8, and what it means to say about the Church of Christ subsists in the Catholic Church.[1] Sullivan says that the one Church of Christ continues to exist perfectly in the Catholic Church, and is present imperfectly in other churches and ecclesial communities. However, he thinks *LG* 8 also enables us to say that the many churches, non-Catholic and Catholic, are all in the one Church of Christ, since to say the one Church of Christ subsists in the Catholic Church means no more than "continues to exist in" the Catholic Church. In this way, he denies the identity of the one Church of Christ with the Catholic Church. We argue that while it is true there is "ecclesial reality" outside the Catholic Church, in that there are elements of truth and sanctification outside of her, the one Church of Christ of which the Second Vatican Council expressly speaks is the Church with all the gifts of unity and all the instruments for salvation with which Christ endowed her. The Catholic Church is not contained in any larger divinely willed and dominically instituted ecclesial reality; she is without qualification the one Church of Christ, and the one Church of Christ is without qualification

---

* A version of this essay appeared in Lawrence J. Welch and Guy Mansini, O.S.B, "*Lumen Gentium* No. 8, and *Subsistit in*, Again," *New Blackfriars* 90 (September 2009): 602–17.

[1] Francis A. Sullivan, S.J., "The Meaning of *Subsistit in* as Explained by the Congregation for the Doctrine of the Faith," *Theological Studies* 69 (2008): 116–24. See his earlier "A Response to Karl Becker, S.J., on the Meaning of *Subsistit in*," *Theological Studies* 67 (2006): 395–409.

the Catholic Church. In what follows, we first state Sullivan's view as we understand it. Second, we try to show why it is unsatisfactory.

Sullivan's Position

Point 1. For Sullivan the non-identity of the Church of Christ with the Catholic Church depends very much on how one understands *subsistere.* It depends, he holds, on taking *subsistere*, with Karl Becker, to mean "to remain, to be perpetuated in."[2] He thinks that if *subsistere* is given a more philosophical sense, such that one is warranted in speaking of one "subsistence" of the Church of Christ and according to which *LG* 8 would mean that in the Catholic Church the Church of Christ has " 'being' in the form of an independent agent" (quoting Ratzinger), or such that one is warranted in saying that "there is only one subsistence" of the Church of Christ, and that in the Catholic Church (quoting the CDF), then it is impossible to maintain (coherently, anyway) the non-identity of the Church of Christ with the Catholic Church, and that it is impossible (coherently) to speak of other churches outside the Catholic Church.[3] Therefore, since *LG* 15 does speak of separated churches (as does *Unitatis Redintegratio* [*UR*], the Decree on Ecumenism, number 15), and since we presume coherence, *subsistere* must mean "continues to exist in." It cannot mean "has its concrete existence in"—these formulations are very different for Sullivan.

His argument for this last point is as follows: "If it is in the Catholic Church that the church of Christ 'is concretely found on earth,'[4] how could

---

[2] Sullivan, "The Meaning of *Subsistit in*," 117–18; idem, "Response to Karl Becker," 396–97; Karl Becker, "The Church and Vatican II's '*Subsistit in*' Terminology," *Origins* 35 (January 19, 2006): 514–22, at 519. This article first appeared in *L'Osservatore Romano* (December 4–5, 2006).

[3] Sullivan, "The Meaning of *Subsistit in*," 118, 121; idem, "Response to Karl Becker," 408. See Joseph Cardinal Ratzinger, "The Ecclesiology of the Constitution *Lumen Gentium*," in *Pilgrim Fellowship of Faith: The Church as Communion* (San Francisco: Ignatius Press, 2005), 123–52, at 147 (he also says "concrete agent"). For the CDF's Notification of March 11, 1985, on Leonardo Boff's *Church, Charism, and Power* (New York: Crossroad, 1985), see *AAS* 77 (1985): 756–62, at 758–59: "Il Concilio aveva . . . schelto la parola 'Subsistit' proprio per chiarire che esiste una sola 'sussistenza' della vera Chiesa, mentre fuori della sua compagine visibile esistono solo 'elementa Ecclesiae' che—essendo elementi della stessa chiesa—tendono e conducono verso la Chiesa cattolica." Sullivan, "The Meaning of *Subsistit in*," 117, 118, links talk of "one subsistence" to the German translation of *LG* 8, "hat ihre konkrete Existenzform in" ("has its concrete form of existence in").

[4] This is the claim of the CDF in "Responses to Some Questions regarding Certain Aspects of the Doctrine of the Church" (June 29, 2007), at question 2; see *Origins* 37 (2007): 134–36, at 135.

there be any concretely existing 'true particular churches' except the particular Catholic churches?"[5] The argument seems to be that, if the Church of Christ is "concrete" only in the Catholic Church, then not only can it not be "concrete" in non-Catholic churches, but these "churches" cannot even really be churches. How does this conclusion follow? He seems to be supposing that a particular, concrete church, in order to be a church, must be contained within the concrete Church of Christ. Thus, if only the Catholic Church is this Church of Christ, concretely, then all other non-Catholic "churches" are both outside the Church of Christ and not even really churches.

Point 2. Sullivan thus thinks that *subsistere* does in fact mean "continues to exist in," and not "has its concrete existence in," although he grants that of course the Church of Christ exists fully only in the Catholic Church. He would allow us to say, further, that while the Church of Christ subsists in non-Catholic churches, it does not do so fully or perfectly.[6]

Point 3. Sullivan thinks as well that saying that "elements of sanctification and truth" are to be found outside the Catholic Church is compatible with recognizing that there are true particular churches outside the Catholic Church. But he thinks saying that "only elements of sanctification and truth" exist outside the Catholic Church is not compatible with saying that there are true particular churches outside the Catholic Church. Saying "only elements" is therefore equivalent to saying that the Church of Christ "has its concrete existence" only in the Catholic Church. Since this is false, we should not say "only elements," and the CDF misspoke in its Notification on Leonardo Boff in 1985.[7]

Point 4. Sullivan thinks it true to say that the Church of Christ "continues to exist in," is "present and operative in," the non-Catholic churches (and ecclesial communities), although of course it exists fully only in the Catholic Church.[8] He thinks this way of speaking fits with saying the

---

5 Sullivan, "The Meaning of *Subsistit in*," 121; similarly, "if the church of Christ 'has its concrete existence' in the Catholic Church, and therefore the Catholic Church is its 'one and only subsistence,' it would follow that outside the Catholic Church there can be no other churches, but only 'elements of church'" (ibid., 118); idem, "Response to Karl Becker," 403.

6 Sullivan, "The Meaning of *Subsistit in*," 120, 121; idem, "Response to Karl Becker," 403. The Church of Christ is present in non-Catholic churches and ecclesial communities to the extent that elements of sanctification and truth are present in them, see John Paul II, *Ut Unum Sint*, no. 11.

7 Sullivan, "The Meaning of *Subsistit in*," 118; idem, "Response to Karl Becker," 407–8; idem, *The Church We Believe In*, 30–31.

8 Sullivan, "The Meaning of *Subsistit in*," 119–20; idem, "Response to Karl Becker," 407–8.

Church of Christ "continues to exist in" the Catholic Church, but not with saying it "has its concrete existence in" the Catholic Church, for with the latter sense, remember, for Sullivan, there are no churches outside the Catholic Church, and so no churches outside the Catholic Church for the one Church of Christ to be operative in.

Point 5. Sullivan thinks that, because *subsistere* means what he says it does (and because it is not true that only elements exist outside the Catholic Church), then the one Church of Christ can be said to be "in and from" all of the particular churches, Catholic and non-Catholic.[9]

Point 6. He thinks this is implied by *UR* 15, too.[10] If one says that *subsistere* means "subsistence" in the philosophical sense, however, one cannot say this.

Why Sullivan's Position Is Unsatisfactory

The Church is not formed out of non-Catholic churches (ad 5). We begin with the fifth point. Sullivan wants to say that the universal Church, the one Church founded by Christ, is both in and formed from churches that are not in communion with Rome. He argues from *LG* 23, which teaches that the universal Church is both present in and formed from particular churches. Then, he notes that Eastern churches are recognized as churches by the Council and in post-conciliar documents. Therefore he concludes that the universal Church is formed out of both Catholic and non-Catholic churches. In this way, the universal Church, the Church founded by Christ, is a container within which both the Catholic Church and the Eastern churches are encompassed. Moreover, this recognition that non-Catholic churches are churches and compose the one Church of Christ is the very reason, according to Sullivan, that the Council said "subsists in," and not "is" in *LG* 8. This asserts, and was meant to assert, the non-identity of the Catholic Church and the universal Church, the Church founded by Christ.

However, Sullivan's use of *LG* 23 is illegitimate. *Lumen Gentium*, number 23, is speaking of Catholic particular churches, Catholic dioceses. The universal Church, the Church founded by Christ, is both present in them and comprised of them, that is, comes from them: "in and from which churches comes into being the one and only Catholic Church."[11] That is, it

[9] Sullivan, "The Meaning of *Subsistit in*," 123.

[10] Sullivan, "Response to Karl Becker, 406–7.

[11] Here is the statement in context: "This collegial union is apparent also in the mutual relations of the individual bishops with particular churches and with the universal Church. The Roman Pontiff, as the successor of Peter, is the perpetual and visible principle and foundation of unity of both the bishops and of the faithful.

is from Catholic dioceses, each of which recognizes the primacy of Peter, each of which enjoys that catholic unity willed by Christ the founder (*UR* 3),[12] that the one, universal Church is constituted, constituted in the very way Christ constituted it, and with all the endowments with which he graced it.

However, the Eastern churches cannot be said to be particular churches from which the universal Church is similarly constituted. For these churches do not recognize the primacy of Peter, which *UR* 3 envisages as one of the means of salvation with which the Church of Christ is endowed.[13] And therefore, the universal Church, the Church founded by Christ, constituted in the very way he constituted it, is certainly not formed out of them. The Church founded by Christ, continuing to exist as he founded it, can be formed only from churches that preserve the unity he gave to it—Catholic unity—and from churches that embrace the Petrine ministry as Catholics understand it, for the Church Christ founded he entrusted to Peter and his successors.

The appeal to UR *15 (ad 6).* In number 15 of the Decree on Ecumenism, the Eastern churches seem to be spoken of as comprising the one Church. It is Sullivan's inference that they are so spoken of. However, we think the inference he draws does not follow as simply and necessarily from the text as he seems to think.

The individual bishops, however, are the visible principle and foundation of unity in their particular churches, fashioned after the model [*ad imaginem*] of the universal Church, in and from which churches comes into being the one and only Catholic Church. For this reason the individual bishops represent each his own church, but all of them together and with the Pope represent the entire Church in the bond of peace, love and unity." All quotations in this chapter of the documents of the Second Vatican Council are taken from www.vatican.va.

12 "Nevertheless, our separated brethren, whether considered as individuals or as Communities and Churches, are not blessed with that unity which Jesus Christ wished to bestow on all those who through Him were born again into one body, and with Him quickened to newness of life—that unity which the Holy Scriptures and the ancient Tradition of the Church proclaim. For it is only through Christ's Catholic Church, which is 'the all-embracing means of salvation,' that they can benefit fully from the means of salvation. We believe that Our Lord entrusted all the blessings of the New Covenant to the apostolic college alone, of which Peter is the head, in order to establish the one Body of Christ on earth to which all should be fully incorporated who belong in any way to the people of God. This people of God, though still in its members liable to sin, is ever growing in Christ during its pilgrimage on earth, and is guided by God's gentle wisdom, according to His hidden designs, until it shall happily arrive at the fullness of eternal glory in the heavenly Jerusalem." Cf. *Dominus Iesus*, no. 17; CDF, "Letter to the Bishops of the Catholic Church on Some Aspects of the Church Understood as Communion," no. 17.

13 Sullivan recognizes just this point in *The Church We Believe In*, 52.

Yes, it seems that the Eastern churches and the Catholic Church are spoken of at least indirectly as comprising the one Church of God (*UR* 15): "Through the celebration of the Eucharist of the Lord in each of these [Eastern] Churches, the Church of God is built up and grows in stature." For the Eucharist certainly builds up the particular church, and if in doing that it is building up the one Church of God, how can that particular church not in some way help comprise the one Church of God?

The answer is that they might "comprise" it only "imperfectly," which would be an attempt to say what is better said in other language: that they are in only imperfect communion with the one Church of God as founded by Christ. Thus, it should be said that the Eucharist of the Eastern churches can certainly build up the one Church of God, even if the Church of Christ does not subsist in them. Why must we put things this way? If the one Church established by Christ subsisted in the Eastern Orthodox churches, we would find in them all the things Christ gave the Church he established. However, we do not; for we do not find the ministry of Peter exercised in them. Therefore, we cannot speak of the one Church of Christ as subsisting in them.

What we can do is take the language the Council used for individuals, speaking of "full incorporation" and therefore implying that there are degrees of incorporation (*LG* 14; *UR* 3), and use it of separated churches.[14] If however we say that these churches are simply "incorporated," or "fully incorporated" into the Church of Christ, then, like saying the Church of Christ subsists in them, we will imply that the Petrine ministry can both be and not be recognized as belonging to the Church established by Christ. In still other words, we can speak of these churches as in "imperfect communion" with the Catholic Church, as does *Ut Unum Sint*, number 11. We can speak, as Sullivan does, of degrees of "theological communion."[15] This way of speaking both preserves the uniqueness of the

---

14 This way of speaking elides the question of membership as classically posed by such theologians as Robert Bellarmine and Francisco Suarez, for whom membership was an "all or nothing question." Walter Cardinal Kasper has pointed out that careful attention to the conciliar acts and to the various redactions of *LG* prior to final approval show that the word *membrum* was intentionally dropped and replaced by the expressions *plene incorporare* (*LG* 14) and *coniungere* (*LG* 15). These changes were made for ecumenical reasons because it was thought that the notion *membrum* was incapable of expressing sufficiently the various degrees and levels of intensity of belonging to the Church. It was Cardinal Augustin Bea who persuaded the Council Fathers that *LG* should use terminology open to various nuances of belonging to the Church. See "Canon Law and Ecumenism," *The Jurist* 69 (2009): 171–89.

15 Sullivan, *The Church We Believe In*, 57, 60.

Catholic Church as the only place where the Church of Christ continues to be found in its wholeness and respects the real relation of separated churches and non-Catholic Christians to the Catholic Church.

Thus, it is important that the way of speaking in *UR* is only indirect. The Council nowhere says directly that the one Church of Christ, the universal Church, is composed of Catholic and non-Catholic particular churches. It nowhere gives the impression that the universal Church is being thought of as a container in which all the churches (and much less all the ecclesial communities) are placed in the same way.

The Catholic Church is not contained (*ad 2*). If we say that the one Church is formed out of Catholic and non-Catholic churches, therefore, we are thinking of the one Church as a container, within which there is, among other things, the Catholic Church. This is the direction in which Sullivan's articles seem to lead. The magisterial documents since the Council have consistently refused this proposal, and have instead spoken of the one Church being present or operative, according to degrees, in non-Catholic churches and communities. The implications of the first way of speaking are worth developing.

If we say the one Church founded by Christ is formed out of Catholic and non-Catholic churches and ecclesial communities, then it is possible to be in one part of it, some non-Catholic part, and not discover things like the papacy or the sacrament of orders or the sacrament of reconciliation. And yet, one is supposed to be in the one Church established by Christ. Can this one Church both have and not have a Petrine office? We will, perhaps, seek more simply for the things held in common. Such things as the Petrine office, then, do not necessarily belong to the one Church established by Christ. They might be thought to be for the *bene esse*, but not the *esse* of the Church. If this is not acceptable, however, then it is not acceptable to think of the one Church as a container in which, among other things, there is also the Catholic Church.

Then again, if non-Catholic churches and communities are in the one Church, then it would seem not only that their members have a real and positive relation to the Church of Christ, but that they simply and without qualification are incorporated in this one Church. It would seem, in other words, as if the talk of degrees of incorporation enabled by the Council is unnecessary—all Christians of whatever communion are fully incorporated in the one Church.

The Church of Christ is operative in non-Catholic churches and communities (ad 4). It is indeed legitimate to say, as Sullivan wants, that the universal

Church, the Church founded by Christ, is present and operative in non-Catholic churches (and ecclesial communities).[16] But it is not legitimate to say, we have argued, that the universal Church, the one Church founded by Christ, is formed "from" them.

However, we should observe that saying that the Church of Christ is in or operative in non-Catholic churches is the same thing as saying that the Catholic Church is in or operative in them,[17] if indeed the Church of Christ—the Church as founded by Christ—is formed out of particular Catholic churches, and those alone (since those alone have all gifts with which Christ endowed the Church).

As we have said, Sullivan thinks that the Council could not have said "churches" in *LG* 15 if "only elements" were said (as it was not in fact said) or meant (as we think the case, see below) in *LG* 8. Now, when *LG* 15 speaks of the Church's relation to non-Catholics, it says that the Church recognizes the sacraments they receive in "their own churches." The "their own" (*propriis*) seems significant. "Their own" is not "our." Since the churches of these non-Catholics are "their own," it cannot be supposed that the Church is being thought of as relating to some part of herself. That is what would follow, however, if the Church of Christ subsists in the Catholic Church and the Church is comprised of all groups that are called "churches." So, since the first is undeniable, the second must be false; and

16 *Ut Unum Sint*, no. 11. It might be noted that this passage seems to assume quite naturally the identity of the Church of Christ and the Catholic Church: "To the extent that these elements are found in other Christian Communities, the one Church of Christ is effectively present in them. For this reason the Second Vatican Council speaks of a certain, though imperfect communion. The Dogmatic Constitution *Lumen Gentium* [no. 14] stresses that the Catholic Church 'recognizes that in many ways she is linked' with these Communities by a true union in the Holy Spirit."

17 *UR* 3 seems to have something of this point in mind, which is easier to see in the Latin text: "Proinde ipsae Ecclesiae et Communitates seiunctae, etsi defectus illas pati credimus, nequaquam in mysterio salutis significatione et pondere exutae sunt. Iis enim Spiritus Christi uti non renuit tamquam salutis mediis, quorum virtus derivatur ab ipsa plenitudine gratiae et veritatis *quae Ecclesiae catholicae concredita est.*" The same point is apparent in the official English translation, although less so because it drops the word *catholicae* in reference to the Church. Walter Abbot—whose own translation is more faithful to the Latin—notes that the word *catholicae* was inserted into the Latin text at the insistence of Pope Paul VI. See Abbot, *Documents of Vatican II*, 346n17. The official English translation published on www.vatican.va is as follows: "It follows that the separated Churches and Communities as such, though we believe them to be deficient in some respects, have been by no means deprived of significance and importance in the mystery of salvation. For the Spirit of Christ has not refrained from using them as means of salvation which derive their efficacy from the very fullness of grace and truth entrusted to the Church."

calling the Eastern churches "churches" does not mean that in *LG* 15 the Council thinks the Church is speaking of parts of herself.

That it is not incorrect to represent the Council's teaching by saying that "only elements" exist outside the Church (ad 3). When Sebastian Tromp proposed to the rest of the Doctrinal Commission that the text say that the Church of Christ subsists in the Catholic Church rather than that it is the Catholic Church, he said at the same time that this is meant "exclusively," and that "only elements" are found outside the one Church.[18] The text of *LG* says merely that "elements" (not "only elements") exist outside the Church. As we have seen, Sullivan thinks this difference is important. For him, to say "only elements" as Tromp does would mean nothing can be called a church except the Catholic Church. This can seem plausible. For the 1962 schema, which has the *est*, remember, says that only the Catholic Church can be rightly (*iure*) called "Church." Contrariwise, the text that first introduces *subsistit in*, and says "elements" (but not "only elements"), in speaking of non-Catholics says that their sacraments are received "in their churches or ecclesial communities," and this survives to the final text at *LG* 15.[19] On the other hand, and to the contrary, when the Commission defends this usage, it says that it is right to say "churches" because the *elementa* that the Catholic Church recognizes as possessed by non-Catholics "not only regard individuals but also communities," and goes on to remark that "pontifical documents speak generally of the separated Eastern 'churches.' "[20] The "elements" were understood from the beginning to be possessed by individuals and also by communities. Thus, it seems that for the Commission, anyway, saying simply "elements," and even saying "only elements," would not mean another group cannot be called a church.[21]

It can be observed that the text of 1962, where it is said that only the Catholic Church can rightly be called "Church" means, in context, the Church given over by Christ to be ruled by Peter and his successors. That is, it means "the Church founded by Christ and as founded by Christ."

---

18 Becker, "The Church," 517.

19 See Francisco Gil Hellín, *Lumen Gentium. Constitutio Dogmatica de Ecclesia Concilii Vaticani II Synopsis in ordinem redigens schemata cum relationibus necnon patrum orationes atque animadversiones* (Vatican City: Libreria Editrice Vaticana, 1995), the third schema, at nos. 7 and 15.

20 Ibid., third schema at no. 15, note D: "Elementa . . . non tantum individuos respiciunt, sed etiam communitates. . . . Documenta pontificia passim de 'Ecclesiis' orientalibus separatis loquuntur."

21 Sullivan quotes this text twice in "Response to Karl Becker" (400, 401), but does not seem to notice that saying "elements" supposes such things as he thinks can be indicated only by saying "ecclesial elements" or "churches."

There is a certain sense, therefore, in saying that only that Church can rightly (*iure*) be called "Church." That is, in context, what is being spoken of is the Church of Christ with all the instruments of sanctification he gave it, and with the unity he desired for it.[22]

What it means to call the churches "churches" and ecclesial communities "ecclesial" (ad 5). For the churches, it is necessary to recall the observation of Henri de Lubac that the Church makes the Eucharist and the Eucharist makes the Church.[23] Wherever there is a full and valid celebration of the Eucharist, therefore, there must be a "church." Defects there may be, of either the theological or moral order, or both, but it cannot be that while "the whole treasure of the Church" is made present at Mass and the assembly there gathered is "called" to its Lord, we yet refuse to say "church."

As for "ecclesial" communities in which "elements" of the Church were recognized, we have forgotten how liberating these words were at the time of the Council, since the distinction between such communities and the Church preserved the sense that, after all, we are bound to confess that it is the Lord who by his gifts defines the Church in her fullness and perfection, and so defines what counts as "Church," and yet, at the same time, can recognize and name those elements of Protestant communions that really are from the Church, really do lead to the Church, really do have their efficacy from the Church, and so provide a basis from properly ecumenical discussion between Christian bodies. As the Doctrinal Commission said in explaining that the *elementa* regard communities, "precisely in this is located the principle of the ecumenical movement."[24]

What "subsists in" means (ad 1 and 2). Becker and Sullivan say it means "continues to exist in." Maximilian Heim and Ratzinger say it means "has its subsistence in," "exists concretely in."[25] Becker and Sullivan argue that Tromp, a master of classical Latin, would have taken *subsistere* in its classical sense—"to continue to exist it." Heim says that Tromp, a professor of fundamental theology, must have intended the word to have its scholastic sense, indicating a substance's manner of being, whereby it possesses its being in

---

22 See Sullivan, *The Church We Believe In*, 28.

23 Henri de Lubac, *The Splendor of the Church*, trans. Michael Mason (San Francisco: Ignatius Press, 1986 [French, 1953]), chap. 4. See also the second chapter of the encyclical *Ecclesia de Eucharistia*. Cf. CDF, "Responses," at question 4; see *Origins* 37 (2007): 135–36.

24 Hellín, *Lumen Gentium*, third schema at no. 15, note D: "in hoc praecise situm est principium motionis oecumenicae."

25 Maximilian Heim, *Joseph Ratzinger: Life in the Church and Living Theology* (San Francisco: Ignatius Press, 2007), 314–16; Ratzinger, "Ecclesiology," 147–48.

itself, and not in another.[26] Ratzinger says that all the Council Fathers, trained as they were *modo scholastico*, would have understood immediately that *subsistere* is narrower in meaning then *esse*, and that it indicates the way of being that the Greeks styled an *hypostasis*.[27] Moreover

> [*s*]*ubsistere* is a special variant of *esse*. It is "being" in the form of independent agent. This is exactly what is concerned here. The Council is trying to tell us that the Church of Jesus Christ may be encountered in this world as a *concrete agent* in the Catholic Church.[28]

Ratzinger's observation, coming as it does from a participant in the Council, seems weighty.[29] Even so, it remains that the Doctrinal Commission did not express itself with all the fullness we might now desire on the meaning of the change. We are not, however, without resource. It may well be that the word has the sense Sullivan says it does, but that, in the larger context of *LG*, it has also the sense Ratzinger thinks nicely captured in the scholastic vocabulary.

So, first, as to "concrete existence." The text of *LG* has it that "the sole Church of Christ, the one "entrusted to Peter's pastoral care," the Church "constituted and organized as a society in the present world," the Church previously characterized in the immediately foregoing sub-paragraph as a "complex reality," visible and spiritual, "structured with hierarchical organs"—this is the Church that subsists in the Catholic Church. But then, as organized in a society, visible, the Church in question seems to be quite concrete, visible, structured. And so, if it subsists in the Catholic Church, it presumably subsists "concretely," which is to say "has its concrete existence" there.

Second, as to the Church of Christ being thought of as an "agent," this is everywhere presupposed where there is talk of the Church speaking, doing, acting, as in the next sub-paragraph of *LG* 8.

But the *concreteness* of the existing, and the characterization of the Church as *agent*—we submit that these are the only two conceptual notes that Ratzinger's understanding of "subsists" adds to Sullivan's.

---

[26] Heim, *Joseph Ratzinger*, 315n458.

[27] Ratzinger, "Ecclesiology," 148n18.

[28] Ibid., 147.

[29] See Christian Geyer's interview with Ratzinger, "Ratzinger on *Dominus Iesus*," *Inside the Vatican* 9 (2001): 112–18, at 114: "I was present during the Second Vatican Council when the word *subsistit* was chosen and I can say that I understand the expression quite well." The interview originally appeared in the *Frankfurter Allgemeine Zeitung* (September 22, 2000): 51–52.

Therefore, whether Tromp was thinking of Gredt's *Elementa Philosophiae Aristotelico-Thomisticae* (as Heim suggests[30]) or whether he contented himself more modestly with some lexicon of classical Latin (as Sullivan suggests), it does not make any difference, since from the context of *LG* we end up with the notion proposed by Ratzinger, by Heim, and by the CDF in its Notification on Boff and elsewhere. It could not be said, therefore, that the CDF in its Notification (1985), *Dominus Iesus* (2000), or Responses to Some Questions regarding Certain Aspects of the Doctrine of the Church (2007) has either derogated from the teaching of the Council or been confused as to what was really meant.

Identity and non-identity (ad 1). If *subsistere* means "has its concrete existence in," Sullivan holds, then the Church of Christ is identical with the Catholic Church, and there are no non-Catholic churches. There is, however, more than one way to conceive non-identity. There is the non-identity of a part and a whole. That is how Sullivan seems to shape things up. The Catholic Church is not exactly the same thing as the Church of Christ because she is only a part of it.

There is also the way the Council conceives of non-identity. The Church founded by Christ and as founded by Christ subsists in the Catholic Church, but the Catholic Church does not exhaust, as it were, absolutely all ecclesial reality; no, elements of the Church and sometimes even churches exist outside her. There is ecclesial being outside the one and unique Church. But there is no subsistence of the one and *unique* Church founded by Christ except singularly, uniquely. And that is in the Catholic Church. The elements are not self-sustaining, and so one is tempted to think of the distinction between substance and accident. That is not quite right, however, since the elements are "outside" the one Church, the one subsistence. It is a distinction, one may say, whose difficulty matches the difficulty of thinking coherently about a reality marred by sin.[31]

Sullivan's proposal is in the interest of respecting non-Catholic Christians. If there are churches and ecclesial communities outside the Catholic Church then we cannot interpret *subsistit* to mean that the Church of Christ is fully identical with the Catholic Church. We agree, but only if that means that the Council acknowledges the existence of ecclesial reality outside the Catholic Church.[32] There is true ecclesial reality outside the boundaries, social and institutional, of the Catholic Church. Because of

30 Heim, *Joseph Ratzinger*, 315.

31 Ratzinger, "Ecclesiology," 148.

32 This is how Ratzinger speaks in Geyer, "Ratzinger on *Dominus Iesus*," 114: "The Council Fathers thus wished to say that the being of the Church as such is a broader

this, however, Sullivan also wants also to deny that the Church of Christ subsists only in the Catholic Church. We do not agree at all. The Church of Christ subsists in the Catholic Church, and only there, and in this sense, moreover, is fully identical with the Catholic Church. True, the Church of Christ must continue to be present and operative, in some degree, in particular churches and ecclesial communities separated from the Catholic Church.[33] However, saying that the Church of Christ subsists only in the Catholic Church because she alone has all the things that Christ gave the Church, does not mean that every church and ecclesial community outside the Church is not really a church or is not really an ecclesial reality.

The observations of Cardinal Ratzinger written in 1982 are helpful:

> No translation can fully capture the sublime nuance of the Latin text [of *Lumen Gentium*] in which the unconditional equation of the first conciliar drafts—the full identity between the Church of Jesus Christ and the Roman Catholic Church—is clearly set forth: nothing of the concreteness of the conciliar concept of the Church is lost—the Church is there present where the successors of the Apostle Peter and of the other apostles visibly incorporate her continuity with her source: but this full concreteness of the Church does not mean that every other Church can be only a non-Church.[34]

The understanding that the meaning of "subsists" still includes conceiving of the full identity between the Church of Christ and the Catholic Church can be put in terms of the unicity of the Church. To deny that there exists only one subsistence of the Church of Christ is to deny the unicity of the Church. The commentary on the "Responses" document makes this very point stating that the unicity of the Church

---

entity than that of the Roman Catholic Church, but that in this last the Church's being acquires, in an incomparable way, her true and proper character as subject."

33 Sullivan, "The Meaning of *Subsistit in*," 123–24.

34 Joseph Cardinal Ratzinger, "Ecumenism at a Standstill? Explanatory Comments on *Mysterium Ecclesiae*," in *Principles of Catholic Theology: Building Stones for a Fundamental Theology*, trans. Mary Frances McCarthy (San Francisco: Ignatius Press, 1987), 228–37, at 230; *Theologische Prinzipienlehre: Baustein zur Fundamentaltheologie* (Munchen: Erich Wewel Verlag, 1982), 243: "Keine deutsche Übersetzung kann die sublime Nuance des lateinischen Textes voll auffangen, in dem die bedingunglose Gleichung der ersten konziliaren Entwurfe, das volle Gleichheitszeichen zwischen Kirche Jesu Christi und römisch-katholischer Kirche differenziert wurde: Nichts von der Konkretheit des Kirchenbegriffs wird weggenommen—die Kirche ist da, wo die Nachfolger des Apostels Petrus und der ubrigen Apostel die Kontinuität mit dem Ursprung sichbar verkorpern; aber diese volle Konkreheit der Kirche heisst doch nicht, dass alles andere dann nur Nichtkirche sein kann" (footnote omitted).

> would be compromised by the proposal that the Church founded by Christ could have more than one subsistence. If this were the case we would be forced, as the Declaration *Mysterium Ecclesiae* puts it, to imagine "the Church of Christ as the sum total of the Churches or the ecclesial Communities—which are simultaneously differentiated and yet united," or "to think that the Church of Christ no longer exists today concretely and therefore can only be the object of research for the Churches and the communities." If this were the case, the Church of Christ would not any longer exist in history, or would exist only in some ideal form emerging either through some future convergence or through the reunification of the diverse sister Churches, to be hoped for and achieved through dialogue.[35]

Either we affirm the one subsistence of the Church of Christ in the Catholic Church or we end up denying that the Church that Christ founded remains and lives today with all the gifts that he gave it—including its unity—from the beginning. If we think of multiple subsistences of the Church of Christ then we will think that the one Church of Christ does not have the unity that Christ willed it to have, and we will, in turn, misconceive the primary reason for ecumenism as having to do with overcoming this lack of unity in the one Church of Christ.[36]

Furthermore, to affirm multiple subsistences is to overlook the fact that the Church of Christ cannot lose its unity without losing something essential to its mission. How can the Church of Christ lose the unity that Christ intends it to have and still remain in the nature of a sacrament and an instrument "both of a very closely knit union with God and of the unity of the whole human race" (*LG* 1)? The unity of the Church willed by Christ is bound up with the indefectability of the Church. It is indefectible, in part, because it will never be lacking in what it needs to fulfill its mission. Unity is necessary for the Church's mission; otherwise, it cannot be the saving sacrament of unity.

---

35 CDF, Commentary on the Document "Responses to Some Questions Regarding Certain Aspects of the Doctrine of the Church;" see *Origins* 37 (2007): 136–39, at 137.

36 Sullivan comes very close to saying this in *The Church We Believe In*, 65: "If the Church is to be found even where ecclesial communion is not as full as it ought to be, we have to admit that the Church, as it exists today, does not have the unity that Christ wants it to have. However, if we have to admit that the Church is not as holy as it ought to be, can we not also admit that it is not as one as it ought to be? Indeed, is not this admission the basic reason for the ecumenical movement?"

Conclusion

The Council Fathers taught in *UR* 4 that the gift of unity Christ bestowed on the one Church was something that remained in the Catholic Church and could never be lost:

> [W]hen the obstacles to perfect ecclesiastical communion have been gradually overcome, all Christians will at last, in a common celebration of the Eucharist, be gathered into the one and only Church in that unity which Christ bestowed on His Church from the beginning. We believe that this unity subsists in the Catholic Church as something she can never lose, and we hope that it will continue to increase until the end of time.

Sullivan acknowledges that the Catholic Church has the unity and the institutional integrity that Christ wants the Church to have but affirms at the same time that the Church of Christ does not have the unity that Christ wants it to have because the Church of Christ is still found where ecclesial communion is not as full as it should be in particular churches and ecclesial communities.[37] Then it follows that if there is but one subsisting of the Church, it subsists as something incoherent, or that there are many subsistences. This second alternative leads one to think of the Church of Christ as existing in fragments, and of the ecumenical task having to do with reassembling those fragments so that the Church of Christ might regain its lost unity and oneness.

On the contrary, the disunity among Christians does not shatter the unity of the Church of Christ but hampers the Church's pursuit of the fullness of catholicity. Therefore we read in *UR* 4:

> Nevertheless, the divisions among Christians prevent the Church from attaining the fullness of catholicity proper to her, in those of her sons who, though attached to her by Baptism, are yet separated from full communion with her. Furthermore, the Church herself finds it more difficult to express in actual life her full catholicity in all her bearings.

And in *Dominus Iesus*, number 17:

> The lack of unity among Christians is certainly a wound for the Church; not in the sense that she is deprived of her unity, but "in that it hinders the complete fulfillment of her universality in history."[38]

---

37 Sullivan, *The Church We Believe In*, 65.

38 Quoted here is the letter of the CDF, "Letter to the Bishops of the Catholic Church on Some Aspects of the Church Understood as Communion," 17; *Dominus Iesus* also refers the reader to *UR* 4.

Holding firmly to the one subsistence of the Church of Christ in the Catholic Church helps us to see and understand that the task of the ecumenical movement bears upon the Church's catholicity. "Full unity and full Catholicity," in the words of Pope Benedict XVI, "go together."[39]

We forget today how at the time of the Second Vatican Council the recognition of ecclesial elements outside the Catholic Church was thought to be a great breakthrough of positive ecumenical significance; maintaining only the subsistence of the Church of Christ in the Catholic Church was thought to be sober and newly modest. Today, on the other hand, it seems that every attempt to recognize the continued perfect and full and identifiable existence of the Church of Christ, and this in accordance with the promises of Christ, is thought to be yet another exercise of Roman imperialism.

We think the position we have outlined—the position we think to be that of the CDF—is coherent. It respects the ecclesial reality of non-Catholic churches and communities. It is the opposite of ecclesial relativism and so accepts the dominical promises to the Church at face value. It both makes ecumenical discussion possible and calls for it.

Postscript

In his "Further Thoughts on the Meaning of *Subsistit in*,"[40] Sullivan argues that Ratzinger and the CDF have issued contradictory interpretations of *LG* 8, some denying and some affirming the identity of Christ's Church with the Catholic Church. He does this because he does not distinguish the assertion of a "total identity" of the Church of Christ with the Catholic Church from the assertion of the "full identity" of the Church of Christ with the Catholic Church. The first, "total identity," would mean there is no ecclesial reality outside the Catholic Church—which is not true, which was not in fact asserted by Pius XII, and which was expressly denied by Vatican II. "Full identity," on the other hand, means that the Church of Christ, as established by Christ, with all the instruments of sanctification and the kind of unity he desired for it, continues to exist concretely in the

---

39 Pope Benedict XVI, Address "Apostolic Journey to Cologne on the Occasion of XX World Youth Day," Ecumenical Meeting, www.vatican.va/holy_father/benedict_xvi/speeches/2005/august/documents/hf_ben-xvi_spe_20050819_ecumenical-meeting_en.html (accessed March 20, 2010). See also his homily for the Solemnity of Saints Peter and Paul on June 29, 2005, www.vatican.va/holy_father/benedict_xvi/homilies/2005/documents/hf_ben-xvi_hom_20050629_sts-peter-paul_en.html (accessed March 20, 2010).

40 Francis A. Sullivan, S.J., "Further Thoughts on the Meaning of *Subsistit in*," *Theological Studies* 71 (March 2010): 133–47.

Catholic Church, and only there—although there is ecclesial reality outside the visible confines of the Catholic Church, namely, elements of truth and sanctification, and even in true particular churches, where there are valid orders and so also the Eucharist. The CDF never speaks of a total identity but of *plenam identitatem* (full identity).[41] Ratzinger speaks of *restlos identifizierende* (total identity), which he rejects, and *das volle Gleichheitszeichen* (the full identity).[42]

Sullivan also wants to say that the CDF in *Dominus Iesus* (2000) follows the ordinary meaning of the phrase *subsistit in* in classical Latin: "continues to exist." This meaning does not entail a metaphysical understanding whereby the Church of Christ is thought to have its concrete form of existence in the Catholic Church. What Sullivan calls the "metaphysical" meaning of *subsistit in*—the meaning the term came to have in Christology—entails affirming that there is only one subsistence of the Church of Christ. To speak of one subsistence supposedly denies the existence of separated particular churches outside the Catholic Church. Sullivan attributes this metaphysical meaning to the "Notification on Leonardo Boff" (1985) and "Responses to Some Questions regarding Certain Aspects of the Doctrine on the Church" (2007). Thus we are to believe that the CDF gives us contradictory and competing interpretations of *subsistit in*. Sullivan advises Catholics to adhere to the interpretation given by *Dominus Iesus* and to avoid the one given in "Responses."[43]

Now Sullivan may make this kind of a sharp distinction between a classical meaning and metaphysical meaning of *subsistit in*, but it is clear that the CDF does not. It can explain *subsistit in* as meaning "to continue to exist" and as also meaning that the Church of Christ has its concrete form of existence in the Catholic Church without denying the existence of particular churches separated from full communion with the Catholic Church. Catholics are not faced with the quandary Sullivan thinks they are. See, for example, the "Responses" which cites *Dominus Iesus*, number 16.3 (where "subsists" is explained as "continues to exist") in support of its claim that "in number 8 of the Dogmatic Constitution *Lumen Gentium* 'subsistence' means this perduring, historical continuity and the permanence of all the elements instituted by Christ in the Catholic Church, *in which the Church of Christ is concretely found on this earth*."[44] It should be pointed out as well that in

41 www.vatican.va/roman_curia/congregations/cfaith/documents/rc_con_cfaith_doc_20070629_responsa-quaestiones_lt.html.

42 For the former, see Joseph Ratziner, *Das Neue Volk Gottes* (Dusseldorf: Patmos-Verlag, 1969), 236. For the latter, see his *Theologische Prinzipienlehre*, 243.

43 See Sullivan, "Further Thoughts," 147.

44 CDF, "Responses," at question 2; 135, emphasis added.

"Responses" the CDF affirms the full identity of the Church of Christ and the Catholic Church, and at the same time states:

> It is possible, according to Catholic doctrine, to affirm correctly that the Church of Christ is present and operative in the churches and ecclesial Communities not yet fully in communion with the Catholic Church, on account of the elements of sanctification and truth that are present in them. Nevertheless, the word "subsists" can only be attributed to the Catholic Church alone precisely because it refers to the mark of unity that we profess in the symbols of the faith (I believe . . . in the "one" Church); and this "one" Church subsists in the Catholic Church.[45]

Affirming the full identity between the Church of Christ and the Catholic Church need not have the nefarious consequences that Sullivan fears.

[45] Ibid.

CHAPTER 7

Priestly Identity and the Headship of Christ

IN HER ARTICLE "Priestly Identity: Sacrament of the Ecclesial Community," Susan Wood takes up the important question of the identity and sacramentality of the ordained priesthood.[1] She argues that the ordained priest is the representative sign of the ecclesial community. Her understanding of sacramental representation sees the Church as the sacramental referent in the sacrament of orders. The ecclesial community is understood primarily as the *totus Christus*, the Body of Christ, Head and members. The priest stands *in persona Christi capitis*, but only because he represents the *totus Christus*, the members of the mystical body in union with Christ the Head. Therefore the priest stands *in persona Christi capitis* only indirectly. The ecclesial representation has priority over the Christic representation. Why? Because sacraments sign and cause to be present an ecclesial reality, the *res et sacramentum*. The *res et sacramentum* has both a Christic and an ecclesial aspect, and for Wood, the Christic occurs in and through the ecclesial. Thus, because of his ordination, the priest is the sacramental sign of the ecclesial community, the *totus Christus*. The ordained minister sacramentally represents and recapitulates the ecclesial community, and thereby acts in the person of Christ the Head. The difference between the common priesthood and the ordained priesthood is found in the ordained minister's relationship to the Church, not in an imaging of Christ.

In this essay I will first indicate points of agreement with Susan Wood's analysis. Next, I will argue that Christ is the source and Head of his Church, and that this priority of Christ as Head is sacramentalized in the Eucharist

[1] Susan Wood, "Priestly Identity: Sacrament of the Ecclesial Community," *Worship* (March 1995): 109–27.

and in the sacrament of orders. This entails an understanding of orders where the priest's standing in the person of Christ as Head has priority over his standing in the person of the Church. This priority is rooted in the reality that the Church's worship has its source in Christ's worship of his Father. A complete and sound theology of orders must be fully informed by the truth that Christ is the principal agent in liturgical worship, and that without Christ, the Church cannot turn toward the Father in prayer. Sacramental worship is through Christ, or it is not sacramental worship at all.

Wood argues, rightly, that if Eucharistic presidency is separated from pastoral leadership then a flawed, a non-sacramental understanding of the Church is sure to follow. She observes also that if pastoral leadership is authorized in a purely juridical manner and not by sacramental ordination, there is the real danger of conceiving of orders as involving merely the juridical communication of powers that are unrelated to the Church. The historical experience of the Church shows that Wood's observation is correct. The separation of jurisdiction from sacramental orders in the Middle Ages contributed in no small way to a theology that understood the Church and the sacrament of orders in highly juridical categories rather than in terms of communion and sacrament. Likewise, the isolation of Eucharistic presidency from pastoral leadership went a long way toward a theology that understood priesthood chiefly in terms of the power to transubstantiate bread and wine into the Body and Blood of Christ. It followed for this line of thinking that the ordination of a bishop was not sacramental but primarily involved the conferral of greater juridical power essentially distinct from sacramental power. Ordained ministry then tended to be individualized and its character as *communio* was greatly obscured.[2] Wood is right to warn that similar consequences will follow in our time to the extent we understand and implement ministry in a juridical fashion.

Wood correctly rejects a congregationalist model that understands ordained ministry simply as a representation of the general ministry of the community. This model imagines that the ecclesial community extends its ministry by delegating certain functions to individual ministers. In the congregationalist model the ritual forms and liturgy of the assembly lack objectivity and authority because they are thought of as something caused and created by the assembly itself. The only real differentiation between lay and ordained ministry has to do with what the ministers can do rather than with what the ministers are. Thus ministry is defined in terms of

---

[2] For a succinct account of this see Joseph Cardinal Ratzinger, *Principles of Catholic Theology*, trans. Sister Mary Frances McCarthy (San Francisco: Ignatius Press) 242–44, 254–57.

functionality.[3] Against this model Wood insists, rightly, upon the sacramentality and the ecclesial dimension of the office of bishop. Indeed, the sacrament of orders does produce a relationship between a bishop and a particular community, and a relation between one bishop and the other bishops of the college, together with its head. The Church as a communion of communions is, to be sure, manifested in the sacrament of orders. This insight, recovered at Vatican II, has not been completely assimilated into the life and pastoral activity of the Church.

Wood also argues that ministry today must not be defined in terms of function but rather in terms of identity, because the former leads to this congregationalist model. It is here that problems begin. It is one thing to reject an understanding of ministry that sees it simply as pure "function"; it is something else to say that ordained ministry needs to be defined in terms of identity rather than function. One must guard against assuming a dualism between ontology and functionality. We ought not be willing to concede to the congregationalist model that we should speak of ministry simply in terms of "functioning" without implying that person's being is profoundly affected by what a person does. We must keep in mind that what a person does constitutes, in part, an identity. While John Zizioulas, upon whom Wood relies, insists that through ordination a priest becomes a related entity, he is equally insistent that we cannot speak about function without speaking about being.[4]

Secondly, it is one thing to point out that ordination creates an ecclesial relation and to call for the full implementation of a sacramental understanding of orders; it is another thing to claim that the Church is the sacramental referent of orders.[5] In the beginning of her article Susan Wood acknowledges that while the priesthood of the baptized and the ordained priesthood share a number of things in common there is still a need to distinguish precisely what it is that differentiates them. Here she has in mind *Lumen Gentium*

---

[3] Wood, "Priestly Identity," 111.

[4] See John Zizioulas, *Being as Communion* (Crestwood, NY: St. Vladimir's Seminary, 1985), 226–27. "In the light of the *koinonia* of the Holy Spirit, ordination relates the ordained man so profoundly and so existentially to the community that in his new state after ordination he cannot be any longer, as a minister, conceived in himself. In this state, existence is determined by *communion* which qualifies and defines both 'ontology' and 'function.' Thus it becomes impossible in this state to say that one simply 'functions' without implying that his being is deeply and decisively affected by what he does. In the same way, it becomes impossible to imply in this state that one 'possesses' anything as an individual."

[5] Indeed, it is impossible to reconcile this claim with the teaching of either *Presbyterorum ordinis* (*PO*) or *Pastores dabo vobis* (*PDV*), and Wood makes no attempt to do so.

(*LG*) 10, which says that the two priesthoods differ essentially and not only in degree. She thinks that *LG* 10 itself does not identify this difference but only describes it in terms of "function." Wood also holds that it is not enough to claim that the ordained priest stands *in persona Christi*, for it is not clear how this is different from the baptized who have put on Christ and participate in his death and Resurrection. Thus for Wood the difference is that the ordained sacramentally represent Christ in his relation to the ecclesial community as Head. However, "the very notion of headship is related to the ability to stand instead of and sacramentally represent the community."[6]

There is a problem with this account of headship. If the term "head" simply represents the whole it is truly hard to see how "head" refers to anything distinct from the body, as something superior over the other bodily members. After all Christ, the Head of the Body, is the source of the Body's unity. But in Wood's scheme the priest only represents the Head indistinctly, which is not really to represent the Head as "head." The parts of a whole, for example, bodily parts, are manifested and signified distinctly only in articulation from one another.

Wood's understanding of headship does not adequately explain the uniqueness of Christ's headship in relation to the Church. This weakness leaves her presentation unable to account for how the Head gives the Body its life and unity. The price of this weakness is a high one. It leaves Wood's presentation open to thinking that the union of the head with the body is brought about by the action of the body whereby the head somehow represents the unifying action of the body. In other words, her presentation forgets the radical dependence of the Church, the Body, on Christ, the Head, and so stands wide open to a sort of ecclesial Pelagianism. If the priority of headship is forgotten, Christ as Head appears to be just another member of the Body and it is hard to see how he can be the source of the life and unity of the body.[7] Put simply, Wood's presentation does not completely integrate the truth, which she herself recognizes, that Christ is the principal agent of ecclesial acts.[8]

---

[6] Wood, "Priestly Identity," 115.

[7] This understanding of headship is emphasized in the Epistle to the Ephesians. For example, in Ephesians 4:15–16: "Rather, living the truth in love, we should grow in every way into him who is the Head, Christ, from whom the whole Body, joined and held together by every supporting ligament, with the proper functioning of each part, brings about the Body's growth and builds itself up in love." Clearly according to the author of the Letter to the Ephesians, headship involves more than representing the body.

[8] In her acknowledgment of the traditional doctrine as stated in *PO* 2, that the priest acts in the person of Christ as Head, Wood writes: "In this view of the sacrament, the ordained person is 'ordered' to Christ. This view is obviously important for all our

Any response to Wood that wants to uphold the primacy of the headship of Christ will be careful to explain how that headship enables the action of the Body and how that action is joined to that of the Head. It is not enough to simply assert that Christ's headship is superior to the body. When there is not a proper differentiation and distinction of the head from the body, and a clear understanding of the relationship between them, then there is also the danger of a kind of ecclesial Monophysitism whereby the action of Christ the Head absorbs the action of the members of the body—a collapse of the Church into Christ or an identity of the Head with the Body. If the ordained priest, *in persona Christi capitis*, is understood to represent this kind of principal agency, the agency of the Body is eliminated, or completely taken over by the priest.

Headship as Participation in Christ's Office as Mediator

The priest's standing *in persona Christi capitis* is based upon a distinctive form of participation in the priesthood of Christ. Wood's view of headship does not sufficiently take this into account. *Lumen Gentium* 10 points directly to this distinctive participation in Christ's priesthood when it says that "the common priesthood of the faithful and the ministerial or hierarchical priesthood are nonetheless related to one another; *each of them in its own special way is a participation in the one priesthood of Christ*."[9] Those who are ordained share in an aspect and dimension of the priesthood of Christ that the rest of the baptized do not.

No less a scholar than Alois Grillmeier observed that the unique nature of the ordained ministry has to do with a special participation in the mediatorship of Christ. In his commentary on *LG* he remarked specifically on number 10:

> The consecrated priesthood is not to be understood merely as an intensification and heightening of the dignity and mission of the common priesthood, but represents a new type of priestly dignity and power, even though it is based on the common priesthood. But of their nature, the common and the special priesthood are ordained to each other by virtue of their common participation in the priesthood of Christ which they share in a different way. Thus the two forms of priesthood are defined in the light of their relationship to Christ the high priest. . . .

sacramental theology since it is Christ who acts in the sacraments." Wood's presentation does not seem to realize the full implications of this important truth. See "Priestly Identity," 112.

9 Austin Flannery, O.P., *Vatican Council II: The Conciliar and Post Conciliar Documents* (Collegeville: The Liturgical Press, 1992).

> The ordained priest has a function within the people of God as a whole, which represents a special participation in the mediatorship of Christ and hence has an ascending and descending component. By virtue of the authority and mission of Christ the consecrated priest has the task of forming and uniting the "priestly people" by giving instruction and guidance. It is to be noted that the authority to teach, the task of proclaiming the word, is mentioned in the first place. Later, the Constitution will bring out and maintain the precedence of the ministry here indicated. Salvation begins with revelation, the word of God who discloses himself, imparts himself and calls, as he speaks from on high. The authority to represent Christ the Head in preaching and guiding is the first gift bestowed on the consecrated priest. It comes to him in a special symbolic action and belongs to him alone. But just as the priesthood of Christ shows a movement from below to on high in the sacrifice of the Cross, so too does the consecrated priesthood, in the power of celebrating the Eucharistic sacrifice in the person of Christ, in the midst of and in the name of the Christian people. Hence *this special quality and nature of the official priesthood must be defined in terms of this special participation in the mediatorship of Christ as it goes from above to below and below to above. To be placed at the point of this junction is a special vocation.* The faithful are drawn into this process of sacred exchange and the full priestly reality of the people of God results from the cooperation of the special and common priesthood."[10]

This special share in the mediatorship of Christ does not exclude speaking in the name of the Church. Gisbert Greshake, in *The Meaning of Christian Priesthood*, points out that the twofold activity of the priest who acts *in persona Christi* and/or *in persona Ecclesiae* is grounded upon a twofold movement that marks the entire process of salvation.[11] On the one hand, there is the downward (katabatic) movement, where Christ comes to the human race for the purpose of reconciliation and sanctification. On the other hand, there is the upward (anabatic) movement where humanity is given the power (the power of the Spirit) to go along with Christ in his sacrifice to the Father. The unity of this double movement is grounded in the person of Christ who is the mediator between the Father and humanity. As mediator Christ is sent to us from the Father and also gathers us together and ascends with us to the Father. Thus, Greshake observes, there is always a certain duality at work in the process of salvation and in preparation for

[10] Alois Grillmeier, "Dogmatic Constitution on the Church, Mystery of the Church," *Commentary on the Documents of Vatican II*, ed. Herbert Vorgrimler, vol. 1 (New York: Herder and Herder), 158, emphasis mine.

[11] Gisbert Greshake, *The Meaning of Christian Priesthood*, trans. Peadar MacSeumais (Westminster, MD: Christian Classics, 1989), 82–83.

communion with Christ in word and sacrament: the word and the response of faith, the sanctifying action and the response of self abandonment and surrender. "In other words: the word of Christ becomes the answering word of belief of the Church."[12] Now this duality should not be understood as if there are two elements that lie close to one another, side by side. On the contrary, there is an intrinsic and essential unity between them because salvation is not simply an act of God upon humanity but a drawing and gathering of human persons into the movement of Christ toward the Father. Put simply, the Church worships through the perfect worship of Christ. Our access to the Father is mediated through Christ. When Christ mediates he does so as our representative in a way that invites our participation in his worship so that we might be joined to him in his self-abandonment to the Father.

Greshake thinks this twofold duality reveals the twofold face of the Church: the Church as the body and the Church as spouse. The former expresses the profound communion with Christ and the latter expresses the Church's difference from Christ. Moreover:

> The twofold view point from which Church office is to be regarded corresponds exactly to this dual unity of aspects. *In persona Christi* the priest is a messenger in place of Christ: as one distinct from the community he is the expression of that difference, the Church receiving from the Lord all that it possesses. But at the same time he is also a *minister ecclesiae*, an organ of the believing, praying and offering Church. As such he acts *in persona ecclesiae* when he proclaims the faith of the Church celebrates its sacraments and works for the formation of Christ in the Church. Ordination consequently not only means a mission and authority received from Christ to act in his place: it also means authority and power to act *in persona ecclesia* as a permanent "servant of the Church." This power is also sacramental and symbolic. That is: the priest is acting not in place of the Church as if he were someone delegated by it—we are not in the juridical sphere—but as that organ through which and in which the Church is present and acting."[13]

The priority of the Christic representation takes nothing away from the ecclesial. The dimension of Church office, *in persona ecclesiae*, is absolutely crucial and is required for a complete and fully fruitful celebration of the Eucharist. It gives concrete expression and shape to the fact that in the Eucharist the salvific divine action has the purpose of realizing

[12] Ibid., 83.
[13] Ibid., 83–84.

the unity of human persons with one another in Christ. The priest speaks in the name of a community that wishes its prayer and offering to be joined to Christ's. This action of course has to do with the upward (the anabatic) movement of the process of salvation—the Church ascends with Christ to the Father.[14] Acting *in persona Christi*, the priest expresses the difference between Christ and the Church, which has to do with the fact that what the Church possesses comes entirely from her Lord. The priest represents Christ who comes to sanctify us and make us capable of being united with him in the offering and self-donation of himself to his heavenly Father. This is parallel with the downward (katabatic) movement of the process of salvation—Christ comes to prepare himself a body.

Difference between Head and Members in the *Totus Christus*

Susan Wood sees the problem of the relation between the ecclesial and Christic dimensions of Church office as inseparable from ecclesiology, from the relationship between the Head and the members of the Body of Christ. What is not completely addressed, at least in her presentation, is the precise difference between the Head and members. Insufficient attention paid to the difference between the Head and members leads to an under-appreciation and realization of Christ's role as the principal agent in the Church's liturgical action. Wood, who interprets the priesthood as a representative sign of the community, proposes that the priest represents in his actions the principal agency of the *totus Christus*. But this really camouflages the problem because the *totus Christus* contains more than one subject or agent. So the problem remains: who does the priest represent in his distinctive actions?

How are we to avoid affirming an ecclesial Pelagianism that reduces the action of the Head to representing the body, effectively making the Head just another member of the Body and thereby denying the unifying action of the Head? On the other hand, how are we to avoid an ecclesial Monophysitism, in which the action of the Head is that only action effectively absorbing the action of the Body, the Church?

It must be, as Grillmeier and Greshake point out, that the priest represents what Christ does for the Church. Christ the Head is the principal

[14] St. Thomas Aquinas recognized this, for example, when he taught that humanity's unity in Christ, that is the unity of the mystical body, is not realized in the Eucharist celebrated by a priest who has separated himself from the Church and can no longer act in the name of the Church. See *ST* III, 82, art 9, ad 2. Wood is right to claim that this ecclesial aspect of Church office has not been fully integrated (or worse, forgotten) in certain theologies of orders today.

agent who moves the Church and enables her to turn with him toward the Father. Thus John 14:6: "No one can come to the Father except through me." Christ is the Head of his Body as its source and cause of its unity. It is in this sense that there is a priority of Christ, the Head, in relation to his Body, the Church. *LG* 7 referred to this priority of Christ, the Head of the body, in the language of 1 Colossians 1:15–18: "He is before all creatures and in him all things hold together. He is the Head of the body which is the Church. He is the beginning, the firstborn from the dead, that in all things he might hold the primacy." And in an allusion to Ephesians 1:18–23, *LG* 7 teaches: "By the greatness of his power he rules heaven and earth, and with his all-surpassing perfection and activity he fills the whole body with the riches of his glory."[15] Thus the priest represents Christ in this distinctive action as Head. While it is true to say that the ordained minister speaks in the name of Church, it must be remembered that he does so only in the sense that the Church is enabled to do so by Christ.

Totus Christus and Maritally Structured Covenant

How do we understand the unity between the Head and members of the Body of Christ? Do we conceive of this unity as something physical or organic, the way a head is joined to a body? This conception is not uncommon, but it cannot correctly explain the unity between the head and body because it makes it a necessary union rather than a free one. The unity between the Head and Body, between Christ and the Church, is not a necessary one but a free one, because it is a union of love. This is how St. Paul understood the unity of the Body of Christ, and we should follow his lead.

The Pauline theme of nuptiality clearly expresses not only the difference between Christ and his Church but their free union as well (2 Cor 11:2). This is the image of the Church as Bride who is one flesh with her husband and Bridegroom (Eph 5:22–33). Put simply, the relation of Christ the Head to his Body should be understood nuptially or maritally as union of one flesh. The relationship between Christ and his Body is a marital kind of union where each subject exists in a union that is freely chosen but does not dissolve or collapse the two subjects, bride and bridegroom into one another.

> The Church is the Body of Christ in the way in which the woman is one body, or rather one flesh, with man. Put in other terms, the Church is the Body, not by virtue of an identity without distinction, but rather by means of the pneumatic-real act of spousal love. Expressed in yet another way, this means that Christ and the Church

[15] Flannery, *Vatican Council II.*

> are one body in the sense in which man and woman are one flesh, that is, in such a way that in their indissoluble spiritual-bodily union, they nonetheless remain unconfused and unmingled.[16]

The image of the Church as Bride makes evident the difference between Christ the Head and his Body and Bride while maintaining their unity. This marital symbolism highlights the interpersonal character of the communion between Christ and the Church, and hence the free nature of that communion.

To embark any further upon the important question of nuptial-spousal symbolism with regard to Christ's relation to the Church is beyond the scope of this short essay.[17] What I want to suggest is that a complete theology of orders ought to be based on an ecclesiology that has fully integrated the truth that Christ as head is the cause and the source of his sacramental body that is the Church. As Head of the Church, Christ represents his body, his bride, to the Father. Christ is the principal agent of the Church's liturgical actions. The body, which is the Church, is capable of turning and praying to the Father only because of Christ. It is this reality that accounts for the priority (not domination!) of the Christic over the ecclesial. At the same time this ecclesiology is also informed by a nuptial-marital conception of unity that makes evident the difference of Christ's headship in relation to the Church and the free nature of ecclesial unity in Christ, thus avoiding the danger of collapsing the Church into Christ or vice versa.

A conception of priestly identity that sees the priest as first in *persona ecclesiae* and indirectly in *persona Christi* is not capable of sacramentalizing Christ's relationship to the Church as Head and mediator, and thus the cause and source (not the result), of his body. In other words, what is stake in the priority of the Christic representation over the ecclesial representation is the sheer gratuity of the grace of Christ.[18] Only a theology of

---

16 Ratzinger, *Called to Communion*, 142.

17 It should be pointed out, though, that the sacramentality of marriage is completely dependent on the spousal relationship between Christ and the Church. See *CCC* 1659–60.

18 Pope John Paul has noticed this in "I Will Give You Shepherds" (*PDV* 16). "And so the priest, on account of his very nature and sacramental mission, appears in the structure of the Church as a sign of the absolute priority and gratuity of that grace which is conferred by the risen Christ on the Church. And through the ministerial priesthood, the Church acquires an awareness of herself in faith, that she has her origin not from herself but from the grace of Christ in the Holy Spirit. The apostles and their successors—since they exercise an authority which is not their own—but one which has been received from Christ the head and shepherd, through their ministry occupy a position facing the Church. And this ministry is nothing but the

priestly identity that understands the priest to sacramentalize the headship of Christ as the source of the Church and a headship of grace will be able to avoid the self-willed autonomy of an ecclesial Pelagianism.

Priority of the Christological Dimension

This essay has argued that it is because the ordained minister stands in the person of Christ that he can stand in the person of the Church. The priority of the Christological dimension of the ordained ministry in relation to the ecclesial dimension is grounded in Christ's relationship to the Church as Head and principal agent. This priority in no way denies that the sacrament of orders involves speaking in the name of the Church or that ordained ministry creates a relational link between a bishop and a particular church, as well as a bond with the college of bishops and the pope. The priority of the Christological does nothing to undermine the reality that the sacrament of orders symbolizes the relationship that constitutes and concretely expresses the Church as a communion of communions. On the contrary, the priority of the Christological brings out the full force of the relational link between the ordained and the Church. Lastly, this essay has claimed that the sacramental referent of the sacrament of orders is first and foremost the distinctive headship of Christ, a headship that is the source and cause of his Body, the Church. The difference between the common priesthood and the ordained priesthood lies in the ordained priesthood's participation in this dimension of Christ's high priesthood.

---

sign, as well as the sacramental and visible continuation, of Christ himself, who faces the church and world as the one author and source of an abiding and always new salvation, since he alone is himself the savior of the body." I have reworked the official English translation of this passage, which does not, in my judgment, accurately convey the meaning of the Latin original. For example, the official translation renders "Apostoli autem eorumque successores, cum potestatem non suam sed a Christo Capite et Pastore receptam habeant, locum coram Ecclesia occupant" into: "The apostles and their successors, inasmuch as they exercise an authority which comes to them from Christ, the head and shepherd, are placed with their ministry—*in the forefront of the Church*" (emphasis mine). "In the forefront" does not capture the sense of the Latin original (*locum coram Ecclesia occupant*), which tries to express the distinctive nature of Christ's headship and hence the ministry of the apostles and their successors as involving an authority that addresses or faces toward the Church. "In the forefront" suggests not an addressing or facing toward the Church but a position of addressing and facing with the Church. For the Latin original of this passage see *AAS* 84 (August 3, 1992): 682. For the official English translation see *Origins* 21 (April 16, 1992): 718–59.

CHAPTER 8

For the Church and within the Church: Priestly Representation*

DAVID COFFEY'S 1997 essay on the common and the ordained priesthood[1] has proved to be an influential one for theologians interested in the theology of priestly representation. A number of studies on the subject have drawn on Coffey's work and have come to the conclusion that the priest is capable of acting in the person of Christ the Head because he first represents the Church.[2] What has been lacking is any investigation of whether Coffey's central claims are well founded.

Coffey's article aims at developing a pneumatological understanding of the priesthood of Christ, and what Coffey calls the "priesthood of the Church" as a "distinct category," in the interest of reaching a new clarity with regard to the relation of the ordained and the common priesthood.[3] In the course of his article, one of the conclusions that Coffey reaches is that there is a priority of the ecclesial to the Christological in the priestly representation of

---

* A version of this essay appeared in *The Thomist* 65 (October 2001): 613–37.

1 David Coffey, "The Common and the Ordained Priesthood," *Theological Studies* 58 (June 1997): 209–36.

2 Most notably Thomas Rausch, "Priestly Identity: Priority of Representation and the Iconic Argument," *Worship* 73 (March 1999): 169–79; see also Paul Philibert, "Issues for a Theology of Priesthood: A Status Report," in *The Theology of Priesthood*, ed. Donald Goergen and Ann Garrido (Collegeville, MN: The Liturgical Press, 2000), 30–31. Both Rausch and Philibert draw on an earlier essay by David Coffey, "Priestly Representation and Women's Ordination," in *Priesthood: The Hard Questions*, ed. Gerald P. Gleeson (Newtown, New South Wales, Australia: E. J. Dwyer, 1992), 79–99.

3 Coffey, "The Common and the Ordained Priesthood," 213.

Christ's headship. To represent Christ as Head is primarily the ability to represent the *totus Christus*, the Head and members.[4] This conclusion is undergirded, it seems to me, by two claims Coffey makes in the same 1997 essay. These amount to the following: (1) Vatican II wrongly assumed the ordained priesthood could be understood directly in Christological terms and thus gave the mistaken impression that the common priesthood was understandable first in ecclesiological terms;[5] and (2) if the ordained priesthood is understood immediately in terms of the headship of Christ, then the priest appears as above the Church or apart from the Church.[6] In other words, if the ordained priesthood is understood first in terms of a new configuration to Christ, then the priest is elevated to some position outside of the rest of the Church. As a consequence, the rest of the baptized, though called priestly and regarded as "members" of Christ, are effectively envisioned as "other" than Christ, that is, "simply" the Church.

I will limit my criticism to these two central claims and the conclusions that Coffey deduces from them. I maintain that these claims cannot be reconciled with the Council documents and the intentions of the Council Fathers as evidenced in the official *Acta*. Furthermore, they are not congruent with how recent Church teaching has interpreted Vatican II. Sara Butler[7] and Samuel Aquila[8] have shown how crucial it is to consult the *Acta* in order to interpret Vatican II's teaching on the ordained priesthood and priestly representation. The *Acta* of a council is of prime importance in determining what a council intended to teach and why it intended to teach what it did. A careful reading shows that Vatican II affirmed a Christological priority for both the common and the ordained priesthoods while strongly asserting the ecclesiological dimensions of both. Far from separating the ordained priesthood from the Church, the Council envisioned it as something for the Church but within the Church—a visible sign of Christ the Head who fills up his Church with life.

Laypersons are presented in the documents of Vatican II not as passive recipients of Christ's activity but as active participants in his threefold office. It is through this participation that the baptized mediate Christ's

---

4 Ibid. Coffey also comes to this conclusion in his earlier essay "Priestly Representation and Women's Ordination," 88.

5 Coffey, "The Common and the Ordained Priesthood," 211.

6 Ibid., 235.

7 Sara Butler, "Priestly Identity: 'Sacrament' of Christ the Head," *Worship* 70 (July 1996): 290–306.

8 Samuel Aquila, *The Teaching of Vatican II on "In Persona Christi" and "In Nomine Ecclesiae" in Relation to the Ministerial Priesthood in the Light of the Historical Development of the Formulae* (Rome: Licentiate tessina, Pontificium Athenaeum Anselmianum, 1990).

gift in their own way. The baptized, united with Christ and made sharers in his priesthood in their own condition, must carry out his threefold office in the Church and in the world. The priesthood of the baptized is not a matter of simple union with Christ or simple belonging to Christ, because the common priesthood is ordered to mission.

This essay will unfold in five parts. First, I will compare the idea that the priest acts *in persona Christi capitis* because he first acts in the name of the Church with recent Church teaching after Vatican II, especially *Pastores Dabo Vobis* (*PDV*), Pope John Paul II's 1992 post-synodal apostolic exhortation.[9] Second, I will give a brief description of Coffey's position. Third, in the longest part, I will show how Coffey's interpretation of Vatican II's teaching on the ordained priesthood and the common priesthood cannot be sustained. Fourth, I will show that what Vatican II teaches concerning the priest representing the headship of Christ does not somehow place the priest above or apart from the Church. Last, I will conclude with a summary of my argument and a suggestion for the direction of further research.

Priestly Representation and Recent Church Teaching

A number of theologians hold that there is a priority of the ecclesial over the Christological in priestly representation.[10] These theologians contend that a priest can act *in persona Christi* because he first acts *in persona ecclesiae*. It should be pointed out that recent magisterial teachings—by both the ordinary universal magisterium[11] and the papal magisterium[12]—have taught the opposite. The *Catechism of the Catholic Church* (*CCC*) teaches that "[i]t is because the ministerial priesthood represents Christ that it can represent the Church" (no. 1553). While strongly affirming *that* reference to the Church is necessary in defining priestly identity, *PDV* teaches that there is a Christological priority in the ordained priesthood. It explains, in its second chapter, that "[t]he priest's relation to the Church is inscribed in

[9] This exhortation was issued after the Eighth Ordinary General Assembly of the Synod of Bishops (1990), which treated the topic of the formation of priests.

[10] For example, Susan Wood, "Priestly Identity: Sacrament of the Ecclesial Community," *Worship* (March 1995): 109–27. Rausch, "Priestly Identity"; Philibert, "Issues for a Theology of Priesthood"; David Power, "Representing Christ in Community and Sacrament," in *Being a Priest Today* (Collegeville, MN: The Liturgical Press, 1992), 97–123.

[11] For example, *CCC* 1553.

[12] See *PDV*; Congregation for the Doctrine of the Faith (CDF), "Declaration on the Question of the Admission of Women to the Ministerial Priesthood" (*Inter Insignores*) (1976), promulgated during the pontificate of Paul VI; and Pope Pius XII's encyclical on the Sacred Liturgy *Mediator Dei* (November 20, 1947).

the very relation which the priest has to Christ, such that the 'sacramental representation' to Christ serves as the basis and inspiration for the relation of the priest to the Church. . . . And so the priest, on account of his very nature and sacramental mission, appears in the structure of the Church as a sign of the absolute priority and gratuity of that grace which is conferred by the risen Christ on the Church."[13]

At the same time, one of the strengths of *PDV* is its statement that the nature and the mission of the ministerial priesthood must be defined in light of the "multiple and rich interconnection of relationships which arise from the Blessed Trinity and are prolonged in the communion of the Church, a sign and instrument of Christ, of communion with God and of the unity of all humanity."[14] In the light of this, it must be admitted that those theologians who are not convinced by the Church's teaching on the priority of the Christological dimension for priestly representation nevertheless share an important concern with recent magisterial teaching: that the ordained priest is not to be understood or seen as existing apart from the Church.[15]

Pastores Dabo Vobis also states that the synod's summary of the nature and mission of the ordained priesthood—which the second chapter of *PDV* itself claims to summarize—is a faithful presentation of the Council's teaching.[16] If this is true, it is hard to see how the idea that the priest can act *in persona Christi* because he can first act *in persona ecclesiae* can be reconciled with the teaching of Vatican II.

Coffey on the Priority of Priestly Representation

Coffey is of the opinion that Vatican II left us with the mistaken impression that the ordained priesthood is Christological, while the common priesthood, rooted in baptism and communicating an orientation to worship, is ecclesiological.[17] He makes this claim on the basis of what he thinks are the pneumatological and ecclesiological dimensions of the common and the ordained priesthood. He argues that *Presbyterorum Ordinis* (*PO*), number 2, which speaks of the priest as acting in the person of

---

[13] John Paul II, *PDV* 16 (translation mine). For the Latin text see *AAS* 84 (1992): 682.

[14] John Paul II, *PDV* 12. For the English translation see *Origins* 21 (April 16, 1992).

[15] *PDV* 16 also states that the ordained priesthood "arises with the Church" and that "consequently, the ordained priesthood ought not to be thought of as existing prior to the Church, because it is totally at the service of the Church. Nor should it be considered as posterior to the ecclesial community, as if the Church could be imagined as already established without this priesthood" (ibid.).

[16] The Pope refers here to the summary of the work of the synod collected in the "propositions" that were forwarded to him at the conclusion of the synod.

[17] Coffey, "The Common and the Ordained Priesthood," 211–12 and 235.

Christ the Head, "assumes" that the ordained priesthood should be understood immediately in Christological terms. Subsequent magisterial documents, he says, make the same assumption.[18] However, according to Coffey, deeper reflection shows that this assumption is mistaken. The headship of Christ is an ecclesial function and can only be exercised in the Church. In Coffey's words, "therefore statements about it [Headship], even one invoking Christ the priest, whether they be magisterial or simply theological are directly ecclesiological and only indirectly Christological."[19] Similarly, Coffey says that the common priesthood is directly ecclesiological and indirectly Christological because the common priesthood "is that of the members of the Mystical Body" and the Mystical Body is the Church.[20] Both priesthoods possess "properly an ecclesiological nature"[21] because

---

18 Ibid., 211.

19 Ibid.

20 Ibid. Coffey tries to correct Vatican II with *Mediator Dei*. He cites the following English translation of *Mediator Dei*, number 88, by the Catholic Truth Society: "[B]y reason of their baptism Christians are in the Mystical Body and become by a common title members of Christ the Priest; by the character that is graven upon their souls they are appointed to the worship of God, and therefore, according to their condition, share in the priesthood of Christ himself." Coffey interprets this to mean that the encyclical makes an ecclesiological statement about the faithful—by baptism they are members of the Body of Christ—and infers from it the Christological statement that the faithful are members of Christ the Priest. This passage of the encyclical, in the eyes of Coffey, gives an unambiguous ecclesiological reference for the common priesthood—one that Vatican II did not embrace as a conclusion. The serious problem with this claim is that Coffey relies on a faulty English translation. It only partially translates the phrase "generali titulo christiani in Mystico Corpore membra efficiuntur Christi sacerdotis." The original Latin text does not allow a disjunction between the Mystical Body and Christ the Priest. Rather, according to *Mediator Dei*, baptism makes the faithful members of the Mystical Body of *Christ the Priest*. The American-English translation in the Vatican Library translation series released by the National Catholic Welfare Office (Washington, DC, 1947) is more faithful to the Latin: "By the waters of Baptism, as by common right, Christians are made members of the Mystical Body of Christ the Priest, and by the 'character' which is imprinted on their souls, they are appointed to give worship to God. Thus they participate, according to their condition, in the priesthood of Christ." For a similar translation see Gerald Ellard, ed., *On the Sacred Liturgy: Encyclical Letter "Mediator Dei" of Pius XII* (New York: America Press, 1948), 44. See also Gerald Treacy, *"Mediator Dei" on the Sacred Liturgy* (New York: Paulist Press, 1948), 41. There is nothing in the encyclical that somehow places the Mystical Body in an antecedent position to Christ the Priest. Furthermore, Coffey's interpretation seems to require us to think that the encyclical supposes the sacramental character of baptism to be ecclesial rather than Christological. On the contrary, there is no reason to believe that *Mediator Dei* conceived of the character as having an ecclesial priority over the Christological.

21 Coffey, "The Common and the Ordained Priesthood," 225.

"they exist and operate as God's gifts to the Church,"[22] albeit as different and distinct gifts. Both forms of priesthood, however, do have "Christ's priesthood as their ontological ground."[23]

Coffey urges us to understand the common priesthood as "a dynamism of faith, of divine sonship or daughterhood," and the ordained priesthood as "a charism, of official witness, which the common priesthood is not."[24] Vatican II was not able to reconcile the two priesthoods in the person of Christ owing to what Coffey believes was an incomplete pneumatological understanding of the priesthood of Christ. The upshot is that the Council clung to the understanding that the ordained priesthood refers immediately to the headship of Christ and this did "nothing to correct the popular perception of the priest as above the Church rather than as part of it."[25] For Coffey, only on the foundation of a sound pneumatology is it possible to reconcile the common priesthood and the ordained priesthood and describe their intrinsic relation. Thus, on the basis of the anointing of the Spirit of Sonship, the common priesthood is said to be a "dynamism of incorporation into the Church" and the ordained priesthood is a particular charism.[26] Coffey describes the intrinsic relation between the ordained priesthood and the common priesthood as "the relation of sharing in Christ's headship over against simple union with him through faith, or the relation of official witness (apostolic leadership) in the Church over against simple belonging to it through faith and baptism."[27] The headship of Christ is a gift for the Church. It is not exercised above the Church, and must be seen as directly ecclesiological.

Priority of Priestly Representation: The Documents of Vatican II

Having described Coffey's interpretation of Vatican II, I will now examine two of his primary claims: (1) that Vatican II assumed that the ordained priesthood should be understood directly in Christological terms, and (2) that it thus gave the impression that the common priesthood was directly ecclesiological.

22 Ibid., 212.
23 Ibid.
24 Ibid, 235.
25 Ibid.
26 Ibid.
27 Ibid.

The Common Priesthood

The conciliar texts and the *Acta* show that the Fathers regarded the common priesthood and the ordained priesthood both as directly Christological. Both priesthoods participate in Christ's priesthood, mission, and triple office. The problem that faced the Fathers at Vatican II was how to specify and identify the difference between the priesthoods, given the fact that both were presented as directly Christological. They did so by specifying the differentiation of roles and functions between the two priesthoods. The diverse roles and functions are rooted in a particular sharing in Christ's life, or, to put it differently, in a particular ontological participation in Christ's life. The distinction that is made between the two priesthoods in *Lumen Gentium* (*LG*), number 10—that they differ essentially and not only in degree—should not be isolated from the explanation of it that is given in chapters 3 and 4.

Careful observation of chapter 4 of *LG* will show that the Council Fathers clearly taught that the common priesthood was directly Christological. *Lumen Gentium*, number 34, teaches that "since the supreme and eternal Priest, Christ Jesus, wills to continue his witness and service through the laity too, He vivifies them in His Spirit and unceasingly urges them on to every good and perfect work."[28] Thanks to the outpouring of the Spirit in baptism, the laity share in the mission of Christ as priest, prophet, and king. The lay faithful's activity in this threefold office is possible because of their profound union with Christ. It is telling that *LG* 34, 35, and 36 affirm that Christ continues his priestly, prophetic, and royal witness and service through the laity. Thus Christ himself continues his priesthood through the spiritual sacrifices of the laity who consecrate the world to God. Christ is said to "fulfill" (*adimplet*) his prophetic office not only through the hierarchy who teach in his name but also through the laity who witness and proclaim the Gospel in word and action (*LG* 36). The Lord desires to spread his kingdom through the laity who must "learn the deepest meaning and the value of all creation and how to relate it to the praise of God" (ibid.). The laity are said to be charged with the responsibility to permeate the world with the Spirit of Christ and to conform the conditions and institutions of the world to the norms of justice. There can be no doubt here that Vatican II understood that the laity, anointed by the power of the Spirit, act because of their union with Christ, the Priest. He alone is the origin of the lay faithful's priestly activity.[29] Coffey objects that

---

[28] All quotations from *LG* and *PO* in this chapter are taken from Abbot, *Documents of Vatican II*.

[29] The apostolic exhortation *Christifideles Laici* calls attention to this very point. Commenting on *LG*'s affirmation of the laity's participation in the triple office of Christ,

even if we can conclude that through their common priesthood the lay faithful act because of their union with Christ, "this would still not be readily recognized as a Christological reference, since in the body metaphor that it implies only the Head was identified as Christ, and therefore the members almost by definition would be other than him."[30] He also contends that even if *LG* did teach that the common priesthood is a participation in the priesthood of Christ, this is not sufficient to place the common priesthood into a Christological framework. According to Coffey this was due to a failure to put forth a model for the common priesthood comparable to that of the ordained priest who acts in the person of Christ the Head.

In reply, it should be pointed out that the head-body symbol must be read in its context and should not be abstracted from the careful presentation in chapters 3 and 4 about the differentiation of the two forms of priesthood. It does not do justice to the text of *LG* simply to assert that it taught that the common priesthood is a participation in the priesthood of Christ. The Council clearly spells out in chapter 4 that Christ acts through the lay members of his Body because he continues his life, his mission, and his threefold office through them. It is true that the laity does not share in the headship of Christ, but this does not mean that they are almost by definition other than Christ. It is because the lay members, by the power of the Spirit, are conformed and likened to Christ in baptism that they can be the mystical and historical extension of his Body. In the conception of the Church as the Body of Christ, Head and members must be understood in light of *LG*'s repeated affirmation that there is a differentiation of roles in the building up of Christ's Body and in the continuation of his mission.

A careful reading of the texts of *LG* cannot sustain the interpretation that Vatican II presented the common priesthood as directly ecclesiological and only indirectly Christological. The Council Fathers taught that the common priesthood is directly Christological, having its origin in Christ, in its own distinct way. The baptized are active participants in Christ's threefold office. United with Christ and made partakers of his priesthood, the baptized actively carry out his threefold office in the Church and especially in the world, where they mediate Christ's gifts. It is not sufficient to

---

Christifideles Laici, no. 14, states: "Clearly we are the Body of Christ *because* we are all 'anointed' and in him are 'christs,' that is, 'anointed ones,' as well as Christ himself, 'the anointed one.' In a certain way, then, it happens that with the head and body the whole Christ is formed" (emphasis mine; Eng. trans. in *Origins* 18 [February 9, 1989]: 562–95).

30 Coffey, "The Common and the Ordained Priesthood," 225.

describe the common priesthood as a matter of simple union with Christ or simple belonging to him because the priesthood of the baptized is ordered to Christ's mission.

The Ordained Priesthood

Coffey's claim that Vatican II "assumed" that the ordained priesthood should be understood directly in Christological terms is focused especially on the texts that deal with Christ's headship.[31] I contend that these texts should not be read in isolation from what is said about the ordained priesthood being rooted in Christ. It is not the case that the texts on headship "assume" that the ordained priesthood is directly Christological because these texts, such as *LG* 28 and *PO* 2, are grounded upon what is taught in the entire third chapter of *LG* (esp. 18–21). In this chapter, the ordained priesthood is presented, step by step, as rooted in a unique participation in the priesthood of Christ or, in other words, as "directly Christological."

According to *LG* 18, "Jesus Christ, the eternal Shepherd, established His holy Church by sending forth the apostles as He Himself had been sent by the Father (cf. John 20:21). He willed that their successors, namely the bishops, should be shepherds in His Church." *Lumen Gentium*, number 20, asserts that whoever listens to them listens to Christ. *Lumen Gentium*, number 21, explains that the bishops possess the fullness of the ordained priesthood and that "[i]n the bishops, therefore, for whom priests are assistants, the Lord Jesus Christ, the supreme High Priest, is present in the midst of those who believe." Thanks to their ordination, bishops exercise the triple office of Christ in *eius persona*. Morever, *LG* 21 states "it is clear that, by means of the impositions of hands and the words of consecration, the grace of the Holy Spirit is so impressed, that the bishops in an eminent and visible way undertake Christ's role as Teacher, Shepherd, and High Priest, and that they act in His person." *Lumen Gentium*, number 25, explains that bishops are "authentic teachers, that is, teachers endowed with the authority of Christ." In these ways, the bishop, and thus the ordained priesthood, has the unique capacity of representing Christ to the Church. It is Christ who continues his work and service of teaching, sanctifying, and shepherding through the ordained priesthood. It is true, of course, that this activity of the ordained priest is a gift of service for the Church, and in the Church, but the Council understands that the origin of this activity and service is Christ. Butler's research is helpful here. She calls attention to the fact that Vatican II's strong statements about the participation of the laity in Christ's priesthood necessitated a

---

31 Ibid., 211.

further specification of the distinctiveness of the ordained priesthood. This further specification of the ordained priesthood in terms of the formulas *in persona Christi* and *in persona Christi capitis*, served not only to clarify its distinctiveness but also to illuminate "the sacramental ordering of the Church as a body in which diverse functions bring about a vital unity."[32]

The text of *LG* 28 presents the ordained priesthood's participation in the priestly office of Christ as encompassing the three *munera* of teaching, leading, and sanctifying. Furthermore, the *relatio* clarifying the final text explains something of how the Council Fathers understood the relation between the Head and Body of the Church. The passage from *LG* 28 reads:

> Although priests do not possess the highest degree of the priesthood, and although they are dependent on the bishops in the exercise of their power, they are nevertheless united with the bishops in sacerdotal dignity. By the power of the sacrament of orders, and in the image of Christ the eternal High Priest (Heb 5:1–10; 7:24; 9:11–28), they are consecrated to preach the gospel, shepherd the faithful, and celebrate the divine worship as true priests of the New Testament. Partakers of the function of Christ the sole Mediator (1 Tim 2:5) on their level of ministry, they announce the divine word to all. They exercise this sacred function of Christ most of all in the Eucharistic liturgy or synaxis. There, acting in the person of Christ, and proclaiming His mystery, they join the offering of the faithful to the sacrifice of their Head. Until the coming of the Lord (cf. 1 Cor 11:26), they represent and apply in the Sacrifice of the Mass the one sacrifice of the New Testament, namely, the sacrifice of Christ offering Himself to His Father as a spotless victim (cf. Heb 9:11–12).

Butler points out that this text is particularly important because, according to the *Acta*, the editing of it forced a clarification of the phrase *in persona Christi*.[33] The first draft of the text did not present priest-presbyters as participating in the *munera* of teaching and leading when they acted *in persona Christi*. The use of the term *in persona Christi* in regard to priest-presbyters was restricted to the *munus* of sanctifying, that is, offering the Eucharistic sacrifice of the Mass and administering the sacraments. As for the other *munera*, priest-presbyters were said to be under the authority of the bishop and were to cooperate with the bishop in his shepherding of the people. The second draft, on the other hand, related the *munera* of teaching and guiding the faithful with acting in the person of Christ. This connection was solidified and expanded in the final draft, quoted above,

---

32 Butler, "Priestly Identity," 305.

33 Ibid., 298.

which became the approved text. Acting *in persona Christi* is not restricted to the celebration of the Eucharist. Priest-presbyters are said to be consecrated "to preach the Gospel, to shepherd the faithful and celebrate the divine worship." The sacrament of orders, which gives the priest-presbyter a share in the priestly office of Christ, includes the three *munera* of teaching, leading, and sanctifying. Butler writes: "The Council connects Eucharistic presidency and pastoral leadership on the grounds that in both the priest acts in the person of Christ."[34] Still, having made this strong connection, the Council Fathers teach that it is in the Eucharistic liturgy that priest-presbyters exercise their sacred functions in a preeminent way. The text of *LG*, at this point, footnotes the twenty-second session of the Council of Trent (Denzinger 1743) and the encyclical *Mediator Dei*, 84 (Denzinger 3850).[35] After warning against certain errors[36] the text from *Mediator Dei* states: "But we deem it necessary to recall that the priest acts for the people only because he represents Jesus Christ, Who is Head of all His members and offers Himself in their stead."

The citation of this passage from *Mediator Dei* also discloses something about how the Fathers at Vatican II understood the relationship between the ordained priesthood and the common priesthood, as well as the relationship between the Head and Body of the Church in the Eucharist. The priest can act for the people, for the common priesthood, only because he represents Jesus Christ, who is Head of all the members. It is Christ who speaks for us to the Father and draws us by the power of the Spirit into his worship of the Father. The ordained priest in the Eucharist sacramentally represents Christ presenting his Body, the Church, to the Father. He represents Christ doing for us what we cannot do by ourselves alone. Thus, it is because the priest acts in the person of Christ as Head that he can speak *in nomine ecclesiae*.

Aquila notices that there was another addition to the final text of *LG* 28 that contributed to the clarification of the term *in persona Christi:* "Exercising within the limits of their authority the function of Christ as Shepherd

---

34 Ibid., 298, citing also *Acta Synodalia*, vol. 2, pars 2, 213; see Aquila, *The Teaching of Vatican II*, 91.

35 The *relatio* on *LG* 28 and 29 explains "the office by which the priest acts 'in persona Christi' especially in Eucharistic worship is shown by the words of Trent and confirmed by the words of the encyclical 'Mediator Dei.'" The Council of Trent taught in its twenty-second session that it is Christ who offers the Eucharistic sacrifice for us. For the text of the *relatio* see *Acta Synodalia*, vol. 2, pars 2, 213. I give the translation in Aquila, *The Teaching of Vatican II*, 91.

36 *Mediator Dei*, no. 83 warns against the error of thinking that a "priest only acts in virtue of an office committed to him by the community."

and Head, they gather together God's family as a brotherhood all of one mind and lead them in the Spirit, through Christ, to God the Father." Aquila notices, rightly, that this addition is important because it connects the *munus* of the priest to Christ's function as Shepherd and Head of the Church.[37] This emphasis is further developed in *PO*.[38]

Summing up thus far: careful study guided by the *Acta* shows that *LG* 28 clarified the phrase *in persona Christi* by teaching that the priest-presbyter acts in the person of Christ not only in Eucharistic presidency but in pastoral leadership as well. In both instances, the priest-presbyter shares in the function of Christ the sole Mediator. It is in the Eucharist that the priest-presbyter acts in the person of Christ *par excellence*. There, he represents the sacrifice of Christ and acts for the faithful joining their sacrifices to the sacrifice of Christ the Head. Priest-presbyters participate in the function of Christ as Head and Shepherd, gathering together the faithful into God's family and leading them in the Spirit through Christ to the Father.

In *LG* 28 the essential difference between the ordained priesthood and the priesthood of the baptized cannot simply be distinguished by its "public" character. The ordained priest has a different relationship to Christ. He shares in the mediatorship of Christ in a special way because he represents Christ facing the Church announcing the word of the gospel and joins the sacrifice of the faith to Christ's sacrifice. In this way, *LG* 28 understands the ordained priesthood as directly Christological and as a gift for the Church.

Presbyterorum Ordinis builds upon what is taught about the ordained priesthood in *LG* 28. The first paragraphs of *PO* 2 state that all the baptized share in the consecration and mission of Christ and that in Christ all the baptized are made into a holy nation and a royal priesthood. It is recalled that the Lord, in order that the baptized might be joined together into one body, set up certain ministers and gave them the power to offer sacrifice and forgive sins. This priestly office is carried out for the faithful in the name of Christ.

Butler points out that the *Acta* show that the Fathers of Vatican II were concerned to clarify further still the theological nature of the distinctiveness of the ordained priesthood. *Presbyterorum Ordinis*, number 2, sets out to do precisely this. It declares that priests share in the authority of Christ to build up his Body, the Church, and act *in persona Christi capitis*:

> Inasmuch as it is connected with the episcopal order, the priestly office shares in the authority by which Christ Himself builds up, sanctifies,

---

[37] Aquila, *The Teaching of Vatican II*, 93.

[38] Understood in this context, the reference to headship in *LG* 28 is far more important than Coffey thinks. He dismisses it as "theologically insignificant" (Coffey, "The Common and the Ordained Priesthood," 211).

> and rules His Body. Therefore, while it indeed presupposes the sacraments of Christian initiation, the sacerdotal office of priests is conferred by that sacrament through which priests, by the anointing of the Holy Spirit, are marked with a special character and are so configured to Christ the Priest that they act in the person of Christ as Head. . . . Through the ministry of priests, the spiritual sacrifice of the faithful is made perfect in union with the sacrifice of Christ, the sole Mediator. Through the hands of priests and in the name of the whole Church [*nomine totius ecclesiae*], the Lord's sacrifice is offered in the Eucharist in an unbloody manner until He Himself returns.[39]

The Council Fathers were not satisfied with simply saying that the priest represents Christ; they wanted to specify how the priest represents Christ differently from the rest of the baptized. The specific difference between the priesthood of the baptized and the ordained priesthood is that the priest acts in the person of Christ the Head. But the Fathers went even further, clearly affirming that the participation in Christ's headship is given for the purpose of building up the Church and directing her growth.

By the time this text reached its final form, it had undergone several revisions. Butler calls attention to the official *relatio*, which explains that the presbyter "is configured in a special way to Christ the priest, so that, having become a sharer in the episcopal mission, he is able to act in the person of Christ the Head, Teacher, Priest, and Ruler . . . in the building up of his body, which is the Church."[40] The connection between headship and mission here is clear.

The next revision of the text and the accompanying *relatio* supply further insight into how the Council Fathers understood *in persona Christi capitis*. The revision—pertinent to the second sentence of the text quoted above—relates and differentiates the sacraments of initiation and the sacrament of orders. The ordained priesthood is grounded in the sacraments of initiation, but it is bestowed by the distinct sacrament of orders. Thanks to the anointing of the Holy Spirit, the priest-presbyter is given a unique character that configures him to Christ. It is this special sacramental character, which is Christological, that enables the ordained man to accomplish his mission *in persona Christi capitis*. In other words, if priests are marked with a special configuration to Christ, then this is basis of their action *for* the Church. Understood in this way the ordained priesthood

---

39 *The Documents of Vatican II*, ed. Walter Abbot, S.J. (Baltimore: Follett Publishing, 1996).

40 *Acta Synodalia*, vol. 4, pars 6, 390. I give Aquila's translation in *The Teaching of Vatican II*, 106.

cannot be spoken of as first ecclesial, because the source of priestly action comes not from the Church but from Christ.

The *relatio* notes the addition of the phrase *nomine totius ecclesiae*. The final text asserts that the faithful participate in the Eucharistic sacrifice through the ministry of the ordained priest. This is, of course, affirmed elsewhere in the documents of Vatican II,[41] but here the spiritual sacrifices of the faithful are said to be consummated in union with Christ's sacrifice which is offered through the hands of priest-presbyters in the name of the whole Church (*nomine totius ecclesiae*). The priest can pray in the name of the Church because he represents Christ, the Head of the Body, who gathers together the prayers and sacrifices of the members, joins them to his prayer and sacrifice, and presents them to the Father. It is this relationship of Christ to the Church that is sacramentalized in the ordained priesthood in which the priest stands *in persona Christi capitis*. Thus, when the priest prays *in nomine eccleisae*, he does so not only in the name of the local church community, but also in the name of the whole Church because he represents Christ, the Head who presents his Body, the Church, to the Father. The *relatio* sheds additional light on how *in persona Christi capitis* was understood because it explains that the mission of the priest-presbyter is distinct from the one given to the laity: the former has its source in the mission Christ gave to the apostles and through the apostles to the bishops.[42]

The understanding of headship, *in persona Christi capitis*, in the documents of Vatican II is different from the conception that Coffey proposes. He understands headship to be directly ecclesiological and indirectly Christological because it is an ecclesial function and can only be exercised in the Church. The difference between the ordained and common priesthood for Coffey ultimately rests upon an ecclesiological difference. He thinks of headship as the ability to represent the members of the Church.

In the documents of Vatican II, on the other hand, the essential difference between the ordained priesthood and the common priesthood is not simply ecclesial but Christological. The ordained priesthood and the com-

---

[41] See for instance *LG* 10; *Sacrosanctum Concilium*, no. 48. Here we can appreciate the logic of the latter document which teaches that since the faithful offer "the immaculate victim, not only through the hands of the priest, but also with him, they should learn to offer themselves too. Through Christ the Mediator, they should be drawn day by day into an ever closer union with God and with each other, so that finally God may be all in all." The point of the text is not to assert some narrow approach to the liturgy that would monopolize it in favor of the priest but rather to affirm the priority and gratuity of Christ who wants to unite the Church to his worship.

[42] *Acta Synodalia*, vol. 4, pars 6, 342.

mon priesthood each involve a different participation in the priesthood of Christ and a different participation in Christ's mission. The Council Fathers could affirm, deliberately, this Christological difference while at the same time asserting that both the common priesthood and the ordained priesthood, each in its own way, are given for the service of the kingdom of God and the Church. But again, this service issues from a certain participation in Christ's priesthood—something that not even the Church can give by her own power or ability alone.[43]

The Meaning of Headship

We turn now to Coffey's other claim, that if the ordained priesthood is understood immediately in terms of the headship of Christ, then the priest appears as above the Church or apart from the Church.

It is certainly true, as we have seen above, that Vatican II understands the source of the ordained priest's action for the Church as a participation in Christ's headship. However, this does not isolate the priest from the Church or put him in a position above the Church. The share of the ordained priest in the headship of Christ is given for the Church and is ultimately intelligible only in reference to the Church. In the documents of Vatican II headship is an inherently relational concept. Recall how *LG* and *PO* describe and explain the *munera* of the ordained priesthood in terms of sanctifying, shepherding, leading, preaching, and teaching. These things only make sense in relation to the Church—not apart from or outside of her. In other words, the priest understood as *in persona Christi capitis* represents Christ the Head in his relationship to the Church. This relationship—thanks to the indissoluble union between the Head and members of the Body—is not outside of the Church but within the Church. The Church lives in her Head and from her Head who is the

[43] It is interesting to note that Vatican II's understanding of the common priesthood and the ordained priesthood bears a certain correspondence with what St. Thomas teaches about the sacramental character being the character of Christ in *ST* III, q. 63, a. 3. After stating that a character marks something as being ordained to a specific end, St. Thomas says: "Secondly, each of the faithful is deputed to receive, or to bestow on others, things pertaining to the worship of God. And this, properly speaking, is the purpose of the sacramental character. Now the whole rite of the Christian religion is derived from Christ's priesthood. Consequently, it is clear that the sacramental character is specially the character of Christ, to Whose character the faithful are likened by reason of the sacramental characters, which are nothing else than certain participations of Christ's Priesthood, flowing from Christ himself" (translation taken from the English Dominicans [Chicago: Benziger Bros., 1947]).

source of her life.[44] Christ the Head lives with her and in her. Headship is constitutive of the Church and therefore cannot be other than within her.

It is because Vatican II affirms the Christological priority of orders—in terms of *in persona Christi capitis*—that it understands the ordained priesthood as "for others." The ordained priesthood is "for others" because it is a special participation in Christ's priesthood which, by its very nature, is ordered to the common good of the Body, the Church.[45] Thus, Vatican II understands that when a man is ordained a priest-presbyter he is given a new relationship to the Church within the one Body because he participates in a new way in the priesthood of Christ. The new relationship, which occurs within the Church, makes visible and effective sacramentally the reality of Christ's priestly office for the baptized.

This presentation of headship in the documents of Vatican II is consistent with the Council's profound sacramental understanding of the Church and orders. Christ's ongoing love for the Church, in which he calls, gathers, sanctifies, builds up, and unifies his Body, the Church—that is, his activity as Head and Shepherd—should be recognizable in a visible sign. This headship, whereby Christ faces the Church, is visible and identifiable in the ministry of the ordained priesthood. It is a sign of the sheer gratuity and priority of the grace of Christ. It is Christ with the power of the Holy Spirit who unites and fills up the Church with the divine life.[46]

---

[44] Cf. *CCC* 708.

[45] Although he did not use the later terminology of *in persona Christi capitis*, Augustine saw something of this relationship of the priesthood to the baptized as one of "with and for" in a sermon marking one of his anniversaries as a bishop: "Where I'm terrified by what I am *for you*, I am given comfort by what I am *with you*. For you I am a bishop, with you after all, I am a Christian." "Sermon 340," in *The Works of Saint Augustine: A New Translation for the 21st Century (WSA)*, ed. John E. Rostelle, vol. 3/9, *Sermons (306–340A) on the Saints*, trans. Edmund Hill (Hyde Park, NY: New City Press, 1990), 292, emphasis added.

[46] It is also worth noting that Vatican II's understanding of the headship of Christ—as the source of growth, order, and life—reflects something of what the Letter to the Ephesians and the Letter to the Colossians proclaim about the headship of Christ. Heinrich Schlier, commenting on the term *kephale* in Eph 1:22f, 4:14; 5:23; Col 1:18, 2:10, 2:19, observes that Christ is presented as Head of the Church "in the sense that from this Head the body grows up to this Head." In this schema, Schlier states, "the Head is not present without or apart from the body, nor the body without or apart from the Head. The Church is the earthly body of the heavenly Head." Moreover, "[i]n this unity of Christ and the Church the headship of Christ is manifested in the fact that He directs the growth of the body to Himself. The *kephale* determines not merely the being of the body but also the fulfilment of its life. . . . He is the effective 'whence' of the activity of the body whereby it edifies itself though gifts given to its members. As the *kephale* He is thus the concrete principle of the bodily growth of the Church. He is the *arche*, Col 1:18." See Heinrich Schlier, *Theological*

In the concern to present the ordained priesthood as existing within the Church, it is easy to confuse the question of context with that of representation. To be sure, both the common and the ordained priesthoods exist within the Church, not outside of her. To that extent, they are both ecclesial. It is also true, as we have seen, that both priesthoods have Christ the Priest as their origin. To that extent they are both Christological. But only the ordained priesthood, not the common priesthood, requires the sacramental representation of Christ.

A further difficulty is that Coffey fails to apply to his understanding of the ordained ministry the truth that Christ is the source of life in the Church. This failure leads to a faulty understanding of headship that equates headship with leadership or "official witness."[47] A fully sacramental

---

Dictionary of the New Testament, vol. 3, ed. Gerhard Kittle, trans. Geoffrey W. Bromiley (Grand Rapids, MI: Eerdmans, 1964–1976), s.v. "*kephale*," 680. Schlier also comments that "*kephale* implies one who stands over another in the sense of being the ground of his being. Paul could have used *arche* if there had not been a closer personal relationship in *kephale*" (ibid., 679). The exegete Markus Barth observes that Paul preferred to employ the verb "to fill" to describe how Christ the Head governed the Body. "If Christ is the head then he is the 'greatest power,' the 'source', the 'beginning' or the 'rule' (*arche*), the 'acropolis' of all members. Thus it is impossible to assume that they 'fill' him. He alone fills them" (Markus Barth, *Ephesians: Introduction, Translation and Commentary* [Garden City, NY: Doubleday, 1974], 190–91).

47 For example, recall Coffey's description of the relationship between the ordained priesthood and the common priesthood. "Depending on whether christological or ecclesiological terms of reference are chosen, it can be called the relation of sharing in Christ's Headship over simple union with him through faith, or the relation of official witness (apostolic leadership) in the Church over against simple belonging to it through faith and baptism. While both possibilities are correct, the second is the more appropriate, as it is expressive of the actual context in which the priesthood exists and operates" (Coffey, "The Common and the Ordained Priesthood," 235). David Power runs into a similar difficulty when he writes: "Hence his [the priest's] action *in persona Ecclesiae* is a cultic action wherein the Church's devotion and spiritual sacrifice is expressed. This distinguishes the action of the Church in giving homage from its action, through a minister, as instrument of Christ's sanctifying power, though the latter properly occurs in the context of the former" ("Representing Christ in Community and Sacrament," 101). Here are contrasted two situations. In the first, the Church through the priest gives homage to the Father, and the priest acts *in persona ecclesiae*. In the second, Christ acts through the Church, and the Church acts through the priest to sanctify. The difficulty with this is that it camouflages an equivocation with respect to "Church." In the first situation, the assembly expresses its devotion through the prayers said by the priest. In the second situation, does the assembly moved by Christ express its sanctifying action through the priest? On the contrary, Christ acts for the people through the priest. It is true that the action of the priest is an action of the Church but in a different sense than in the first situation.

understanding of headship is of a different kind. It is exercised only by the authority of Christ and in his person. It involves a special participation in the mission and mediatorship of Christ whereby Christ, the source of life, nourishes and builds up the Church. The ordained priesthood is a gift to the Church, instituted by Christ, neither prior nor posterior to the Church but within her. The rest of the baptized may designate the one to occupy this office, but they do not confer on him the authority to act *in persona Christi capitis*.

Coffey does, at one point, appear to come close to a sacramental understanding of headship that represents Christ as the source of the Church's life. After quoting some comments from an essay by Georg Hintze about priestly representation,[48] Coffey argues that the ordained priest sacramentally represents Christ's headship and that this headship is drawn not from the members of the Church but from Christ.

It is necessary to add only that the priest does not represent Christ and the Church in exactly the same way. He represents Christ in that he sacramentally makes visible and active in the Church an invisible reality, Christ in his headship. This is not the case with his representation of the Church, for in a real sense the Church is visible already. But in this case he adds headship, apostleship, or leadership to the action of this group of believers, in order to constitute them as Church in the full sense. Apart from his presence and ministry they are only a group of believers, unable of themselves to represent the Church. But at the same time, the fact that he represents them by no means renders their presence and action superfluous, for just as their faith is positive and active, so too is their priesthood. Thus it can be

---

Sanctifying the elements is not an action of the congregation. To be sure, the Church regulates the exercise of the priest acting as Christ's instrument. Still, the sanctifying action of Christ does not pass as it were from Christ to the assembly and then to the priest. Nor does the liturgy signify anything like this. It is relevant to note that during the discussion of the drafting of *PO* 2 the *relatio* explains that the addition of the words *nomine totius ecclesiae*, in reference to the priest, was made to show forth the nature of the sacrifice of the Mass. A Council Father proposed that the text should be emended so as to describe presbyters as "ministers of the Church." The theological commission responsible for overseeing revisions to the text rejected the request explaining that the text already spoke of the priest-presbyter speaking in "*nomine totius ecclesiae*." Furthermore, the *relatio* replied, "Presbyters act not as ministers of the Church but as ministers of Christ." The *relatio* cited *LG* 10 and 28: *in persona Christi agentes*. See *Acta Synodalia*, vol. 4, pars 7, 123–24. Here again we see the Council's intention to affirm the Christological priority of the priest representing Christ as Head.

48 Georg Hintze, "Das gemeinsame Priestertum aller Gläubigen und das besondere Priestertum des Dienstes in der ökumenischen Diskussion," *Catholica* 45 (1991): 44–77.

seen that, even though the priest represents a reality that is already at least partially visible, his is truly a sacramental, and not merely juridical, representation. (If, *per impossibile*, it were only of the latter kind, his priesthood would differ only in degree, not in kind, from theirs.) But what he adds is drawn not from them, but from Christ. And it is precisely this contribution that, along with theirs, truly constitutes the Church, and therefore the Church at prayer, that is, the priesthood of the Church.[49]

This affirmation that the ordained priest's sacramental representation of headship is derived directly from Christ does not seem to be integrated into Coffey's wider analysis of the nature of the ordained priesthood. Throughout his article,[50] except for the passage quoted above, he claims,

> For the headship of Christ as exercised in the only place where it can be exercised, namely, the Church, is clearly an ecclesial function, and therefore statements about it, even ones invoking Christ the priest, whether they be magisterial or simply theological, are directly ecclesiological and only indirectly Christological.[51]

But how can this headship, which the ordained priesthood sacramentally represents, be only indirectly Christological and directly ecclesiological *if*, as Coffey says, headship is drawn from Christ and *if* it is precisely this contribution that, together with the common priesthood, constitutes the Church, particularly the Church at prayer? There seems to be a failure, as described above, to grasp Vatican II's point that the sacramental representation of the headship of Christ has to do with representing Christ as source of the life of the Church, evident in the actions of sanctifying, teaching, and shepherding the Church.[52] Or in the words of *PDV* 16, "And so the priest, on account of his very nature and sacramental mission appears in the structure of the Church as a sign of the absolute priority and gratuity of that grace which is conferred by the risen Christ on the Church" (translation mine). A closer

---

49 Coffey, "The Common and the Ordained Priesthood," 233–34.

50 He comes to the same conclusion in his earlier essay "Priestly Representation and Women's Ordination," 96. Here Coffey states: "However, the priest's primary and direct representation is of the earthly church, and it is only insofar as he represents it that he is able to represent Christ and the whole Church."

51 Coffey, "The Common and the Ordained Priesthood," 211.

52 Here again, Vatican II's view of Christ's headship seems to be well-informed by the Pauline understanding. Markus Barth argues that "Paul could ascribe to the head more than a representative and dominating function. He could attribute to it the power to perceive, to interpret, to coordinate, and to unify all that went on in the body and its several members. Because the head is the 'greatest power' of the body, causation and coordination can be ascribed to nothing else" (Barth, *Ephesians*, 190).

reading of the documents of Vatican II together with the *Acta* would have assuaged Coffey's entirely legitimate fear that the sacramental representation of Christ's headship might be seen as isolating the ordained priest from the Church and placing him in a position apart from the Church or above her. *Lumen Gentium* and *Presbyterorum Ordinis* present the ordained priesthood (and the common priesthood) in a strong relational and Christological framework, understanding the ordained priest as sacramentally representing headship within the Church and for the Church.

Conclusion

Vatican II successfully avoided a juridical interpretation of priestly identity as well as a juridical understanding of the term *in persona Christi* that would isolate the priest from the Church. It affirmed a strong Christological priority of priestly identity in terms of a sacramental representation *in persona Christi capitis*. This inherently relational sacramental imaging of Christ in terms of headship firmly placed the ordained priest within the one Body, the Church, and thus made reference to the Church absolutely necessary for defining priestly identity. The ordained priesthood is a gift to the Church, instituted by Christ, neither prior nor posterior to the Church. The concern that scholars such as Coffey have for the ecclesial dimension of a contemporary theology of priestly identity is well placed. While not denying these concerns, this presentation has called attention to the priority of the gratuity of the grace of Christ and the gift of communion that Christ gives to the Church.

In persona Christi capitis is understood in the documents of Vatican II as a sacramental representation of the priority of Christ's activity whereby he gathers and builds up his Body, the Church, and draws the Church into his worship and his sacrifice. The ordained priest's ability to represent the Church and to pray in the name of the whole Church is based on his participation in this function of Christ as sole Mediator. The priest's representation of the Church and speaking *in nomine ecclesiae* is situated within *in persona Christi capitis*. The former has its foundation and its reason in the latter. It is Christ who first offers himself; the Church is only able to offer herself because of his offering. The Church gives homage and offers her sacrifice of praise through Christ. In this way, Christ, the Head of the Body, acts in the name of the whole Church and represents the whole Church to the Father. It is on this basis that we can distinguish two distinct forms of representation—distinct but always united. On the one hand, the priest represents Christ the Head who sanctifies his Body the Church and directs her growth. On the other hand, the priest represents the whole

Church by speaking *in nomine ecclesiae*, just as Christ does, representing her faithful response to the Father through the sacrifice of Christ.

The Christological priority of priestly representation is well established in Church teaching. I would suggest that the direction of further research might be well served if it moved beyond the issue of the priority of priestly representation. In *PDV* 12 we read that priestly identity, "like every Christian identity, has its source in the Blessed Trinity, which is revealed and is communicated to people in Christ, establishing, in him and through the Spirit, the Church." The exhortation goes on to observe that both the nature and the mission of the ordained priesthood cannot be defined except through this multiple and rich interconnection of relationships that arise from the Blessed Trinity and are prolonged in the communion of the Church, as a sign and instrument of Christ, of communion with God and of the unity of all humanity. I believe scholars might find it fruitful to take up the task of probing the interconnection of these relationships that constitute the identity of the ordained priest.

CHAPTER 9

In Conformity to Christ*

On November 29, 2005, the Congregation for Catholic Education in Rome released an instruction concerning the admission of men with homosexual tendencies to seminaries.[1] Barring men "who practice homosexuality, present deep-seated homosexual tendencies or support the so-called gay culture,"[2] the instruction was immediately subjected to endless commentary about what it means by "deep-seated homosexual tendencies."[3]

Gradually, the questions shifted to what the document means by "affective maturity"—but there are other important theological issues raised by the instruction that have yet to receive the attention they merit. One is an issue of moral theology. The second is a concern of theological anthropology or the "theology of the body." The third is an issue in the theology of orders. And the last concerns marriage.

Within the instruction, "deep-seated tendencies" are contrasted with "homosexual tendencies" that are "only the expression of a transitory problem—for example, that of an adolescence not yet superseded."[4] So, deep-seated tendencies are relatively permanent, not transitory. Deep-seated

* A version of this essay appeared in *First Things* (April 2006): 13–16.

1 Congregation for Education, "Instruction Concerning the Criteria for the Discernment with regard to Persons with Homosexual Tendencies in view of their Admission to the Seminary and to Holy Orders", www.vatican.va/roman_curia/congregations/ccatheduc/documents/rc_con_ccatheduc_doc_20051104_istruzione_en.html.

2 Ibid., 2.

3 Ibid., Introduction.

4 Ibid., 2.

tendencies are not some developmental glitch that one grows out of or past, as it were. They are "seated" deeply in the person and are not so much a passing product of environment or situation but something the person brings with him to every situation and environment. The instruction is saying that the bare presence of such "deep-seated tendencies" is reason enough to bar a candidate from the seminary. It is not what the person makes of such tendencies but the fact of the tendencies themselves that, according to the instruction, is a problem.

Some—even several in the American hierarchy—suggest the instruction is concerned not with the tendencies but with the place the person gives them in his own sense of himself, his personal identity.[5] This interpretation understands the instruction to mean that the problem is not the presence of homosexual tendencies but one's self-definition. Those men who have deep-rooted tendencies cannot be called by the Church to priesthood because their self-identification revolves around being gay. In this way, the problem of "deep-seated tendencies" is moved toward what the instruction identifies as "the so-called gay culture"—for the adherents of which, typically, a homosexual orientation is indeed taken to define a person and to be the most important fact about themselves. And it is said that part of the problem with such a self-definition is that it may lead to homosexual activity.

Some who subscribe to this interpretation have even gone so far as to identify or equate the problems of homosexual and heterosexual candidates.[6] They argue that if a man's heterosexual orientation dominates his self-definition and personality and therefore makes him unable to live the celibate life, then he, like the man with deep-rooted homosexual tendencies, would be disqualified from ordination as well. In these ways, the category of possessing "deep-seated homosexual tendencies" is moved to the other categories of being homosexually active or of engaging in gay culture. At the same time, the psychologies of heterosexual and homosexual men are put on par with each other, suggesting that they face the same prospects with the same chances for affective maturity.

Now, it may be that deep-seated tendencies turn out to be uncontrolled or uncontrollable. But "deep-seated" does not mean "uncontrolled or uncontrollable." Nor does it mean "desires I have chosen or allowed to be central or predominating in my sense of identity." The instruction is speaking of desires that are not situational or transitory (as perhaps in adoles-

5 See for example, "Bishop Says Edict Allows Some Gay Priests," *Washington Post*, (November 30, 2005): A01.

6 Ibid., see for example the comments of Bishop William Skylstad and Bishop Matthew Clark.

cence, in the case envisioned by the instruction). Some American seminaries may find attractive the notion that the problem is "self-definition," because it would not require them to do anything different from what they are doing now. Even now, no seminary enrolls men who are actively homosexual or who live a gay lifestyle. This sort of interpretation, in fact, would make the instruction completely unnecessary, and all could say, as several have done, that all the instruction demands of us is that we carry on as usual.

As for the psycho-sexual parity of heterosexual and homosexual men, a standard American Catholic seminary practice is indeed to suppose with the American Psychiatric Association that a man can possess affective maturity, of which psycho-sexual maturity is a part, while at the same time having deep-seated homosexual tendencies.

The instruction, however, supposes no such thing. For the instruction, an affectively mature man may once have had homosexual tendencies; but if so, they were transitory and he has grown—to maturity—out of them. Affective maturity is thus a more foundational issue than parsing "deep-seated homosexual tendencies." If we paraphrase and speak of "tendencies that won't go away," then the real difference is whether such tendencies all by themselves are compatible with affective maturity or not. Those for whom the problem is self-definition think they are; the instruction thinks they are not. This is clear enough, really, from the letter of the document. It is also clear from the comments of Cardinal Grocholewski, the prefect of the congregation that issued the instruction.[7]

Consistency with Moral Theology

This important psychological issue, however, is intimately and ineluctably related to a matter of moral theology. Affective maturity requires the consolidation of a man's passions and emotions into stable patterns that are congruent with and cooperate with moral virtue. So, a heterosexual man who has reached affective maturity and is ready for orders is serenely chaste, and the stable pattern of his passions and emotions does not spontaneously and precipitously bring him to the brink of immoral action: he not only wants to be chaste, but his sexual desires and emotional responses are chastened—disciplined, schooled—and therefore ordinate; they cooperate with his moral decision to be chaste, whether as a married man or as a celibate.

---

[7] See the Catholic News service story reporting on his comments during the press conference at which the instruction was presented, "Homosexuality and the Priesthood Revisted" *Catholic News Service Blog*, 31 October 2008, www.cnsblog.wordpress.com/2008/10/31/homosexuality-and-the-priesthood-revisited.

Affective maturity does not prohibit affections, of course; it means having good affections: ordinate and well-tempered affections. A man of deep-seated homosexual tendencies can certainly attain to chastity, refraining from all sexual behavior that is intrinsically disordered. He can be chaste, in that his sexual desires and tendencies are not unruly in the sense of regularly bringing him to the brink of immoral sexual activity. He may be chaste to the extent that his sexual desires do not preoccupy him. Nonetheless, if homosexual activity itself is always intrinsically immoral, and if homosexual tendencies are therefore always objectively disordered because inclining to what is always intrinsically immoral, then it makes good sense to say that his sexual affections, as such, are not good. They do not bear on the feminine, which is the target of mature male psychosexual desire. And therefore, since they are deep-seated, they prevent "affective maturity," which means, if it means anything, having good desires rightly ordered.

In fact, if a man of deep-seated homosexual tendencies can be affectively mature, then it cannot be said that homosexual tendencies are objectively disordered. And, obversely, if homosexual tendencies are objectively disordered, then no man with deep-seated homosexual desires can ever be affectively mature. In this light, it is hard to see how such a position that understands the problem to be one of self-definition can be in line with the Letter on the Pastoral Care of Homosexual Persons of 1986 from the Congregation for the Doctrine of the Faith (CDF).

Further, if homosexual tendencies are not *objectively* disordered, then there can be nothing *intrinsically* disordered about their satisfaction—and therefore one could not agree with the Declaration on Certain Questions concerning Sexual Ethics of the Congregation for the Doctrine of the Faith of 1975.[8] Nor could one agree with the *Catechism of the Catholic Church* (*CCC*).[9] Those who make self-definition the problem may not have expressly denied the teaching about either homosexual tendencies or homosexual acts, but they cannot consistently assert this teaching and at the same time read the instruction as they want to and take affective maturity in the way they want to take it.

Theological Anthropology and Spiritual Fatherhood

Also at stake in the faulty reading of the instruction is theological anthropology—attached to what the instruction calls the "spiritual paternity" the priest is supposed to exercise. Affective maturity requires a disciplining of

[8] www.vatican.va/roman_curia/congregations/cfaith/documents/rc_con_cfaith_doc_19751229_persona-humana_en.html.

[9] *CCC* 2357–58.

sexual desire and affection, and the priesthood requires a kind of sublimation or redirection of a man's natural sexual orientation to the service of the Church, the spouse of Christ, and to spiritual paternity in bringing forth children of God from the laver of baptism. In this, the heterosexual man does not have to suspend or abstract from what would be his felt and conscious choice of "sexual object," were he sexually active. The celibate priest has renounced something that nonetheless, on a different plane, the symbolic and ecclesial, finds expression; he has embraced something—the Bride of Christ, the Church—which is in harmony with what he has renounced.

The instruction indicates this framework for understanding its teaching in its very first section. For affective maturity, it directs its readers to *Pastores Dabo Vobis* (*PDV*). But for "spiritual fatherhood," the instruction sends us to the Directory on the Ministry and Life of Priests of 1994 from the Congregation for the Clergy, and this document in turn sends us to the paragraph on celibacy in *Presbyterorum Ordinis* (*PO*), the Decree on the Life and Ministry of Priests of the Second Vatican Council. Through celibacy, the Council teaches, priests "more expeditiously minister to his [Christ's] Kingdom and the work of heavenly regeneration, and thus they are better fitted to accept paternity in Christ more widely" (*PO* 16). The text also puts celibacy in the context of the nuptial relation of Christ and the Church. Priestly celibacy in the service of Christ and the Church is therefore properly that of a man, a male—it is an exercise of "paternity." The priest's maleness, his sexuality, his sexual psychology, is a part of his conformation to Christ.

In priestly celibacy there is a form of life in which the meaning of sexual difference for self-gift—nuptiality—is lived, and in which the specific finality of sexuality in fruitfulness is preserved. In this, the priest is configured to Christ. Because of celibacy, moreover, which makes the gift of self to the Church total, there is even greater configuration to Christ, as John Paul II pointed out in *PDV*. But this realization of nuptial self-gift occurs in its characteristically masculine form. The theologian Sara Butler has noted the priority of the love of God relative to our love, the initiative that characterizes the love of Christ and the love of God and which makes their figuration as masculine appropriate: "This priority in loving can be compared to a *masculine mode of loving*, of self-donation," she writes, "when considered in light of the 'nuptial meaning of the body' and the active role of the husband in the marital embrace."[10] Feminine and masculine modes of loving are coordinate; they complement and evoke one another, but they are distinct.

---

[10] Sarah Butler, "The Priest as Sacrament of Christ the Bridegroom," *Worship* 66 (1992): 511.

Presbyterorum Ordinis therefore envisages a seamless integration of the psycho-sexual and affective with the sacramental and spiritual. The priest renounces ordinary paternity, but he gives himself to spiritual paternity. He renounces something good, and something to which he is by nature directed, and something for which he may have felt and conscious desire. And yet, in its own way and at its own level, spiritual paternity expresses the truth of the body. All is harmonious, and there is no discord between one's own identity, affectivity, and sexuality—and the representation of Christ, the Bridegroom of the Church, his Bride.

Masculine Maturity and the Theology of Orders

There is thus a sort of "affective" conformation to Christ that priestly mission and life calls for. Ordination, to be sure, effects a conformation to Christ at a sacramental level, making the priest an instrument of Christ. But just as there is a prior conformation to Christ required of the candidate at the level of the body, at the level of the moral virtues, and at the level of charity, so also at the affective level. It is not, therefore, merely that the man of deeply seated homosexual tendencies cannot be affectively mature, but also that his affective immaturity, since it fails of *masculine* maturity, prevents him, at that level, from conformation to Christ. Claiming that a man with deep-seated homosexual tendencies is an apt candidate to exercise spiritual paternity means emptying it of any meaning specific to maleness.

If we are going to ordain to the priesthood men of deep-seated homosexual tendency, we will have to excise from spiritual fatherhood anything that connects it to actual sexual desire, sexual differentiation, and bodiliness. For the same reason that there is nothing to prevent a child in a modern family having "two daddies" or "two mommies," there will be nothing to prevent a homosexual man from exercising spiritual fatherhood. But then, it will be hard to see why it is that only men can be ordained to the priesthood, contrary to the universal practice of the Church as confirmed by *Ordinatio Sacerdotalis*. If a priest does not have to be psychologically masculine, why should a priest be somatically male? It will follow as well that there can be no significance to the manhood of Jesus of Nazareth. In the end, we will have to practice a studied ignorance of all paternity, even that of the Father of Lights, from whom every fatherhood in heaven and earth takes its name.

The Connection to Marriage

Marriage, too, must be among the casualties of the neglect of the natural order of desires and affections that ignoring the plain sense of the instruction implies. The relation of Christ and the Church is the great sacrament of which the relation of husband and wife in Christ is the little sacrament. If the manhood of Christ is theologically insignificant, then sexual differentiation must be immaterial to the little sacrament as well. It cannot become irrelevant for one without becoming irrelevant for the other. If *spiritual* paternity is whatever we want it to be, then marriage—with its own paternity and maternity—is whatever we want it to be, too. We land squarely in the post-modern sensibility about matters sexual and marital.

There are serious implications to the attempt by some commentators to interpret the recent instruction as concerned primarily with self-definition. There are implications for the morality of homosexual acts. There are implications for the psycho-physico-spiritual unity of man. There are implications for the theology of orders. And there are implications for marriage, as well. All these implications are contrary to the established, universal, and constant teaching and practice of the Church.

CHAPTER 10

The Augustinian Foundations of Nuptial Theology of the Body: "He Who Created Both Sexes Will Restore Both"*

THE PLACE and importance of nuptial sexuality in Christian revelation is greatly questioned today. By nuptial sexuality I mean the reciprocity between man and woman whereby in their sexual existence each one of them is placed in relation to the other in a special way. What special way? I mean the way that both man and woman experience the other as a different personal embodiment of human identity, in that man is made for woman, and woman for man.[1] What some dispute, including some theologians, is whether this nuptial ordering of sexuality is of any importance for Christian revelation.

Embodied Nuptial Sexuality: Does It Matter?

Two Modern Responses

For example, the well-known theologian Elizabeth Johnson thinks, in effect, that nuptial sexuality has very little theological significance.[2] For one thing,

---

* A version of this essay first appeared in *Wisdom and Holiness, Science and Scholarship, Essays in Honor of Matthew L. Lamb* (Naples, FL: Sapientia Press, 2007), 353–74.

1 This reciprocity is asymmetrical in the sense that the sexual difference of the other can never be overcome or transcended by me. In other words, the reciprocal relation between the sexes is between two beings, each of whom has a certain irreducible identity. There can be a union between the two ways of being in the body as man or woman, but this union is not an absorption of one into the other or a union into a third way of being in a body. The other always remains "other" for me. On this point see Angelo Scola, "The Nuptial Mystery at the Heart of the Church," *Communio* 25 (1998): 630–62, at 645.

2 Elizabeth Johnson, *She Who Is* (New York: Crossroad, 1993), 154–55. Johnson also objects to what she calls the "prevailing dualistic model" that imagines each sex as

Johnson argues that we need to go beyond an idea of a human nature that is polarized on the basis of sex, in favor of "one human nature celebrated in a multiplicity of differences" of which sex is one among many.[3] Being a male or female is no more important than many other things that are said to be part of a person's identity. It is "short-sighted" to think of sexuality as more important and more fundamental than the elements of race, of culture, and of politics, as well as a whole host of other elements said to be intrinsic to personal identity. Sexuality is one among many essential anthropological elements that make up personal identity. For Johnson what is important about sexuality is not that it has an enduring theological determination or meaning in Christian revelation but that it is a part of a set of combinations that make up and celebrate the one human nature. According to Johnson, only if sexuality is conceived as integrated into a holistic vision as one anthropological element among many will sexuality avoid being distorted as a "touchstone of personal identity."[4]

Another theologian, David Power, has argued that sexuality is part of the limiting condition of our human enfleshment that the risen Christ now somehow transcends.[5] Thus Power distinguishes between "a historical Jesus from the past," who was sexually determined, from the risen Christ, who is not. At the Resurrection, Christ overcame the negative and limiting conditions of human existence, including that of maleness, and entered into solidarity with the whole human race. Transformed in the Resurrection by the power of the Spirit, Christ takes body in the Church-communion, where there is no male or female, Greek or Jew. Power therefore proposes that it is more fitting to see Christ as the renewed human rather than "as the male unit of a renewed male-female unity in one body." Here again nuptial sexuality is judged to have little if any lasting importance for Christian revelation.

The theological significance of the fact that human persons are created in two different bodily incarnations has been disputed for some time in the history of Christian thought. Already in the fourth and fifth centuries a common view among many of the Fathers of the Church was that

---

"bearing unique characteristics from which the other sex is excluded." She rejects any idea of the complementarity of the sexes as rigidly determining the qualities and roles each should cultivate and play, but sees it as functioning as a "smoke screen for the subordination of women."

[3] Ibid., 155. At least here Johnson does not seem to make much of a distinction between "nature" and "person."

[4] Ibid., 156. Johnson explains that the sexuality of Jesus is important for his personal and historical identity, "but is not theologically determinative for his identity as the Christ nor normative for the identity of Christian community."

[5] See, for example, Power, "Representing Christ in Community and Sacrament," 116.

sexual differentiation was something God in his mercy gave to a humanity threatened by death because of the Fall of Adam. Some of the Fathers thought that originally Adam and Eve were sexless angelic creatures who had no need of reproduction as we know it now. Sexuality after the Fall was important for one reason and one reason only: that the human race might continue to live and that God's command "Be fruitful and multiply" might be obeyed. The role sexuality played in the cosmic drama was temporary and instrumental. This was, albeit with some variation, the view of Ambrose, Gregory of Nyssa, and Jerome.[6]

An Impermanent Reality: Gregory of Nyssa

Gregory of Nyssa was particularly insistent about the temporary nature of sexuality. In his interpretation of the creation of humanity in the Genesis accounts, Gregory distinguished between an ideal, angelic humanity and an actual humanity. In his original design, God saw humanity as a collective whole destined for Christ, in whom there is neither male nor female. In a process unknown to us, humanity would have grown and multiplied in an angelic way, rather than through bodily sexual union. Why then an actual creation of humanity as male and female? Gregory explains that God foresaw that humanity as a whole would sin against its spiritual nature by turning away from God and toward material realities. The human race, no longer existing in an angelic way, would have stopped reproducing and would have faced extinction. Therefore God in his mercy divided humanity into male and female with garments of skin, in order that they might multiply by way of carnal generation like the animals. Thus, for Gregory, sexual differentiation is secondary and temporary. Sexuality and procreation serve God's original design for humanity but only because they prevent the extinction of a sinful humanity.[7] While Gregory

---

[6] Ambrose, *Exhortation on Virginity* 6.36 (*Exhortatio uirginitatis*, PL 16, 197–244). E. Cazzaniga, *Sancti Ambrosii De Virginibus* (Turin, 1948); for an English translation, see *On Virginity*, by Ambrose, *Bishop of Milan*, trans. Daniel Callam (Toronto: Peregrina, 1980). Gregory of Nyssa, *On the Making of Man* 17 (*De opifico hominis*, PG 44, 125–256; SC 6 [1943]); for an English translation, see "Gregory of Nyssa: On the Making of Man," in *A Select Library of the Nicene and Post-Nicene Fathers* (hereinafter referred to as *NPNF*), ed. P. Schaff and H. Wace, vol. 2/5 (Grand Rapids, MI: Eerdmans, 1994 [reprint]). See Jerome, *Against Jovianian*, 1, 29 [*Adversus Jovinianum*, PL 23, 211–338.] For an English translation see *NPNF* 2/6, *Jerome, against Jovinianus*.

[7] The following account is taken from Gregory of Nyssa, *On the Making of Man* 16–17. See also the oration "On Those Who Have Fallen Asleep" 9.63 (*Gregory Nysseni Opera*, ed. W. Jaeger et al. [Leiden: E. J. Brill, 1960]), where Gregory repeats

believes that humanity is created in the image of God, he argues that the creation of humanity as *male and female* in no way pertains to the divine image and likeness.[8] He holds that in the resurrection we will all be one in Christ and that our risen bodies will be divested of all signs of sexual differentiation.[9] In the resurrected state we will leave behind all that we have received with the garment of skin—all those things that we share with the nature of irrational animals. The ideal humanity of God's original design will be fulfilled eschatologically. Ultimately, sexuality is something alien to both the original divine design and the final definition of humanity.

The common element between these theologians, both ancient and modern, is that nuptial sexuality is disconnected from the order of

---

his opinion that the differences between the sexes were given solely for the purpose of procreation. Gregory's views proved to be influential for some of the Greek Fathers that followed him. For instance, Hans Urs von Balthasar cites this interesting passage from Maximus the Confessor: "I repeat what the great Gregory of Nyssa taught me: the first thing to happen when man fell from perfection was that *pathe* were introduced, growing up in the irrational part of man's nature; only then did that manner of procreation enter into human existence that is connected to fleshly pleasure, on the one hand and death on the other." See Maximus, *Questiones ad Thalassium* 1 (PG 90, 296A), quoted in Hans Urs von Balthasar, *Theo-Drama*, trans. Graham Harrison, vol. 2 (San Francisco: Ignatius Press, 1990), 380.

8 In his *On the Making of Man* 16.14, Gregory claims that the distinction between male and female "has no reference to the Divine Archetype, but, as we have said, is an approximation to the less rational nature." See 16.7 where he makes reference to Galatians 3:28 in support of this claim: "We must, then, examine the words carefully: for we find, if we do so, that that which was made 'in the image' is one thing, and that which is now manifested in wretchedness is another. 'God created man,' it says; 'in the image of God created He him.' There is an end of the creation of that which was made 'in the image': then it makes a resumption of the account of creation, and says, 'male and female created He them.' I presume that everyone knows that this is a departure from the Prototype: for 'in Christ Jesus,' as the apostle says, 'there is neither male nor female.' Yet the phrase declares that man is thus divided." For Gregory man, male and female, shares the likeness of animals. See *On the Making of Man* 17.5. For a helpful summary of Gregory of Nyssa's understanding of sexuality, see Verna E. F. Harrison, "Male and Female in Cappadocian Theology," *Journal of Theological Studies* 41 (1990): 441–71, at 465–71. Harrison points out that "[f]or Gregory, this second likeness includes a whole complex of nonrational and biological characteristics—gender and the corresponding mode of reproduction, childhood and old age, nutrition and elimination, passions such as desire and aggressiveness, and mortality itself" (p. 467).

9 For example, see the discussion in his dialogue *On the Soul and Resurrection*, trans. Virginia Woods Callahan, in *Saint Gregory of Nyssa: Ascetical Works* (Washington, DC: Catholic University Press of America Press, 1967), 264–71, especially 266. For Gregory the resurrection will be the return of human nature to its original form, that is, before its division into male and female.

redemption insofar as it is considered to be without any real theological significance in Christian revelation. Whether one thinks of nuptial sexuality as temporary, or a limitation, or just another part of a socially constructed identity, it is supposed that Christ and the redemption he brings has very little to say about something that is important to embodied human existence. Surely this is something of a problem. For instance, if as the Christian tradition teaches us about the resurrection, our whole bodies will rise and not just some part of our bodies, then, our risen bodies will be masculine and feminine. If we will be raised as men and women, then sexuality is in some way a redeemed reality. If sexuality is a redeemed reality, it must bear some theological meaning. Surely, it is the case that at least someone among the Fathers saw this and thought about it. I believe there is someone, but oddly enough someone that many people might least suspect.

Augustine of Hippo and Sexual Differentiation: A Sacramental Reality

An important exception to the understanding in his day of sexuality as a temporary and instrumental remedy against death, and therefore of little or no theological meaning, was Augustine of Hippo. He saw the sexual differentiation of the first couple as a part of God's original creative plan and as something that foreshadowed the unity between Christ and the Church. The idea that Augustine has anything to say of importance to us today about sexuality may strike some as rather odd. After all, we often hear, wrongly I might add, that it was Augustine who taught that sexual relations between a husband and wife always involved at least a venial sin.[10]

The real Augustine was far more complicated. As one of his twentieth-century biographers reminds us, we should not demonize Augustine on the issue of sexuality.[11] Peter Brown has pointed out, rightly I believe, that Augustine's thought on sexuality evolved and developed over time—the result of a long inner journey that the North African saint underwent. I

---

10 Augustine actually held that intercourse for the purpose of procreation was not sinful. He thought that when married couples engaged in intercourse beyond the need for generation it was venially sinful. This may be rigorist, but it is not the same thing as saying all intercourse between married men and women is a venial sin. See *On the Good of Marriage* 5.6, and *On Marriage and Concupiscence* 1.12.13. For an excellent discussion of this issue, see John Hugo, *Augustine on Nature, Sex, and Marriage* (Chicago: Scepter, 1969), 109–15.

11 `Peter Brown, *Augustine of Hippo* (Los Angeles: University of California, 1967, 2000), 502. See also his *The Body and Society* (New York: Columbia University Press, 1988), 399–408.

believe that we can learn something today from Augustine's journey, particularly as it touches on the theological significance of the creation of human persons as sexually differentiated. It shows us that the context for thinking about the place and meaning of nuptial sexuality in Christian anthropology is sacramental. Augustine saw that if marriage is in some sense a sacrament, and if the union between Christ and the Church is understood nuptially, then sexuality cannot be regarded simply as given for biological survival. It has an intrinsic significance to our salvation. I believe that Augustine's journey anticipated, in a way, today's struggle over the sacramental meaning of sexuality.

Augustine's insights to be sure are incomplete. Nevertheless he grasped, with unusual perceptivity, something about how nuptial sexuality is a central part of human existence that is really addressed by divine revelation, really addressed by Christ. In terms of contributing to the current discussion about the significance of nuptial sexuality in Christian revelation, Augustine's journey shows us that to think of nuptial sexuality as theologically neutral is to put in question the sacramentality of marriage and the nature of the relationship between Christ and the Church. It is to put in question sacramental realism; it is to put in question the belief that the sacramental acts of the Church reflect and correspond to the truth of existence as effected by God.

At the same time that Augustine explained the married unity of couples as a sacrament of Christ and the Church, he was also explaining how the unity between Christ and his Church should be understood as a personal unity like that of marriage. There is a real relation between Augustine's theology of marriage and his ecclesiology. Thanks to a number of factors, Augustine's thought was sharpened over time. His rethinking of the significance of the sexuality of Adam and Eve in paradise, as well as his explanation of the relationship between Christ and the Church as a nuptial reality, is an intellectual journey that is instructive for us today.

In what follows I will sketch in broad strokes this journey of Augustine. Of course I will have to be brief. I make no pretense of giving a comprehensive description of Augustine's complicated views on human sexuality. Still, I believe that Augustine can show us some important things.

My presentation will unfold in four parts. In the first part, I will give a brief overview of Augustine's early attempt to articulate the sacramentality of marriage in the history of salvation. He saw that understanding marriage as a sacrament inevitably raised questions about the role of nuptial sexuality in God's plan of creation even prior to the Fall. In the second part, I will describe how Augustine rethought his views on the place and importance of the sexual differentiation of the first couple in paradise, and how he came to the conclusion that the first man and woman foreshadowed the future reality of Christ and the Church. So strongly did Augustine connect nuptial sexuality to the order of redemption that he insisted that the unity between Christ and the Church should be understood in terms of personal unity like that of marriage. Thus, in the third part, I will give a brief overview of how Augustine described Christ and the Church as joined in a bodily union as Bridegroom and Bride. In the fourth and final section of my presentation I will indicate how I believe Augustine's thought is helpful for the contemporary discussion about theological significance of nuptial sexuality.

Augustine and the Sacramentality of Marriage

In 401 Augustine wrote a treatise titled *On the Good of Marriage.*[12] In his *Retractions*, Augustine says that he wrote the work in response to the heresy of the monk Jovinian. The writings of Jovinian rejected the doctrine that the merit of virginity was superior to the merit of marriage. Jovinian argued that to hold virginity as superior to marriage involved a negative, Manichean understanding of marriage. These views of Jovinian were very influential and persuaded some nuns in Rome to give up celibacy for marriage. Jovinian's teachings commanded a following even after they were condemned in 393 by a Roman synod headed by Pope Siricus and by a synod in Milan headed by Ambrose.

Augustine tells us that the supporters of Jovinian bragged that he could only be answered by censuring marriage, not by praising it. Augustine disagreed. For this reason he wrote *On the Good of Marriage.* But there was also another reason. He tells us that there were previous unsuccessful attempts to refute Jovinian. One that Augustine may have in mind was an infamous treatise by Jerome, *Against Jovinian.* Jerome, perhaps the most accomplished Christian polemicist of all time, was so harsh and negative in his rhetoric that his response to Jovinian was rightly regarded by many as an attack on marriage itself. Some of Jerome's friends tried to have copies of his treatise withdrawn from circulation.

Augustine's treatise *On the Good of Marriage* is an effort to sail midway between Jovinian's claim that the gift of virginity is in no way superior to

[12] All quotes from *On the Good of Marriage* are taken from the English translation in *The Works of Saint Augustine* (*WSA*), ed. John E. Rotelle, vol. 1/9, *Marriage and Virginity: The Excellence of Marriage, Holy Virginity, The Excellence of Widowhood, Adulterous Marriages, Continence*, trans. Ray Kearney, ed. David Hunter (Hyde Park, NY: New City Press, 1999), 33–61. Although I make use of this translation in this paper, I have chosen not to follow its translation of the title *De bono conjugali* into the *Excellence of Marriage*. I prefer to translate the title *De bono conjugali* into *On the Good of Marriage*. This has been the more common way of translating *De bono conjugali* in earlier and familiar English translations. For the Latin texts see *De bono conjugali*, PL 40, 373–96; CSEL 41.

marriage and Jerome's belittling of marriage. Augustine argued, on the one hand, that the gift of virginity is of greater merit than the married state and, on the other hand, that marriage was good, holy, and instituted by God.[13] He presented marriage as a form of friendship and "the first natural bond of human society."[14] In defense of marriage, Augustine identified three goods destined to become classic for the Catholic theology of marriage: offspring,[15] mutual fidelity,[16] and the *sacramentum* or the sacramental bond.[17]

It is this third good that is of particular interest for present purposes because the holiness of the *sacramentum* is something specific to the marriage of Christians. While we should be careful not to read back into Augustine's thought a later and more developed understanding of sacraments and sacramental causality, it should be remembered that Augustine's theology of the sacraments was quite advanced for its time and proved to be very influential. He understood sacraments broadly as visible signs that corresponded to an invisible sacred reality.[18] He could also make more precise distinctions with regard to the sacraments such as baptism and Eucharist. Augustine

---

13 Augustine believed that virginity was of higher merit because of its intense eschatological character. Virginity anticipated the life of the world to come. In *On Holy Virginity*, Augustine could describe it as a sharing in the life of the angels (13). Virgins, Augustine contends, preserve in their bodies that spiritual integrity that the whole Church preserves in the faith, imitating the Mother of the Lord. At the same time Augustine says that those who have the gift of virginity need sound instruction so that they might be humble and not become puffed up with pride, so that love might not be offended against. He also points out that the gift of martyrdom is even higher than the gift of virginity (46.46–47).

14 Augustine, *On the Good of Marriage* 1.1.

15 Ibid., 1.1; 6; 24, 32. Thanks to children, who are the worthy fruit of the union of man and wife, human persons are held together in society not only by similarity of race but also by the bond of kinship.

16 Ibid., 4.4; 24, 32. This good of marriage referred to that power of authority each spouse has over the body of his or her partner. A husband or wife was not to abstain from sexual relations except with the approval of his or her spouse. The violation of fidelity, of course, is adultery. Augustine understood husband and wife as giving one another the mutual service of sustaining each other in weakness for the avoidance of illicit sexual union.

17 Ibid., 18.21; 24, 32.

18 See Letter 138 (*Epistula 138*, CSEL 44.131): "It would take too long to discuss adequately the variety of signs which are called sacraments when they applied [pertinent] to divine things" (*St. Augustine: Letters*, Volume III, trans. Sister Wilfrid Parsons, Fathers of the Church 20 [New York: Fathers of the Church, Inc., 1989, 40]). Cf. *City of God* 10.5: "A sacrifice, therefore, is the visible sacrament or sacred sign of an invisible sacrifice." All quotations of the *Civitas Dei* (PL 41; CSEL 40) are taken from *The City of God*, trans. Marcus Dods (New York: The Modern Library, 1950).

could distinguish between the sacramental sign itself (*sacramentum tantum*) and the effect of the sacrament (*res sacramenti*). Water, for example, washes the body and signifies what occurs in the soul.[19] Moreover, Augustine argued that sacraments are not arbitrary sacred signs. They have a likeness to the reality that they signify.[20] Augustine could also speak of a sacrament in terms of a binding oath or sacred religious commitment. In *On the Good of Marriage* Augustine seems to understand the *sacramentum* of marriage in this way, although he sees it too as a symbol capable of signifying a plurality of sacred realities. He could even speak of the polygamous marriages of the Old Testament patriarchs as *sacramentum.* They signified "the plurality of people who would one day be subject to God in all nations of the earth."[21] The many wives of the patriarchs also signified the future churches arising from all nations subject to one husband, Christ. What made the *sacramentum* of monogamous marriages in the Christian dispensation different had to do with the fact that indissolubility was fundamental to it. The holiness or sanctity of the *sacramentum* of Christian marriage did not permit divorce and remarriage even in the case of adultery on the part of one of the spouses or for reason of sterility.

Augustine thought that the Christian signification of marriage brought about an indissoluble bond that was more binding than the bond of non-Christian marriage.[22] What brings about this *sacramentum*, this indissoluble bond? Augustine takes it almost for granted that it comes from Christ in his union with the Church. Although he does not explicitly cite Ephesians 5:31–32—where the one-flesh union of Genesis 2:24 is said to be a "great mystery" in reference to Christ and the Church—this passage lurks in the background of Augustine's discussion of the indissolubility of Christian marriage. Augustine supposes that the union of Christ and the Church is the great *sacramentum* that contains the holiness of indissolubility. This can be seen in a fascinating and often overlooked passage in the eighteenth chapter of *On the Good of Marriage*, where Augustine makes an interesting

---

19 See *Tractates on the First Letter of John* 6.3.11, in *NPNF*, vol. 1/7 (*In epistulam Ioannis ad Parthos*, PL 35; SC 75). "Consequently, the water of the sacrament is one thing: another, the water which betokens the Spirit of God. The water of the sacrament is visible: the water of the Spirit invisible. That washes the body, and betokens that which is done in the soul. By this Spirit the soul itself is cleansed and fed."

20 For example, Letter 98 (*Epistula 98*, CSEL 34.520) in *St. Augustine: Letters*, Volume II, trans. Sister Wilfrid Parsons, Fathers of the Church 18 (New York: Fathers of the Church, 1989), 137–38. "If the sacred rites had no resemblance to the things which they represent, they would not be sacred rites; they generally take their names from the mysteries they represent."

21 Augustine, *On the Good of Marriage* 18.21.

22 Ibid., 24, 32.

argument from the liturgical practice of the Church of his day comparing holy orders to marriage.[23] He explains that after our pilgrimage on earth there will be a perfection of human unity in heaven, where there will be a city of people with a single heart and soul turned toward God. For this reason, he thinks that with the coming of Christ, marriage has been restored to a union of one man and one woman to the extent that a man who has been married more than once should not be ordained. A presiding priest (*antiste*) who is able to symbolize the union of all nations in submission to Christ is a man who has had only one wife or who has not been married at all. Augustine argues that a man who has married more than once, even though he has not sinned, has lost a certain standard or prerequisite for the seal of ordination. He seems to think of him as unable to symbolize the great *sacramentum*, the indissoluble union of Christ and the Church.

It is not too surprising that Augustine almost as a matter of fact assumes in *On the Good of Marriage* that the unity of all nations or the Church with Christ is a nuptial kind of unity. In earlier works Augustine had already spoken of the Church as a wife created from the side of Christ[24] and of "the marriage of the catholic Church to the Lord."[25]

Augustine goes on to say in chapter 18 of *On the Good of Marriage* that this unity of all nations in submission to Christ will be perfected in the future. The sacrament of monogamous marriage, he claims, symbolically signifies this future reality in the heavenly city. But Augustine seems

---

23 Augustine also compares the bond of marriage to the permanency of ordination. See ibid. He makes the point that there are times when one of the purposes of marriage is not achieved and yet the sacrament remains. Something like this can happen with the sacrament of ordination as well. Ordination, the Bishop of Hippo says, is given for the purpose of forming the community of the faithful. Nevertheless, sometimes communities fall apart or cannot be formed. Still, the sacrament of ordination remains. So, too, in the cases where an ordained man is dismissed from the clerical state. The Lord's sacrament still remains, although the unworthy man must answer for his wrongdoing at the judgment. Similarly, if a man or woman divorces his or her spouse and marries another the marriage bond is not broken. The Lord's sacrament is still intact and will remain so until the death of one of the marriage partners. Augustine's comments show that he had some idea that the sacrament of marriage brought about a bond that had certain kind of sacramental objectivity to it.

24 *On Genesis against the Manichees*, 2.24.11 (*De Genesi contra Manichaeos libri II*, PL 34, 173–220; CSEL 91). For an English translation, see *Two Books on Genesis against the Manichees*, trans. Roland J. Teske, Fathers of the Church 84 (Washington, DC: Catholic University of America Press, 1991). This early work was written from 388 to 389. See also *Reply to Faustus the Manichean* 15.3 (*Contra Faustum Manicheum*, PL 42; CSEL 25.1). For an English translation see *NPNF*, vol. 1/4. This theme appears in later works of Augustine as well. For instance, *City of God* 22.17.

25 Augustine, *Reply to Faustus* 15.5.

to suppose too that marriage is able to signify this reality because it signifies the indissolubility of Christ and the Church and in a way participates in it. Augustine thinks of the symbolic signification of Christian marriage in more than one way but always in reference to the Christ-Church unity.[26] That the *sacramentum* of Christian marriage signifies this nuptial reality is an idea that Augustine will return to again in his later works.

Rethinking the Place of Embodied Sexuality in Paradise

A keen interpreter of Augustine's thought once observed that it would have never occurred to Augustine, who was biblical to his fingertips, to use any basis for evaluating marriage other than the history of salvation in its eschatological movement.[27] For eschatological things cast light on first things. This approach also prodded Augustine into raising a question in *On the Good of Marriage* that he answered only in a later work. The question has to do with whether the begetting of children by means of sexual intercourse was a part of God's original plan for the first man and the first woman even if they had not sinned. A number of Church Fathers, as I mentioned earlier, asked the same question and answered it in the negative. Bodily reproduction was thought to be tied up with being a fallen creature. Augustine was not so sure and left the question open in *On the Good of Marriage*, only to answer it later in an important way in another work, *On the Literal Interpretation of Genesis*. Augustine began this commentary on Genesis around 401, soon after he had completed *On the Good of Marriage*. He did not finish his commentary on Genesis until about 415. In this work there is an important shift in his understanding of marriage and sexuality, a shift that put Augustine in stark contrast with some prominent Christian thinkers up to that time. The shift in Augustine's thinking in this work is an important moment in the intellectual movement of his thought about marriage and sexuality.

In an earlier commentary on Genesis prior to 401, Augustine gave a highly spiritualized interpretation of Adam and Eve in paradise. In his commentary *On Genesis against the Manichees*, written around 389, Augustine was more interested in what the first man and woman spiritually symbolize than he was in the meaning of the first couple's corporeal reality. For instance, in one passage, Augustine seems to say that prior to the Fall human souls had

---

[26] One scholar of Augustine has remarked, rightly, that while Augustine "never draws the explicit conclusion that matrimony is a grace-giving sacrament of the New Law, as subsequently has become defined Catholic doctrine, but everything he says on this point has sacramental connotations, and makes such a conclusion almost inevitable." See Augustine Regan, "The Perennial Value of Augustine's Theology of the Goods of Marriage," *Studia Moralia* 21 (1983): 351–76, at 358.

[27] Ibid., 353.

no need for spoken words but drank directly from the Word of God, the fountain of truth.[28] Commenting on the creation of woman (Gen 2:22) Augustine was less interested in the bodily reality of the first man and woman and more interested in how as male and female they symbolized certain parts of the soul and how these parts are related to one another. The first woman illustrates how the soul's appetites should be subject to the virile mind.[29] The command in Genesis 1:28 to be fruitful and multiply, according to Augustine, refers to a spiritual, not a corporeal union, which would produce the fruit of good works.[30] Prior to the Fall the first man and woman would not have produced children in a carnal, fleshly way, in keeping with their quasi-angelic condition. Sexual reproduction was something that happened only after Adam and Eve had incurred the penalty of death for their sin.

But in his *Literal Interpretation of Genesis* Augustine embarked upon a very different reading. He admits that his interpretation in *On Genesis against the Manichees* was overly allegorical and did not explain the text according to its proper historical meaning.[31] Augustine now insists that paradise must not be interpreted in an exclusively spiritual sense. It should be taken to refer to a spiritual and a literal, corporeal sense.[32] He explicitly rejects the opinion of some authors who thought that history properly speaking did not begin until Adam and Eve sinned, fell into tunics of skin, were joined in sexual union, and bore children.[33]

This new approach to reading Genesis allows Augustine to take up the question he had previously left unanswered in *On the Good of Marriage*: whether the begetting of children through sexual intercourse was a part of God's original plan for the first man and woman even if they had not sinned. Augustine now explains that Adam and Eve were fully physical, sexual, and social human beings before the Fall. The bodies of Adam and Eve, although unlike ours and not subject to death, would have been earthly ones, not heavenly, angelic ones.[34]

---

[28] Augustine, *On Genesis against the Manichees*, 2.4.5. Even in his *Confessions* 8.24.37, he interprets Genesis 1:28 as referring to the spiritual production of thoughts produced by the mind.

[29] Augustine, *On Genesis against the Manichees*, 2.11.15.

[30] Ibid., 1.19.30.

[31] Augustine, *On the Literal Interpretation of Genesis* 8.2.5 (*De Genesi ad litteram libri XII*, PL 34, 245–486; CSEL 28.1). For an English translation see *The Literal Meaning of Genesis*, vol. 2, trans. John Hammond Taylor, Ancient Christian Writers 41 (New York: Newman Press, 1992).

[32] Augustine, *On the Literal Interpretation of Genesis*, 8.1.1.

[33] Ibid., 8.1.2.

[34] Ibid., 9.10.17.

Augustine acknowledges that there was no actual sexual union before the Fall of the first couple, but he insists there was nothing in paradise that would have forbidden it. He contends that Adam and Eve chose to sin before they had a chance to know the corporeal union of sexual intercourse.[35] Had they avoided sin, the intercourse they could have enjoyed would have been free from any lust or compulsion. They would not have known of that inner struggle that the Apostle Paul wrote about between the law in our members and the law of our minds making us captive to the law of sin.[36] Childbirth would have been free from any pain and labor. Children would have been born not to make up for dead parents but for the purpose of populating the city of God. Once a certain determined number of people were born, they all would have been given an additional gift: the transformation of their bodies into a new higher, heavenly form of bodily existence without having to first pass through death, the punishment for sin.[37] Far from being asexual souls who fell from an angelic state into a physical one, Augustine now presented Adam and Eve as physical, sexual, and social creatures whom God placed in paradise to establish a people for the city of God. This vision of God's original plan for man before the Fall was a bold one, and very different from the ascetic interpretation of Genesis in which marriage and sexuality were basically alien to the man's original state.

Augustine continues to champion the goodness of marital sexual relations and procreation in paradise in his famous work *The City of God.* In book 14, written around 418–419, shortly after he completed *On the Literal Interpretation of Genesis,* he argues that it is absurd to think that were it not for sin there would be no need for sexual relations and procreation. This is tantamount, he objects, to asserting that sin is necessary to complete the number of saints. No, marriage and children were worthy of the happiness of paradise. Rejecting an overspiritualized interpretation of God's creation of humanity as male and female as described in the book of Genesis, Augustine continues to insist that sexuality, the gift of marriage, and procreation were all instituted by God before Adam and Eve sinned. As proof for this claim he appeals to Christ's reply to the Pharisees concerning divorce: "Have you not read that He who made them from the beginning made them male and female and said, For this reason shall a man leave father and mother, and shall cleave to his wife, and they shall be no longer two but one flesh."[38]

Augustine goes on to a discussion of what sexual relations between Adam and Eve would have been like had there been no sin and no Fall. He

---

[35] Ibid., 9.3.5.

[36] Ibid., 9.10.16.

[37] Ibid., 9.3.5; 9.6.10.

[38] Augustine, *City of God* 14.22.

argues that there would have been a complete harmony between the bodies and souls of Adam and Eve. They would have enjoyed a calmness of mind and integrity of body. There would have been an absence not only of lust but of impotence as well. Augustine draws a picture of the first couple with a freedom, a freedom for the good; that is, a greater freedom where spontaneity is not divorced from the mind. This is something Augustine thinks is largely unknown to us. We know only fallen freedom weighed down by concupiscence, disordered desire.[39]

For Augustine, the sexual existence of humanity as male and female was not limited to the original state and the fallen state. In book 22 of the *City of God* Augustine contends that although there will be no marriage and procreation in heaven, nevertheless, those just men and women who are risen with Christ will keep their sexuality. In chapter 17, "Whether the bodies of women shall retain their own sex in the resurrection,"[40] Augustine refutes those who thought that because Romans 7:29 spoke of human creatures as being "[c]onformed to the image of the Son" it must mean women would rise as men. Against this idea, Augustine says that the trouble is not the existence of women but the existence of lust. He says, "For before they sinned, the man and the woman were naked, and were not ashamed."[41] The woman is a part of the good creation as is the man, and her creation from man expresses that God intends a unity between them. Furthermore, Augustine explains that the creation of woman foreshadowed Christ and the Church. For just as the woman was made from the side of Adam as he slept, so the Church was created from the side of Christ who was asleep in death on the Cross. Augustine goes on to claim, "He, then, who created both sexes will restore both." In other words, if risen bodies were asexual they would not be the resurrection of *our* bodies, the bodies that God made in the good creation.

Augustine has gone far beyond his earlier, highly spiritualized interpretation of the original state of Adam and Eve in *On Genesis against the Manichees*. The contrast with his earlier views could not be more striking. Augustine now presents Adam and Eve in the original plan of God as fully embodied sexual beings who are to procreate and raise up citizens for the city of God. Sexual reproduction is something God intended prior to the Fall. Therefore it is not something that can be simply understood as a merciful remedy against death. Augustine, in affirming sexuality and procreation not only as compatible with paradise but as a part of it, detaches

---

[39] Ibid., 14.23.
[40] Ibid., 22.17.
[41] Ibid.

sexuality and procreation from any necessary link with the Fall. Human sexuality and procreation now have a meaning independent from the Fall and its consequences. While marriage and procreation do not constitute the eschatological future of humanity, nevertheless masculinity and femininity—part of God's good creation—will not pass away in the risen life.

Augustine continues this line of thought in another work, *On Marriage and Concupiscence*, written around 419–420. This work was addressed to Valerius, an officer of the imperial court. In the first book of this work, Augustine repeats his claim that marriage is good and was instituted in paradise prior to the Fall, and that sexual reproduction could have taken place. Marriage after the Fall labors under the burden of concupiscence. This is illustrated by the fact that the sexual organs are not completely obedient to fallen man whether in the case of compulsive copulation or in the case of impotence.[42] Augustine answers his Pelagian opponents who accused him of teaching, in effect, that marriage is sinful because it produces children who inherit the fallen condition of Adam. Against these opponents he is adamant about the fact that even though marriage produces children who have been corrupted by the sin of Adam and need to be reborn in baptism, marriage is nevertheless good. The three goods of offspring, mutual fidelity, and the sacramental bond still mark marriage after the Fall. At one point, Augustine rhetorically interrogates the three goods to show that sin does not arise from them but that they would have been more secure in marriage had sin not wounded them. What is of particular interest for my purpose is what Augustine says about the sacramental bond:

> And then this will be the answer of the sacramental bond of marriage,—the third good: Of me was that word spoken in paradise before the entrance of sin: "A man shall leave his father and his mother, and shall cleave unto his wife; and the two shall become one flesh." This the apostle applies to the case of Christ and of the Church, and calls it then "a great sacrament." What, then, in Christ and in the Church is great, in the instances of each married pair it is but very small, but even then it is the sacrament of an inseparable union.[43]

This passage shows that for Augustine the great nuptial mystery is the one-flesh union of Christ and the Church. The full meaning and significance of the "small" one-flesh union between man and woman is known from the "great" one-flesh union of Christ and his Church. It is *the* paradigm for the nuptial union between the sexes. This is the reason for the indissolubility of

[42] Augustine, *On Marriage and Concupiscence* 1.6.7 (*De Nuptiis et Concupiscentia*, PL 44; CSEL 42). All quotations are taken from *NPNF*, vol. 1/5.

[43] Ibid., 1.23.21.

Christian marriage. In another passage, Augustine explains that married believers as members of the Body of Christ are never permitted to divorce and remarry. Just as there can be no separation or divorce in the case of Christ and the Church, so there can be no separation between married believers while both are still alive. Augustine compares the marriage bond with the sacrament of baptism. Just as the apostate retains his baptism after his apostasy, so the marriage partners retain their marriage bond even if one or both of them sins or divorces and remarries. Clearly, for Augustine, marriage between believers involves a participation in the nuptial union of Christ and the Church, which in turn creates an indissoluble bond between the partners. But again, Christ the Bridegroom and his Bride function as the norm and paradigm for marriage.

In the second book of *On Marriage and Concupiscence*, Augustine makes a short comment about marriage prior to the Fall that builds on this point.[44] It occurs in the course of his answer to his Pelagian opponent Julian of Eclanum, who accused him of teaching that marriage after the Fall was changed into something evil. In defense of his views, Augustine argues again that what is changed after the sin of Adam and Eve is not the nature of marriage but the nature of humanity. He says that marriage was instituted by God in paradise and that marriage remains something instituted by God even after sin. At one point in this explanation, Augustine makes an additional claim about marriage in paradise. He says that the marriage instituted in paradise is a figure of the great mystery between Christ and the Church. Now an important part of the holiness and goodness of Adam and Eve in their nuptial union is that they are a figure of a reality that is to come.[45] The goodness of marriage and sexuality, far from

[44] Ibid., 2.54.32.

[45] It is true that in *On Genesis against the Manichees* 2.24.37 he says what was fulfilled as history in Adam and the woman signifies as prophecy Christ in his one-flesh union with the Church. The important difference between this affirmation and the one in *On Marriage and Concupiscence* is that in *On Genesis against the Manichees* Adam and Eve prophesied Christ and the Church not from the very beginning but only after sin. In 1.19.30 Augustine, commenting on Genesis 1:28, "Increase be fruitful and multiply," claims that the bodily union between Adam and Eve occurred only after the first sin. Prior to sin there would have been a union of virile reason and a lower part of the soul that would have brought forth spiritual children. It would seem then that Adam and Eve did not prophesy Christ and the Church until their one-flesh bodily union and thus after the first sin. This is what Augustine refers to as "what was fulfilled in history in Adam." At least in *On Genesis against the Manichees*, Augustine saw a link between bodily union and procreation and the first sin. On the other hand, this notion is completely absent in *On Marriage and Concupiscence*, where there could have been a bodily union prior to sin and where nuptial relationship between Adam and Eve even before sin prefigured the mystery of Christ and the Church.

being something alien in paradise, is most fitting because it is a figure of how man and woman will be further blessed in Christ.[46] It seems too that here again for Augustine, Christ and the Church is the nuptial union par excellence, the one-flesh union, and the paradigm for every nuptial union.

Totus Christus: *A Nuptial Reality*

There is strong evidence that shows while Augustine rethought his views on sexuality in paradise he was also thinking more deeply about the nuptial union between Christ and the Church. Over 50 percent of the occurrences of the term *sponsa Christi*, referring to the Church as spouse of Christ, are found in works that Augustine wrote between A.D. 401 and 420.[47] For instance in his homilies on the first epistle of John written around A.D. 406–407, Augustine proclaims: "For all the Church is Christ's Bride, of which the beginning and first fruits is the flesh of Christ: there was the Bride joined to the Bridegroom in the flesh."[48] In a passage from *Tractates on the Gospel according to John*, also dated from around A.D. 406–407, Augustine says that the marriage at Cana is a reflection of the virginal marriage between Christ and the Church.[49] Thus even women who vow virginity have a share in marriage, "For they too, together with the whole Church, attain to a marriage, a marriage in which Christ is the Bridegroom."[50]

---

46 In several of his other works written after *On Marriage and Concupiscence*, Augustine continues to proclaim the presence of marriage in paradise. For instance, there is a letter discovered only in 1975, known as Letter 6* (CSEL 88.32–38) in which Augustine wrote to Atticus of Constantinople defending his understanding of marriage and sexuality. Not only does Augustine affirm that marriage and sexuality were a part of God's original plan, he tries to imagine what sexual intercourse might have been like in paradise. Sexual desire in paradise would have been different from sexual desire as man now knows it as there would have been absent any sort of compulsiveness.

47 A search of the entire corpus of Augustine run on the database *Cetedoc Library of Christian Texts* shows 23 out 44 occurrences of *sponsa Christi* occur in works written between A.D. 401 and 420.

48 Augustine, *Tractates on the First Letter of John* 2.2, in *NPNF*, vol. 1/7. "Omnis enim Ecclesia sponsa Christi est, cujus principium et primitae caro Christi est: ibi iuncta est sponsa sponso in carne."

49 Augustine, *Tractates on the Gospel according to John* 9.2.2 (*In Johannis evangelium tractus*, PL 35; CCL 36). "Nor are those women who vow virginity to God, although they hold a higher place of honor and sanctity in the Church, without marriage. For they too, together with the whole Church, attain to a marriage, a marriage in which Christ is the Bridegroom. And for this cause, therefore, did the Lord, on being invited, come to the marriage, to confirm conjugal chastity, and to show forth the sacrament of marriage. For the bridegroom in that marriage, to whom it was said, 'Thou hast kept the good wine until now,' represented the person of the Lord. For the good wine—namely, the gospel—Christ has kept until now."

50 Ibid. In addition to these passages there are also three sermons that speak of the wedding contracts (*tabulae matrimoniales*) between Christ and the Church: sermon

Still more telling at this time is how Augustine appealed to the nuptial, marital relation to explain the nature of unity between the Head and Body of the *totus Christus*. Earlier I asserted my belief that there is a real relation between Augustine's theology of marriage and his ecclesiology. At the center of Augustine's doctrine of the Church is the *totus Christus*, the whole Christ, which encompasses the Head and Body. The eternal Son of God made man is the Head, while the Body is made up of the baptized who are the members. Together the Head and Body is the *totus Christus*. After his death and Resurrection, Christ the Head is present and embodied on earth in the Body that is the Church. The Head and the Body are always united and are never apart or divided. The union of the Body with the Head is a unity that is freely chosen out of love. Tarcisius van Bavel observes that this unity for Augustine is a personal unity like that of a bridegroom and bride:[51] Christ the Head is to the Body as Bridegroom is to Bride.

Van Bavel notices that Augustine makes the point repeatedly in his writings that the Head and Body seem to be two, but they are also one, one flesh, that is. There is a certain unity through identification but not an identity between the Church and Christ. For instance, in a commentary on Psalm 30 (probably written around 411) Augustine says:

> I want you to understand that the Head and body together are called one Christ. To make this quite clear he [the Lord] says, when speaking of marriage, *They will be two in one flesh; so they are two no longer, but one flesh* (Mt 19:5–6). But perhaps it might be thought that he only means this to apply to any ordinary marriage? No, because listen to what Paul tells us: They shall be two in one flesh, he says. *This is a great mystery, but I am referring it to Christ and the Church* (Eph 5:31–32). So out of two, one single person comes to be, the Head and body, Bridegroom and bride.[52]

238.1 (PL 38:1125), sermon 183.11 (PL 38:992), sermon 340A.11 (MA 1:573). On this see David Hunter, "Augustine and the Making of Marriage in Roman North Africa," *Journal of Early Christian Studies* 11 (2003): 63–85. Hunter has pointed out that the argument Augustine makes in all three sermons is the same: "Since Christ is the Bridegroom and the Church is the Bride, their wedding contracts will reveal their true identity and the true nature of their union" (p. 82). The gospels according to Augustine are these wedding contracts and Luke 24:46–47 contains the essentials of these *tabulae matrimoniales*: "Thus it is written the Messiah would suffer and rise from the dead on the third day."

[51] Alan Fitzgerald, ed., *Augustine through the Ages* (Grand Rapids, MI: Eerdmans, 1999), s.v. "Church," 169–79, at 171.

[52] *Exposition of the Psalms* 30.2, 4 (*Ennarrationes in Psalmos*, PL 36–37; CCL 38–40). All quotations are taken from the English translations in *WSA*, ed. J. E. Rotelle, vol. 3/15 (New York: New City Press, 1990). I have also slightly reworked it, eliminating

In another sermon which Augustine preached around 417, he explains that Christ can be understood in the scriptures as named in three ways. The first way is before his assumption of the flesh, as according to the divine nature in which he is God coeternal with the Father. The second way is after the Son assumed flesh and became the Mediator and Head of the Church. Augustine says about the third way:

> The third way is how the whole Christ is predicted with reference to the Church, that is as head and body. Where do we find this, that head and body form one Christ, that is, the body together with its head? In Isaiah he is speaking as if in the singular, [and it is one and the same speaking] and see what is said: "As for a bridegroom he has bound a turban on my head, and as for a bride he has decked me out with ornaments." (Isa 61:10) As bridegroom and bride; he calls one and the same bridegroom with reference to the head, bride with reference to the body. They are seen as two, and are one.[53]

Augustine goes on to say later in the same sermon: "So whether I say head and body, or whether I say bridegroom and bride, you must understand the same thing."[54] What is of interest for the present purpose is that

---

the word "people" where it does not appear in the Latin original. This is Augustine's second commentary on Psalm 30. Augustine's commentary on the Psalms can be hard to date. On the basis of internal evidence, scholars believe that Augustine possibly preached this commentary at a church near Carthage in 411. See *WSA*, vol. 3/15, 324.

53 Sermon 341, 19 (F. Dolbeau, *Vingt-Six Sermons au people d'Afrique* [Paris: Études Agustiniennes, 1996], 22); *WSA*, vol. 3/11. This nuptial understanding of the Head-Body relationship leads Augustine to propose the principle of the one flesh, one voice that highlights the unity hidden in the distinction between the Head and the Body. For instance, in a commentary composed sometime around 414, Augustine wrote about Psalm 34: "We hear Christ's voice in it: the voice, that is of Christ, Head and body. When you hear Christ mentioned never divorce Bridegroom from Bride, but recognize the great sacrament, they will be two in one flesh (Eph 5:31; Gen 2:24). If there are two in one flesh, why not two in one voice?" (*Exposition of the Psalms*, 34.2; *WSA*, vol. 3/16). Similarly commenting on Psalm 30: "Let Christ speak, then, because in Christ the Church speaks, and in the Church Christ speaks, and the body speaks in the Head, and the Head in the body" (*Exposition of the Psalms* 30.2.4; *WSA*, vol. 3/15). We see again how important the nuptial reality is not only for Augustine's ecclesiology but for his interpretation of the psalms as well.

54 Ibid., 20. Augustine also argues that the one-flesh union spoken of in Genesis 2:24 applies to Christ and the Church. We should also understand Christ as referring Genesis 2:24 to the one-flesh union between himself and the Church in Matthew 19:5–6 where Christ says, "They shall be two in one flesh; they are not now two, but there is one flesh."

some of the most profound texts in which Augustine explained the Head-Body relationship in nuptial terms occur around the same time he claimed that marriage was part of God's original plan, and insisted upon its sacramentality. It may well be that as Augustine thought about and explained the eschatological reality of Christ and the Church as nuptial, he was stirred to think about the place of marriage and sexuality in God's original plan. Whatever the case may be, Augustine's claim that the sexual differentiation of created humanity is something that is a part of the eschatological reality of Christ and the Church is absolutely indispensable for Augustine's understanding of the sacramentality of marriage. Sacramental signs for Augustine were not arbitrary. They have a likeness to the reality that they signify. Augustine once explained to a puzzled bishop that "[i]f the sacred rites had no resemblance to the things which they represent, they would not be sacred rites; they generally take their names from the mysteries they represent."[55] The logic of Augustine's thought leads to the conclusion that unless the union between Christ and his Church is in some sense nuptial, unless the bipolarity of man and woman is in some way a part of the Christ-Church relationship, marriage would not be a sacrament.[56] If we look back over Augustine's intellectual journey, from his early work *On Genesis against the Manichees* to his later work *On Marriage and Concupiscence*, we see that his thought evolved from a disinterest in sexuality in the original plan of God to a profound affirmation of the religious significance of the masculine-feminine bipolarity of sexuality that embraces the order of creation and the order of redemption. His thinking about the sacramentality of marriage inevitably raised the question about the place of nuptial sexuality in God's original plan of creation. For Augustine, the complete meaning of the one-flesh union of man and woman written about in Genesis 2:24 is found in the one-flesh union of Christ and his Church (Eph 5:32). Nuptial sexuality is thus sacramental. Ultimately, the truth of sexuality, the truth of masculine-feminine bipolarity of the good creation, is a matter of mystery that is best known and discovered in the light of the eschatological relationship of Christ and his

---

[55] Letter 98 (*Epistula 98*, CSEL 34.520) in *St. Augustine: Letters* 2:137–38. Augustine writes to Boniface, the bishop.

[56] By bipolarity I mean what Angelo Scola means when he writes about a "constitutive polarity": "The reciprocity that springs from sexual difference thus shows that the 'I' emerges into existence from within a kind of constitutive polarity. In order to be able to say 'I' in the fullest sense, I need to take the other into account; I have the possibility of (that is, the resource for) taking the other into account" (Scola, "Nuptial Mystery at the Heart of the Church," 643). See also Hans Urs von Balthasar, *Theo-Drama*, 2:346–94.

Church. This means, of course, that the masculine-feminine distinction is something intrinsic to the new covenant, the new creation in Christ. Finally, by insisting on the created goodness and permanency of sexuality, Augustine could not avoid the conclusion that human persons will enjoy the full perfection of sexuality in heaven that is in the perfected unity of Christ and the Church. Nuptial sexuality is therefore a supernaturally redeemed reality. Augustine, unlike Gregory of Nyssa, could not regard sexuality as instrumental and temporary and as a mere remedy for death.

Embodied Nuptial Sexuality: A Redeemed Reality

What conclusions might be drawn from Augustine's intellectual journey for the current discussion about the theological significance or insignificance of nuptial sexuality? First and foremost, Augustine's thought points us in the direction of sacramental realism. Marriage as a sacrament tells us something real and true about our salvation. If marriage is a sacrament in which the union of one man and one woman *really and truly* signifies and participates in the unity between Christ and his Church, then it communicates the truth that the union between Christ and the Church is a nuptial one. It means, as Augustine knew, that the masculinity and femininity of created humanity is a redeemed reality and ultimately an eschatological reality because its exemplar, its archetype is Christ, the Bridegroom, and the Church, his Bride.

If on the other hand, as some contemporary theologians have proposed, we should think of the unity between Christ and the Church as beyond all masculinity and femininity, then the nuptial relation of man and woman cannot signify it, or any other intrinsically differentiated symbol for that matter. There would be nothing of intrinsic significance in nuptial sexuality with its masculine-feminine bipolarity that would be capable of really and truly signifying a Christ-Church unity that is beyond sexuality that is not nuptial. The only signification of such a Christ-Church relation would be a nominalist one at best. One theologian has pointed out that fallen humanity would have nothing to say to such a Christ-Church union, the most complete union it would presumably know, because it is utterly transcended by it. This theologian remarks: "Sacramental signs have been reduced to programmatic gesturing, of some real social and psychological value but without any intrinsic relation to our salvation."[57]

In other words, there has been for nearly two millennia the sacramental worship of marriage. What would it mean to repudiate nearly two millennia

[57] Donald Keefe, "Sacramental Sexuality and the Ordination of Women," *Communio* 3 (1978): 228–51, at 240.

of worship? But this is what we would have to do if we would think that sexuality is simply one "anthropological element" like race, politics, or culture that makes up human identity, or if masculinity and femininity is some limitation that is overcome in the resurrection. On the contrary, if the man-woman relation in Christian marriage is a sacramentally real and true sign of a heavenly, eschatological reality, then it has a greater meaning and theological importance than the racial, the cultural, and the political.

Close attention to Augustine's journey shows us that if human sexuality with its masculine-feminine bipolarity has no intrinsic relation to the Christ-Church union and therefore no intrinsic relation to our salvation, then sexuality is indeed temporary and instrumental as Gregory of Nyssa, in a more innocent age than ours, envisioned it. On the other hand, if the masculine-feminine bipolarity is of the good creation and if the meaning of it is given and found in the one-flesh union of Christ and the Church, then embodied nuptial sexuality is not only of prime significance for Christian revelation, but its full splendor will be manifested and made known when, in the words of the Second Vatican Council, "that mystical marriage established by God" will be "fully revealed" in the future resurrection.[58]

---

[58] *Presbyterorum Ordinis* no. 16, trans. Austin Flannery, *Documents of Vatican II* (Collegeville, MN: The Liturgical Press, 1992).

CHAPTER 11

Gaudium et Spes, the Divine Image, and the Synthesis of *Veritatis Splendor**

IT HAS BEEN SAID, rightly, that the theological anthropology of *Gaudium et Spes* (*GS*), especially the way it is expressed in *GS* 22, has become emblematic of the pontificate of Pope John Paul II.[1] It is also true and right to say that, in the encyclical *Veritatis Splendor* (*VS*), there is an important development of *GS*'s anthropology. At the heart of this development is a profound integration of Christology, freedom, and communion with the image of God in the human person. To be sure, these things are present in *GS*, but Pope John Paul is able to bring them together and relate them to each other in a way that results in a significant expansion of the anthropological vision of the Pastoral Constitution especially with regard to the *imago Dei*.

This essay is divided into four sections. First, I will briefly discuss the approach of *GS* to anthropology. Second, I will provide an overview of *GS*'s anthropology and teaching on the divine image in the human person. Third, I will describe Pope John Paul's emphasis upon the "original centrality of Christ" that marks his approach to anthropology. This emphasis is operative in *VS* where the Pope develops the anthropology of *GS* with regard to the divine image. Fourth and lastly, I will show how the Pope accomplishes this development in *VS*. In that encyclical Pope John Paul explains the relation of the divine image to freedom and communion as well as the role of the Cross in the reconstitution of the divine image in the human person.

* A version of this essay first appeared in *Communio* 24 (Winter 1997): 794–814.

[1] David Schindler, "A Christology and the Imago Dei: Intrerpreting *Gaudium et Spes*," *Communio*, 23 (Spring 1996): 156–84.

The Approach of *Gaudium et Spes* to Anthropology

Walter Kasper has remarked that before the Second Vatican Council, no Church council had gone so far as to put forth a general outline of Christian anthropology.[2] *Gaudium et Spes* takes the Person of Christ as the clear criterion for its statements and affirmations about anthropology. The conviction that Christ is "the key, the center and the purpose of man's history" is the guiding principle for the Pastoral Constitution. This principle comes to its fullest expression in what is perhaps the key text of the entire constitution: "In fact, the mystery of man is revealed only in light of the mystery of the incarnate Word" (*GS* 22). On the other hand, as Kasper points out, even though Christology is the clear standard for anthropology, *GS* presents anthropology first and then ascends to Christology. Citing the official *relatio* Kasper writes:

> Decisive in this respect was the concern that—in the words of the *relatio* on the text of Arrica—the document proceeds from facts and truths accepted by most people, even non-believers, but in such a way as to arrive gradually at the presentation of the whole revealed truth. Even so, these "natural" truths have to be seen with the eyes of the Gospel—without that reprehensible separation between what belongs to the "purely natural order" and what belongs to the "order of redemption," since even the creation itself is embedded in the order of redemption.[3]

Gaudium et Spes's approach to anthropology was taken in the interest of what the Council Fathers judged to be the demands of dialogue with modern man.[4] The goal of entering into this dialogue was to present Christ as answering what it means to be human. Still, as we shall see below, this approach produces certain tensions in the text, which are not fully resolved.

The Image of God in *Gaudium et Spes*

The anthropology of *GS* begins in chapter 1, number 12, "The Dignity of the Human Person." Given the decision of the Council Fathers to introduce Christ explicitly toward the end of the chapter, it is not surprising that *GS* 12 discusses the divine image in man without any reference to New Testa-

---

[2] See Walter Kasper, "Theological Anthropology," *Communio* 26 (Winter 1996): 129–40.

[3] Ibid., 136–37. Kasper cites *Relatio Generalis*, I, AS IV/1, 523.

[4] Kasper documents how the Council Fathers struggled over the question of the proper relation between anthropology and Christology. See his "Theological Anthropology," 136–37.

ment statements. The starting point for presenting the image of God is Genesis 1:26 and the Old Testament's theology of creation (Gen 1:26–27; Wis 2:23; Sir 17:3-10; Ps 8:5–6). The link between Christ, the second Adam, and the first Adam is only asserted and clarified later in *GS* 22.

Gaudium et Spes 12 presents the divine image as a capacity to know and love the Creator. Man is the being who stands in relation to God as a knower and lover and who is appointed the master or steward of the good creation. As such, man is charged with the responsibility of insuring that the good creation be subdued for the sake of the glory of God. At the same time, the Pastoral Constitution teaches that man is not a solitary being. For God created man from the beginning as male and female. The "companionship" of man, male and female, is "the primary form of interpersonal communion." Man's relationality is constitutive of his humanity, his personhood. Man, male and female, cannot "live nor develop his potential unless he relates to others."[5]

Implicit here is the idea that human relationality and interpersonal communion are constitutive of the divine imaging because the God that is imaged is a divine communion of persons. But this is only implied and not concretely spelled out as Pope John Paul does in his sermons on Genesis.[6] Also important here is the fact that *GS* 12 connects the existence of the human person as male and female to the divine image. Sexual differentiation is not simply a brute biological element in man but something profoundly constitutive of being a human person, and of interpersonal communion. Still, it must be admitted that *GS* 12 does not further specify the connection between sexual differences and the image of God. In sum, *GS* 12 presents the image of God in man, male and female, as having something to do with human relationality and communion as well as the capacity to know and love God.

Another important statement that the Pastoral Constitution makes about the divine image is found in *GS* 17, entitled the "Excellence of Freedom." There it is asserted that freedom is "an exceptional sign of the image of God within man." "For God has willed that men are left 'in the hand of his own counsel' " (Sir 15:14). What is to be made of this statement? First of all, it has nothing to do with a concept of freedom that understands it simply as the ability to choose one thing over another. The Fathers wished to state that God intended man to seek and love him free from all external compulsion. Joseph Ratzinger observed in his 1968 commentary that the

[5] *GS* 12. All quotations of the documents of Vatican II that appear in this chapter are taken from Abbot, *Documents of Vatican II*.

[6] John Paul II, *The Original Unity of Man and Woman: Catechesis on the Book of Genesis* (Boston: Daughters of St. Paul, 1981).

Council Fathers were concerned here for a positive affirmation of freedom on the basis of faith, despite the fact that the contemporary age is subject to great confusion with regard to the idea of freedom.[7] The Fathers offered as a starting point for an authentic notion of freedom the truth that man is the free being who must decide to be himself. They wanted to acknowledge that freedom is at the very center of what it means to be human and at the same time relate it to its source—God. *Gaudium et Spes*, number 17, is anxious to assert that God is not in opposition to freedom and that human freedom flourishes only in the presence of the divine life. Human freedom in some way stands in relation to God. On the other hand, the Pastoral Constitution does not further explain the precise content of freedom and its relation to the image of God. Therefore *GS* 17 affirms a connection between freedom and the divine image but leaves it, for the most part, undefined.

The anthropology and teaching of *GS* on the divine image in man culminates in number 22. The full weight of salvation history and Christology together with pneumatology is brought to bear here, resulting in a very Christocentric view of man. Ratzinger observes, "[W]e are probably justified in saying that in an official document of the magisterium, a new type of Christocentric theology appears."[8] Christ is the last Adam, prefigured by the first, and "fully reveals man to himself and makes his calling clear." *Gaudium et Spes*, number 22 emphasizes that what is truly human can only fully flourish in Christ—who as the perfect man is all that every human person hopes to be.

Gaudium et Spes, number 22, returns again to the subject of the image of God in man. This time it is explicitly discussed in reference to Christology. The framework for understanding the divine image is Colossians 1:15 where Christ is the "image of the invisible God, the firstborn of all creation."[9] For Christ is the one in whom "all things were created through

---

[7] Joseph Ratzinger, "Pastoral Constitution on the Church in the Modern World," in *Commentary on the Documents of Vatican II*, vol. 5, ed Herbert Vorgrimler et al. (New York: Herder and Herder, 1968), 115–63, at 139. Ratzinger is very critical of this section of *GS*, calling it one of the least satisfactory of whole document. He argues that the New Testament doctrine of freedom does not inform this section of the constitution. This makes the consideration of freedom according to Ratzinger "unhistorical." The problem as Ratzinger sees it is that: "[t]he omission of Christology from the doctrine of the image and likeness of God, with which the idea of freedom is linked here, once again imposes its consequences." Ibid., 137.

[8] Ibid., 159.

[9] David Schindler has drawn attention to distinct emphases in *GS* 12 (Gen 1:26) and *GS* 22 (Col 1:15) with regard to the divine imaging. He argues that there cannot be an opposition between the Old and New Testament contexts for understanding the image of God. "Nonetheless, the distinct emphases in two contexts, if

him and for him" (Col 1:16). Christ is the eschatological Adam who is the perfect man and the perfect image of God. Christ shows us what it means to be created in the divine image. As the perfect man and the perfect image of the invisible God, he restores the divine likeness that was disfigured by sin. *GS* 22 presents Christ as accomplishing this restoration through his Incarnation, death and Resurrection, and the gift of the Spirit. The passage treats each of these mysteries.

The Council Fathers affirm that every person is touched by the event of the Incarnation when they state that "by his incarnation the Son united Himself in some fashion with every man." On this point Ratzinger remarks:

> The human nature of men is one; Christ taking to himself the one human nature of man is an event which affects every human being; consequently human nature in every human being is henceforth Christologically characterized. This idea then is extended to the real plane of actual concrete human existence. Human action, thought, willing and loving have become an instrument of the Logos; what is first present on the plan of being also gives new significance to the plan of action, to the actual accomplishment of human personal life.[10]

Ratzinger also comments that this emphasis upon the Son really and truly thinking with a human mind and loving and willing with a human heart is an important nexus between a sound theology of the Incarnation and a sound theology of the Cross. The vision of *GS* has nothing to do with one-sided incarnationalist theology in which the joining of God and man in the Incarnation is regarded as the most important event and where the life and death of Christ can only be secondary. In other words, *GS* 22 carefully avoids an abstract, non-historical essentialism in which Christ tends to be thought of as an essence to which the human race is conformed. On the contrary, Christ himself shows us that man's being is not some "pure essence" and that man only realizes his reality in and through his actions. Put simply, for Christ to be our prototype and exemplar means that he calls us to follow him in the way of his Cross. Thus, the Council Fathers assert that

---

left unintegrated, can lead to significant differences in anthropology—indeed, to the sort of differences which, one might argue, have lain at the source of much of the ecclesial controversy and unrest since the Council." See "Christology and the *Imago Dei*," 158.

10 Ratzinger, *Commentary on the Documents of Vatican II*, 160. Ratzinger writes further about this point: "But since it is made clear that man's being is not that of a pure essence, and that he only attains his reality by his activity, it is once evident that we cannot rest on a purely essentialist outlook. Man's being must be examined in his activities" (ibid.).

> from bondage to the devil and sin, he delivered us so that each one of us can say with the Apostle: The Son of God "loved me and gave himself up for me" (Gal. 2:20). By suffering for us he has not only provided us with an example for our imitation. He blazed a trail, and if we follow it life and death are made holy and take on a new meaning. (*GS* 22)

The divine image that has been disfigured due to sin is renewed by Christ through his Cross since it frees us from sin. By way of the *sequela Christi* man will find that Christ is the answer to one of the most vexing questions of human existence: the problem of suffering and death. This universal "fate" of every human person is transformed into a path to holiness. Walking with Christ along the way of the Cross enables the human to share in the restored and recreated divine image. This emphasis on the Cross is important also for *GS*'s claim that the eternal Son of God has united himself in some way to every human person through his Incarnation. Ratzinger writes:

> To endure in the cross, as the expression of abiding in the "pro me" of Jesus Christ, is thus a concrete result of the way human nature is ontologically affected by the incarnation. Just as, from the point of view of the theology of the cross, the ontological idea takes concrete form in Christ, so also the ontological affirmation that by the incarnation all human reality is affected, must now be understood as a statement concerning personal life. Its concrete meaning is the claim made on me and the consent to its being made on me by the "pro me" of Jesus Christ, and this expresses the concrete spirituality of the doctrine of the two natures. Thus the foundation laid by the theology of incarnation necessarily leads to a spirituality of the cross.[11]

The claim that Christ has united himself to everyone in his Incarnation is not an abstract, non-historical, non-personal one. The Incarnation does not somehow affect human nature apart from the event of the Cross. The Cross addresses each human person personally.

It should be added to these observations of Ratzinger that *GS* links its theology of the Cross to pneumatology. It is the gift of the Spirit that frees us to follow the crucified Christ and be conformed to his likeness, restoring in us the divine image. By the power of the Spirit we become "capable of discharging the new law of love" (*GS* 22). The Spirit effects our renewal in Christ inwardly and outwardly "even to the achievement of 'the redemption of the body' " (Rom 8:23). Our participation in the pattern of

---

[11] Ibid., 161.

Christ's suffering and dying under the sway of the Spirit is also our incorporation in the hope of the Resurrection. The risen body is the fruit of this renovation of man liberated from sin by the Cross. Clearly, for *GS*, Christology does not simply have implications for anthropology; it is constitutive for anthropology.

Another key text in *GS* concerning anthropology is number 24. There the Pastoral Constitution speaks about the communitarian nature of the human person's vocation and the communitarian nature of the image of God. Every human person is called to the same goal and end: communion with the Triune God. God intends the human race to be one family in his Son and calls us to treat one another "in a spirit of brotherhood." The human person realizes his or her vocation in union with his or her brothers and sisters in Christ. There is no question here of the human person having a solitary call from God or participating in the divine life alone, apart from one's neighbor. The personal vocation of every man or woman is also a vocation to communal life. It follows then, according to the constitution, that the love of God and the love of neighbor are inseparable. Human persons are essentially interdependent. The human race as a multitude in unity bears a certain likeness and resemblance to the communion of the divine Persons:

> Indeed, the Lord Jesus, when he prayed to the Father, "that they all may be made one . . . as we are one" (Jn 17:21–22) opened up vistas closed to human reason, for He implied a certain likeness between the union of the divine Persons, and the unity of God's sons in truth and charity. This likeness reveals that man, who is the only creature on earth which God willed for itself, cannot fully find himself except through a sincere gift of himself. (*GS* 24)

Here again, as *GS* 12, we find interpersonal communion connected with the imaging of God. The claim is made here that the human unity in truth and love, which is constituted by persons—who can only find themselves by giving themselves—is grounded in the divine Trinity that subsists in three Persons who are comprised by their mutual relations. The sincere gift of self on the part of individual human persons is absolutely essential for the realization of this resemblance between human unity and the union of divine Persons as well as for realization of the individual's vocation to communal life.

To sum up: in its chapter "The Dignity of the Human Person," *GS* affirms that the divine image in man has a Christological content. This is especially clear, as we have seen, in *GS* 22. The constitution connects Christ's renewal of the divine image with the Incarnation, the Cross, and the gift of the Spirit. *Gaudium et Spes* presents human freedom as an exceptional sign of the divine image, but without offering a discussion of the specific content of freedom. On the other hand, the Pastoral Constitution does not specify precise relationships between these various dimensions of the divine image in the human person. It does not define for instance, the relation between the Cross and human freedom with regard to imaging of God. Similarly, the constitution seems to affirm in *GS* 12 and *GS* 24 that interpersonal communion is constitutive of the divine imaging. *Gaudium et Spes*, number 24, asserts that the sincere gift of self is essential for human interpersonal communion that bears a likeness to the union of the divine Persons. But left unexplained, at least in any detail, is how this interpersonal communion is related to Christ's renewal of the divine image through the Cross. Also left undefined and unexplained is the relation between freedom and communion. The point here is not to fault the Council for failing to do these things. *Gaudium et Spes* left this to later doctrinal and theological development. Its outline of the divine image in man and its anthropology remains a remarkable achievement. This achievement, however, is a beginning, not an end.

Anthropology and the Original Centrality of Christ

Pope John Paul II has approached the anthropology of *GS* as a beginning and an opportunity for a new synthesis. The Pope's thought, as it has taken shape in the writings of his pontificate, is an important development of *GS*'s anthropology and its view of the divine image in man. There can be no question here of a complete discussion of Pope John Paul's anthropology. I want to point out what I think are significant developments in the anthropological vision of *GS* that are found in *VS*. I believe that this development reaches a high point in the third part of *VS*—a section that has not received enough attention by commentators.[12] I also believe *VS* must be read in the context of the Pope's earlier Trinitarian encyclicals and as well as his Marian encyclical, *Redemptoris Mater* (*RM*). There is a clear unity to the Pope's theology. It will be necessary in what follows below to refer back and forth to key passages in the earlier encyclicals.

The development in *VS* of the anthropology of *GS* with its theology of the divine image is firmly linked to a process that begins in the Pope's first encyclical, *Redemptor Hominis* (*RH*), and continues throughout his

---

[12] Raphael Gallagher has recently drawn attention to this fact. See his "The Reception of *Veritatis Splendor* within the Theological Community," *Studia Morala* 31 (1993): 414–34.

later writings. This process involves a further integration of the theology of creation and Christology. Pope John Paul teaches that Christ is the full revelation of the meaning of creation. We are created for Christ by the Father, who planned from the beginning to unite the human race in him. Christ is our model and prototype from the beginning. It is upon this foundation that the Pope reaches in *VS* the height of his development of the anthropological vision in *GS*.

From the very beginning of *VS*,[13] John Paul asserts that a Christological anthropology must inform moral theology. Jesus Christ, "the light of the nations" is the answer to man's questions, especially his moral and religious questions. The Pope does not mean this in a superficial, pietistic sense. In *VS* 2 he makes it clear that his point of departure is *GS* 22: "The truth is that only in the mystery of the incarnate Word does the mystery of man take on light. For Adam, the first man, was a figure of Him Who was to come, namely Christ the Lord. Christ, the final Adam, by the revelation of the mystery of the Father and His love, fully reveals man to man himself and makes his supreme calling clear." The Church, upon whose face Jesus Christ shines, is charged with the mission of offering "to everyone the answer which comes from the truth about Jesus Christ and his Gospel."

These affirmations in *VS* and the Pope's approach to *GS* 22 must be read in continuity with what the Pope has written previously about Christ disclosing the meaning of creation and revealing the Father's plan for all creation. For example, in *RH* 8, he wrote: "The Redeemer of the world! In Him has been revealed in a new and more wonderful way the fundamental truth concerning creation to which the Book of Genesis gives witness when it repeats several times: 'God saw that it was good.' " *RH* is informed by the truth that the primacy of Christ is not limited to redemption but extends to creation as well. Pope John Paul's Christological anthropology seeks to develop and further integrate the claim of *GS* 22 that Christ is the eschatological Adam: "He who is the 'image of the invisible God' (Col 1:15), is Himself the perfect man who has restored in the children of Adam that likeness to God."

Angelo Scola has observed that in *RH* the Pope advances the notion of a "radical and original centrality of Christ."[14] This centrality does not originate in the sin of Adam but is inscribed in the very order of creation itself by the Father. Scola notices that in *RH* 7 the Pope presents Christ as

---

13 All quotations from *VS* and all other papal encyclicals quoted in this chapter are from official Vatican translations.

14 Angelo Scola, " 'Claim' of Christ, 'Claim' of the World: On the Trinitarian Encyclicals of John Paul II, *Communio* 18 (Fall 1991): 322–31.

the Head and cites numerous biblical texts (Eph 1:10, 22; 4:25; Col 1:18; 1 Cor 8:6; cf. Col 1:17; cf. Jn 14:6) that refer to the total primacy of Christ and the primacy of Christ as Redeemer. "We must constantly aim at Him," the Pope writes, ' "who is the head,' 'through whom are all things and through whom we exist,' who is both 'the way, and the truth.' " What the Pope takes seriously in *RH* 7 is the Christ who is the Head and Alpha in whom man is not only redeemed but created in, through, and for. According to Pope John Paul, creation, the beginning, is only fully understood eschatologically. The beginning is only truly and completely known in the light of the end. While the Pope certainly knows that historically Christ was the last Adam, foreshadowed by the first Adam, he also knows of Christ eschatologically, not only as the End, but as the Alpha and the Beginning as well. This must be kept in mind when in *VS* the Pope speaks about Christ as the "decisive answer to man's questions" and about Christ as truth that the Church offers mankind in her efforts to discover the meaning of life. This emphasis upon the eschatological Adam is the background for the claim in *VS* 8: "As the source and summit of the economy of salvation, as the Alpha and Omega of human history (cf. Rev 1:8; 21:6; 22:31), Christ sheds light on man's condition and his integral vocation." It is this same broad eschatological perspective that is behind the Pontiff's claim in *VS* 53 that "Christ is the 'Beginning' who, having taken on human nature, definitively illumines it in its constitutive elements and in its dynamism of charity toward God and neighbor."

These claims, which maintain Christ as the Alpha and the Beginning who reveals the meaning of creation, are not isolated ideas that are stated from time to time in the writings of Pope John Paul. They are firmly connected to the theme of the original centrality of Christ. This theme runs throughout his encyclicals. Scola has drawn attention to how this emphasis on the original centrality of Christ is developed in the Trinitarian encyclicals. For example, in *RH* 9, after claiming that creation is renewed in the mystery of redemption and that we are predestined in the Son and called to love, and, after explaining that love is greater than sin, weakness, and the futility of creation, the Pope writes: "This revelation of love is also described as mercy; and in man's history this revelation of love and mercy has taken a form and a name: that of Jesus Christ." Continuing this emphasis in the encyclical *Dives in Misericordia* (*DM*) the Pontiff contends that Jesus is the incarnation of mercy. In *DM* 2 he says that "Christ confers on the whole of the Old Testament tradition about God's mercy a definitive meaning. Not only does He speak of it and explain it by the use of comparisons and parables, but above all He Himself makes it incarnate and personifies it. He himself is in a certain sense mercy." Christ makes visible the Father's mercy.

In *DM* 4, the Pope examines the concept of mercy in the Old Testament and makes the point that mercy reveals God "who already as Creator has linked himself to his creature with a particular love." This love is primary and fundamental in such a way as to make justice serve love, because God does not despise what he has created. It is Christ, mercy incarnate, who best manifests God's relationship of love with humanity that exists from the beginning in the mystery of creation.[15] Closely linked to the mystery of creation, according to the Pope, is the mystery of election—a mystery that is inclusive of every person in the whole human family. Recalling the words of Isaiah 54:10 that God's steadfast love will not depart nor will the covenant of peace be removed, the Pope declares: "This truth, once proclaimed to Israel, involves a perspective of the whole history of man, a perspective both temporal and eschatological." The mystery of election is inclusive of everyone of course because of Christ, who is the full revelation of God's steadfast love and mercy, and who reveals the Father. "He who has seen me has seen the Father" (Jn 14:9; *DM* 4). Scola observes that for the Pope:

> Creation appears as the plan of the Trinity to give being, outside itself, to sons in the Son; and it thus links itself from eternity to a single and most personal call of all human beings in Christ which, in technical terms, can be defined as predestination.[16]

The Pope emphasizes our election in Christ from the beginning in *RM* 7. The vision of the Letter to the Ephesians looms large in his emphasis on this subject. He quotes Ephesians 1:4–7:

> "Blessed be the God and Father of our Lord Jesus Christ, who blessed us in Christ with every spiritual blessing in the heavenly places" (Eph 1:3). . . . In fact, the God who is the "Father of our Lord Jesus Christ"—these are the next words of the same Letter—"chose us in him before the foundation of the world, that we should

---

15 The Pope's thought here resonates very strongly with that of the Greek Orthodox theologian John Zizioulas, who writes in a similar vein: "Since God knows created beings as the realizations of his will, it is not being itself but the ultimate being of God's love which unifies being and points to the meaning of being. And precisely here is the role of the incarnation. The incarnate Christ is so identical to the ultimate will of God's love, that the meaning of created being and the purpose of history are simply the incarnate Christ. All things were made with Christ in mind, or rather at heart." See John Zizioulas, *Being as Communion* (Crestwood, NY: St. Vladimir's Seminary Press, 1985), 97.

16 Scola, "'Claim' of Christ," 324.

be holy and blameless before him. He destined us in love to be his sons through Jesus Christ, according to the purpose of his will, to the praise of his glorious grace which he freely bestowed on us in the Beloved. In him we have redemption though his blood, the forgiveness of our trespasses, according to the riches of his grace."

The Pope goes on to explain in *RM* 8 that our election in Christ, which includes everyone but retains a special place for the Mother of the Redeemer, is the fruit of the Trinitarian love of God, the Triune God who is love. Our election has to do with God desiring to save us by granting us a participation in the divine life in Christ. In him we are blessed, with every "spiritual blessing" as adopted sons and daughters.[17]

In his encyclical on the Holy Spirit, *Dominum et Vivificantem* (*DV*), the Pope also refers to the primacy of Christ. In *DV* 33 the Holy Father explains the original disobedience "in the beginning" in reference to the Son who is also ' "the first-born of all creation,' 'for in him all things were created . . . through him and for him.' " The disobedience or "turning away from the truth contained in the Word of God" that occurred in the mystery of the beginning occurs again in the Paschal mystery. In both cases, the Pope says, there is "non-faith" in the Word of the Father. All sin for Pope John Paul is sin against the Word. He claims that the Word of God is the eternal law, "the

[17] My interpretation that the Pope develops the anthropology of *GS* 22 with his claim that Christ reveals the truth of creation is further confirmed in *Tertio Millennio Adveniente*, where the Pope explicitly links this claim to *GS* 22: "Christ, the Redeemer of the world, *is the one Mediator between God and men*, and there is no other name under heaven by which we can be saved (cf. Acts 4:12). As we read in the Letter to the Ephesians: 'In him, we have redemption through his blood, the forgiveness of our trespasses, according to the richness of his grace, which he has lavished upon us. For he has made known to us in all wisdom and insight . . . his purpose which he set forth in Christ as a plan for the fullness of time, to unite all things in him, things in heaven and things on earth' (1:7–10). Christ, the Son who is of one being with the Father, is therefore the one who *reveals God's plan for all creation, and for man in particular*. In the memorable phrase of the Second Vatican Council, Christ '*fully reveals man to man himself and makes his supreme calling clear*.' He shows us this calling by revealing the mystery of the Father and his love. As the image of the invisible God, Christ is the perfect man who has restored to the children of Adam the divine likeness which had been deformed by sin. In his human nature, free from all sin and assumed into the divine Person of the Word, the nature shared by all human beings is raised to a sublime dignity: 'By his incarnation the Son of God *united himself in some sense with every man*. He labored with human hands, thought with a human mind, acted with a human will, and loved with a human heart. Born of Mary the Virgin he truly became one of us and, sin apart, was like us in every way' " (*Tertio Millennio Adveniente*, no. 4).

source of every law which regulates the world and especially human acts."[18] Thus, when Christ spoke on the night before he died about the sin of those who did not believe in him, there was a certain echoing of that sin, that non-faith and non-belief, which marks the mystery of creation.

In *VS* references to Christ as the "Alpha and Omega of human history" and Christ as "the Beginning" who definitively illumines the meaning of human nature must be read in the context of the Pope's firm insistence on the original centrality of Christ. This insistence is prominent in the Pope's Trinitarian encyclicals. There is one plan of creation and redemption where Christ is the Beginning and the End. Christ, the Alpha and the Omega, reveals the full meaning of creation. Christ is truly the Lord of history. We are sons and daughters in the Son. Christ shows us that creation "waits with eager longing for the revealing of the sons of God" (Rom 8:19), those whom "God has predestined to be conformed to the image of the Son" (Rom 8:29). It is this truth that Adam turned away from, this Word of the Father that Adam refused to believe; it is this plan that Adam disobeyed and refused to serve. Nevertheless, sin did not frustrate the purpose which the Father had set forth in Christ, "as a plan for the fullness of time, to unite all things in him, things in heaven and things on earth" (Eph 1:9–10). It is upon this firm basis that in *VS* the Holy Father broadens and deepens the anthropological vision of *GS* especially with regard to the divine image in the human person. He accomplishes this development by indicating the relationship between the divine image, freedom and communion, and the role of the Cross in the renewal of the divine image.

Veritatis Splendor, Freedom, and the Divine Image

In *VS* freedom is the point of integration for the development of *GS*'s view of the divine image. The question of freedom especially in relation to truth is raised in the first part of *VS*. In the second part, it is explicitly connected to the divine image in the human creature. In the third part, the Pope synthesizes the insights of parts one and two. He firmly links the question of freedom with Christology and so to the divine image.

[18] It is interesting to compare this claim that the "Word is also the eternal law" with *VS* 45, where the Pope says that the distinction between the positive revealed law and the natural law is a helpful theological distinction. It must be remembered that this distinction is never a matter of separation because "[t]hey have their origin and goal in the eternal, wise and loving counsel whereby God predestines men and women 'to be conformed to the image of the Son (Rom 8:29).'" At the heart of the Pope's theology is a profound awareness of the unity between creation and redemption. This unity, of course, has far-reaching implications for moral theology.

The first part of *VS* is a biblical meditation on Christ's conversation with the rich young man and the question of what we must do to gain life eternal. Christ's reply makes it clear that this search for goodness is connected with the search for God who is the Good itself. To be good is to be God-like. The Ten Commandments are a self-revelation of God; in them God makes himself known as the One who is the Good itself. Walking in the way of the commandments is a way that leads to life with God. Jesus himself puts them forth as a way to eternal life and salvation. To be sure, there is a close connection between eternal life and the commandments. But not even the strictest observance of the commandments fulfills the Law. The rich young man knows something of this truth because there is something that he still lacks. Christ teaches us that fulfillment of the Law comes to us only as a gift. Jesus himself reveals and communicates this gift, which is no less than an offer to participate in the divine Goodness.

The commandment about the good of the person—"You shall love your neighbor as yourself"—is both the "summary and the foundation" of the Decalogue. The Pope explains in *VS* 13 that the commandments "are meant to protect the good of the person, the image of God, by protecting his goods." He goes on to claim that the commandments are only the beginning of freedom; the first step on the way toward full and perfect freedom.

It is Jesus who fulfills the commandments, particularly, of course, the commandment of the love of neighbor. He does this because he interiorizes the demands of the Law and brings about the full meaning and intent of the commandments. Fulfillment of the Law is the ability and capacity to realize what the Law intends. Jesus teaches us that the commandments are not minimum norms but a way that involves a movement toward moral perfection that finds its center in love. Thus the commandment against murder becomes a vocation to a love that champions and protects the life of our neighbor. In other words, unlike us sinners, Jesus is able to fulfill the Law because he has perfectly realized the commandment of love. Pope John Paul writes in *VS* 15:

> Jesus is the living "fulfillment" of the Law inasmuch as he fulfills its authentic meaning by the total gift of himself: he himself becomes a living and personal Law, who invites people to follow him; through the Spirit, he gives the grace to share his own life and love and provides the love and provides the strength to bear witness to that love in personal choices and actions.

It is this total gift of self that we, disfigured by sin, are incapable of offering by our own power. The Pope observes that the rich young man, who kept all the commandments, shows that even he by himself alone does not have the ability or capacity to take the next step. To fulfill the law requires mature human freedom. But freedom is called to mature self-giving. This is the moral perfection that everyone is called to but which no one capable of reaching by themselves alone. Jesus invites us to give up all that we possess and follow him. This invitation discloses the "dynamic of freedom's growth toward maturity." In other words, to fulfill the law is to be conformed to Jesus who became a servant to the point of giving himself up for us on the cross. The following of Jesus then is not simply an outward imitation of him but it is a "holding fast to his person" which "touches man at the very depths of his being." It is sharing in his life and destiny, and a participation in his loving obedience to the will of the Father. Christian morality therefore, finds its "essential and primordial foundation" in the following of Jesus.

To hold fast to the Person of Christ, to live out his love, and to acquire mature freedom is possible only because of the gift of the Spirit. Christ receives the love of the Father and gives it to his disciples. Christ's gift is the Spirit and the first fruit of the Spirit is charity. God's love has been poured into our hearts. It is by the power of the Spirit that we share in Christ's life in the sacraments. The Spirit, in baptism, makes us members of the Body of Christ, that is, the Church. In the Spirit we share in the Eucharist which is the sacramental culmination of our assimilation to Christ (see *VS* 21).

The second chapter of *VS* discusses the need to link freedom with truth in order to overcome the separation between them. Genuine freedom is not somehow autonomous from truth. What is of particular interest is that in this chapter the Pope also discusses freedom and the divine image in man. In *VS* 34 the Holy Father says that the question about morality must be anchored in the issue of freedom. But this raises the question: what kind of freedom? He notes, with *GS* 17, that the contemporary age highly esteems freedom but understands it as a kind of ability to do and choose whatever one pleases. The Pope recalls that *GS* 17 teaches that the human person must pursue a "genuine freedom" and that this sort of freedom is "an outstanding image of the divine image in man." But he understands this genuine freedom as mature self-giving. In *VS* 38 the Pope goes on to explain that the "genuine freedom" spoken of in *GS* 17 has to do with the fact that man's dominion, which is a sharing in God's dominion, "extends to a certain extent over man himself." In other words, genuine freedom is such that man has the spiritual maturity to be master of himself in the sense that man is not divided against himself and dominated by lust.[19] To

[19] This point in *VS* should be compared to the following passage in *RH* 21: "However, one element seems to stand out in the midst of all these riches: the sharing in Christ's kingly mission, that is to say, the fact of rediscovering in oneself and others the special

be genuinely free, a man must be able to give up himself, without that inner struggle whereby he does not do the good that he wills to do, but the evil he does not intend (Rom 7:19). Genuine freedom involves sharing in the kingship of Christ. In *VS* 38 the Pope quotes Gregory of Nyssa:

> The soul shows its royal and exalted character . . . in that it is free and self-governed, swayed autonomously by its own will. Of whom else can this be said, save a king . . . ? Thus human nature, created to rule other creatures, was by its likeness to the King of the universe made as it were a living image, partaking with the Archetype both in dignity and in name.[20]

Pope John Paul continues to develop the meaning of genuine freedom and hence the meaning of the divine image in the human person in the third chapter of *VS*. This has been described as the pastoral chapter of the encyclical, and in it the Pope synthesizes his insights of chapters one and two, especially his Christological treatment of freedom. The Pope's development of the meaning of freedom and its importance for the divine image takes place in the context of his return to the question of the fundamental relationship between freedom and truth.

The Pope states that freedom must be based upon the truth which can be known from our nature that comes from the Creator and from divine revelation. The cultural and social situation of today has largely forgotten the intrinsic links between truth, the good, and freedom. In a text that may surprise some, the Pope argues that the Church's pedagogical power lies in looking constantly to Christ rather than in doctrinal statements and proclamation (see *VS* 85). In this way the Church can best form moral consciences capable of making judgments based on truth. This constantly looking to Christ also shows us the true meaning of freedom. The Pope writes: "The Crucified Christ reveals the authentic meaning of freedom; he lives it fully in the total gift of himself and calls the disciples to share in his freedom."

---

dignity of our vocation that can be described as 'kingship.' This dignity is expressed in readiness to serve, in keeping with the example of Christ, who 'came not to be served but to serve.' If, in the light of this attitude of Christ's, 'being a king' is truly possible only by 'being a servant,' then 'being a servant' also demands so much spiritual maturity that it must really be described as 'being a king.' In order to be able to serve others worthily and effectively we must be able to master ourselves, possess the virtues that make this mastery possible. Our sharing in Christ's kingly mission—His 'kingly function' (*munus*)—is closely linked with every sphere of both Christian and human morality."

[20] The Pope cites Gregory of Nyssa's *De Hominis Opificio*, chap. 4, PG 44, 135–36.

The Pontiff then returns again to the idea that freedom is an essential part of the divine image. Our freedom is weak and fallen, and must be cultivated. In freedom we can detect something of the ancient call from the Creator, from the beginning, for the human person to partake of the divine life. Freedom is ultimately oriented to a life of grace in communion. Thus the Pope says in *VS* 86:

> Within that freedom there is an echo of the primordial vocation whereby the Creator calls man to the Good, even more, through Christ's Revelation, to become his friend and to share his own divine life. It is at once inalienable self-possession and openness to all that exists, in passing beyond self to knowledge and love of the other. Freedom then is rooted in the truth about man and is directed toward communion.

The call of our Creator "from the beginning" to participate in the divine life is realized in Christ. He shows us, in the giving up of himself for our sake, that our freedom is anchored in "this call of our Creator," this "truth about man." True freedom is obtained in love, the sincere gift of self, and leads to communion and sharing in the life of the other, especially the divine Other. The Holy Father continues to emphasize, in *VS* 87, that the complete meaning of freedom is disclosed on the Cross:

> Contemplation of Jesus Crucified is thus the highroad which the Church must tread every day if she wishes to understand the full meaning of freedom: the gift of self in service to God and one's brethren. Communion with the Crucified and Risen Lord is the never-ending source from which the Church draws unceasingly in order to live in freedom, to give of herself and serve.

Thus it is possible to see how the gift of self is related to the divine imaging and why man can only find himself if he gives himself up. For man is created for communion and for sharing in the divine life, but communion is only possible if man in genuine freedom makes a sincere gift of himself. Understood in this way it is clear why freedom is an "outstanding manifestation of the image of God." The Pope makes clear the relation between freedom and communion in the divine image in the human person. Genuine freedom is directed and oriented toward the participation in the Good itself—God. Christ, the last Adam, renews the disfigured likeness to God by restoring to us freedom and communion. In Christ we can share in the interior life of God because our freedom is free for the disinterested gift of self—a gift in the freedom of love—for the sake of the other. Christ reveals to us that the human person, as the creature who images God, does not first exist or "be" and then relate to God and to others. On the contrary, relation, "being for" is fundamental to who we are and fundamental to our imaging of the Triune God. This relationality, this "being for" must be realized in freedom and communion. The union of communion is the perfect fulfillment of our personal subjectivity and the actualization of the divine imaging.

According to Pope John Paul II, Christ renovates the divine image and likeness in action. This theology resonates with those Fathers of the Church who taught that the divine image must be realized into the divine likeness.[21] Robert A. Connor has noticed the importance of this point in the Pope's thought and summarizes it very well:

> Jesus Christ, who is gift of self, assumes as his own the fallen nature of Adam which contradicted the gift of self by willful disobedience which, in turn, imaged the "*non serviam*" of Satan. The impossible is about to take place. That which ceased to be image-in-act, and had been relegated to image as mere capacity for God, now becomes image-in-act as obedience to death on the Cross. That which was in Adam the first of a series now becomes the perfected image of God, the very prototype of divinized man.[22]

For the Pope the culmination of this realization is Christ's sacrifice on the Cross. This emphasis upon the importance of the Cross for the renewal of the divine imaging is a significant development of the claim in *GS* 22 that in the Incarnation the Son of God has united himself to every person. If we accept the idea that it is through the Cross that every person is affected by the Incarnation, and if, as we saw above, the full meaning of freedom is revealed and given to us on the Cross, then the incarnate Son really does touch each human person, because true human freedom is not to be had apart from communion with Christ in his sacrifice on the Cross. The development of the anthropology of *GS* here is unmistakable.

The divine image that Christ refashions is, of course, Trinitarian. We image a God who is a communion of persons. It should be recalled that the Pope has constantly maintained in many of his other writings (for example, his *Theology of the Body*, and *Mulieris Dignitatem*)[23] that human beings

---

[21] For example, Irenaeus of Lyons. For a succinct overview of the thought of Irenaeus on this point see Denis Minns, O.P., *Irenaeus* (Washington, DC: Georgetown University Press, 1994).

[22] Robert A. Connor, "The One Truth of Freedom: Gift of Self," *Communio* 21 (Summer 1994): 367–71.

[23] A good example of how the Pope upholds the communal dimension of the divine image can be found in *Mulieris Dignitatem*, number 7: "The fact that man 'created

image the Triune God most fully and completely as a communion of persons, especially in the spousal relation between man and woman.[24] Christ is the new Adam who in giving himself up unites himself to the second Eve, the Church. The one flesh of the new Adam and new Eve is the reconstitution of the divine imaging that was defaced by the first Adam and the first Eve.

This reconstitution of the Trinitarian divine image and the question of human freedom involves a conformation to Christ. This is made possible by the gift of the Spirit whose first fruit is charity. Pope John Paul affirms that through the Spirit of truth, freedom, and love, we are "enabled to interiorize the law and live it as the motivating force of freedom." Conformed to Christ in his crucified gift of self, we are empowered to fulfill the Law. This participation in his freedom and his renewal of the divine image takes place in us gradually. We must follow Christ step by step in his loving obedience to his Father. The way to freedom, the way ultimately to fulfillment, is an entering into the one sacrifice of Christ. This share in the Cross is mediated of course by the Church and her worship. Thus the priest prays

---

as man and woman' is the image of God means not only that each of them individually is like God, as a rational and free being. It also means that man and woman, created as a 'unity of the two' in their common humanity, are called to live in a communion of love, and in this way to mirror in the world the communion of love that is in God, through which the Three Persons love each other in the intimate mystery of the one divine life. The Father, Son and Holy Spirit, one God through the unity of the divinity, exist as persons through the inscrutable divine relationship. Only in this way can we understand the truth that God in himself is love (cf. 1 Jn 4:16). The image and likeness of God in man, created as man and woman (in the analogy that can be presumed between Creator and creature), thus also expresses the 'unity of the two' in a common humanity. This 'unity of the two,' which is a sign of interpersonal communion, shows that the creation of man is also marked by a certain likeness to the divine communion ('*communio*'). This likeness is a quality of the personal being of both man and woman, and is also a call and a task. The foundation of the whole human 'ethos' is rooted in the image and likeness of God which the human being bears within himself from the beginning. Both the Old and New Testaments will develop that 'ethos,' which reaches its apex in the commandment of love." Cf. John Paul II, "By the Communion of Persons Man Becomes the Image of God," in *The Original Unity of Man and Woman*, 73–74.

24 This spousal imaging of the divine is not limited to those who participate in the sacrament of marriage. Those who have chosen celibacy and virginity for the sake of the kingdom participate in this spousal imaging of God because their state of life always stands in relation to the union of the new Adam and the new Eve. In other words, the choice for continence for the sake of the kingdom is always made in reference to the nuptial meaning of the body. The fullness of this meaning is revealed in the one-flesh union of the new Adam and new Eve. See Pope John Paul II, General Audience of April 28, 1982, in *TOB*, 436–40.

in the liturgy: "Lord, may this sacrifice, which has made our peace with you, advance the peace and salvation of all the world."[25]

Conclusion

Pope John Paul II fully accepted the anthropology of *GS* and approached it as a beginning that opens up the possibility for development. In *VS* the Pope advances the doctrine of the *imago Dei* beyond what is taught in *GS*. He achieves this advance by explaining that our freedom is Christologically grounded and that our freedom is fully realized only in communion.

Gaudium et Spes teaches that freedom and communion are in some sense constitutive of the divine imaging. Freedom, because it is something that only fully thrives in the presence of the divine, stands in relation to God. The sincere gift of self is essential for a communion that bears a likeness to the divine communion of persons. But *GS* does not specify or explain the precise meaning of freedom vis-à-vis Christ. Nor does the Pastoral Constitution define the relationship between freedom and communion in the divine imaging. The relation between the sincere gift of self and freedom is left unexplained. Furthermore, it is not apparent precisely how the Cross is related to the restoration of our freedom and how the Cross makes us capable of communion.

Pope John Paul II is able to explain the meaning of freedom as disclosed by Christ, as well as the relationship between freedom, communion, and the sincere gift of self. He accomplishes this synthesis by emphasizing what some have called the original centrality of Christ. This emphasis is developed in the Trinitarian encyclicals and is present in *VS*. Pope John Paul II observed that God reveals his mercy from the beginning of the history of the chosen people. Mercy is a special power of love that prevails over sin and infidelity. Mercy shows that God has linked himself to creation with a particular love. The Pope identifies Christ with this mercy. Christ, mercy incarnate, manifests God's relationship of love with humanity from the beginning in the mystery of creation. Closely related to the mystery of creation is the mystery of election. The latter has to do with the Father destining us in love to be his sons and daughters in the Son. We are predestined to be conformed to the image of the Son. It is this plan and truth that Adam turned away from and refused to serve. It is this plan and truth that Christ came to serve and complete.

Pope John Paul II's emphasis on the original centrality of Christ deepens the Christocentricism of *GS* and its claim that Christ fully reveals man

[25] Eucharistic Prayer III.

to himself. If we are predestined to be sons and daughters in the Son from the beginning, then it is apparent how profoundly human existence is related to Christ. This original centrality of Christ is presupposed in *VS* when the Pope claims that Christ is the Beginning who definitively illumines the meaning of human nature and the meaning of freedom.

According to the Pope in *VS* our freedom is defined Christologically. This "outstanding manifestation" of the divine image is fully understood only in the light of Christ's death on the Cross. Full authentic freedom is to be found only in the gift of self to God and to one's brothers and sisters. Genuine freedom is oriented toward participation in the Good itself—the Triune God. Freedom and communion are determined Christologically. Christ through his Cross has made it possible to exist in freedom and communion and thus image God, who is a communion of divine Persons. Christ, the new Adam, reforges the divine image in his sacrifice for the sake of his Bride, the second Eve. Our appropriation of this reforged image lies in our following of Christ in his one sacrifice. In this way, Pope John Paul II proclaims that Christ reveals the truth about God and at the same time the whole truth about man.

CHAPTER 12

Affective Maturity and the Spousal Mystery in the State of Consecrated Virginity

IN THE APOSTOLIC exhortation on the priesthood *Pastores Dabo Vobis* (*PDV*), Pope John Paul II wrote eloquently about the human, spiritual, intellectual, and pastoral areas of priestly formation. In the human area, the Pope discussed the kind of affective maturity required of candidates for the priesthood. In fact, the basic affective maturity that the Pope described is necessary for any baptized person who aspires to live one of the states of life in the Church, whether married or in the state of perfect continence and virginity. The Pope explained that affective maturity "requires an awareness of love as having a central role in human life." This is a love that has to do with "the entire person, in all his or her aspects—physical, psychic and spiritual—and which is expressed in the 'spousal meaning' of the human body, thanks to which a person gives oneself to another and takes the other to oneself."[1]

In his many writings on the theology of the body, Pope John Paul offered a fresh perspective on the state of perfect continence and virginity from the standpoint of Christian anthropology and the spousal meaning of the body. As the quote from *PDV* shows the Holy Father believed our understanding of affective maturity must be situated within this standpoint as well.

I want to give an overview of this spousal meaning of the body not only to show its importance for affective maturity but to show how it

---

[1] *PDV* 44. Translations of magisterial documents quoted in this chapter are taken from the Vatican website, www.vatican.va. In this quote, I have slightly reworked the translation so that it more closely follows the words in the Latin text "significationem sponsalem."

sheds a considerable light on the vocation of consecrated virginity. How it helps us to understand this vocation is my primary interest. My presentation is divided into two main parts. First, I give an overview of the spousal meaning of the body from the perspective of redemption in Christ where the full truth about it is revealed. In the second part, I describe, briefly, how Pope John Paul presents the state of perfect continence and virginity within this context and how it is a witness to the truth of the body. Finally, I make some brief observations about how consecrated virginity can come to the aid of married couples and families.

The Truth of the Spousal Meaning of the Body

The spousal meaning of the body is seen in all of its profundity with the eyes of faith, but persons can and should know something of it with the eyes of reason. In our day, with the cultural confusion and even subversion of the true meaning of sexuality, this spousal meaning of the body is harder to grasp than in former times. As the Pope noted, this is especially true when sexuality is reduced to something that is only bodily and a matter of selfish pleasure. An affective maturity that has an awareness of love that is expressed in the spousal meaning of the body is harder to attain in a culture that tells us sexual difference is on the same level as ethnicity or race. The Holy Father made the point that a sound sexual education together with the nurturing of a strong family life leads us to the truth about human love expressed in the spousal meaning of the body (see *PDV* 44).

What is this spousal meaning of the body that affective maturity has a deep awareness of? In the most basic sense it involves the truth that embodied masculine and feminine persons are ordered to one another and that the person is called to make a sincere gift of self according to the distinctive masculine or feminine way of loving.

Now it may be easy to see how this spousal meaning of the body is important for marriage, but why and on what authority should we think that it is equally important for perfect continence for the sake of the kingdom?

As Pope John Paul has reminded us it is the Lord Jesus Christ himself who shows us that perfect continence is inseparable from the spousal meaning of the body. Even in his own teaching, before his death and Resurrection, the Lord connected perfect continence with the truth about man and woman from "the beginning." In the gospel according to Matthew 19:3–12, the Lord's teaching on perfect continence occurs in the same conversation with the Pharisees on the question of marriage and divorce. We all recall the Lord's reply. He referred the Pharisees to "the beginning," where "[t]he Creator created them male and female and said,

'For this reason a man will leave his father and his mother and unite with his wife, and the two will be one flesh. . . .' So it is that they are no longer two but one flesh. Therefore what God has joined let man not separate."[2]

In his teaching on the indissolubility of marriage the Lord shows how marriage was intended to express the truth about the body in its masculinity and femininity. Right away the disciples respond, saying that it is better not to marry. Our Lord does not follow their line of reasoning but speaks of the call to voluntary continence for the sake of the kingdom of heaven. It is surely important that when the Lord spoke of this call his listeners had before them the truth about the spousal meaning of the body in its masculinity and femininity in the mystery of creation. Only later after the Lord's death and Resurrection and the revelation of the spousal relationship of Christ and the Church—which Ephesians 5:25 speaks to us about—does the wealth of meaning contained in the Lord's concise statement about perfect continence become apparent: that the choice of virginity or celibacy is a response to the love of the risen Christ, and that, in its own way and at its own level, expresses the truth of the body. Thus Pope John Paul concluded that the Lord's words about the call to perfect continence are "organically connected with the deep and mature *consciousness of the spousal meaning of the body*" and that it is "only in relation to such a meaning of masculinity and femininity of the human person . . . the call to voluntary continence 'for the kingdom of heaven' find[s] full guarantee and motivation."[3] In *PDV* the Pope goes even further and claims that virginity, even in its renunciation of marriage, makes evident the spousal meaning of the body because virginity involves "human sexuality lived as a genuine sign of and precious service to the love of communion and gift of self to others" (*PDV* 29).

When speaking of the spousal meaning of the body we must keep in mind that the Pope refers not only to how God created us but also to a conscious experience of the body that most everyone knows of at least on some level. He does not mean for us to join him in a reflection about an abstract idea. On the subjective level, the awareness of the spousal meaning of the body can go on behind the mind of the knower. There is an awareness of it that most people have even if they can only explain it with difficulty. They have a sense of it even though there are things that interfere with a proper

---

[2] Pope John Paul II, General Audience of September 5, 1979, in *A Theology of the Body* (*TOB*).

[3] John Paul II, "The Spousal Meaning of the Body as the Foundation of Christ's Call to Continence," General Audience of April 28, 1982, as translated in *TOB*, 438–39. The audiences of April 21, 1982 (p. 432), and March 10, 1982 (p. 412), are also important and relevant here.

conceptual grasp of the conscious experience of it. People can and do, of course, make all kinds of choices that go against its meaning. The eyes of faith are needed to know the full truth about the spousal meaning of the body, and we need grace to live according to it. Still, at a basic level most people know that embodied masculine and feminine persons are ordered toward one another, that love between them makes for human happiness, and that the survival of humanity depends on this reality. Even those who advocate an agenda that would deny the orientation of the sexes to one another must argue against an understanding and experience of man and woman that has been at the basis of human civilization for thousands of years.

To grasp the fullness of truth about the spousal meaning of the body requires a certain spiritual maturity, as the Pope reminded us in *PDV*. Christ not only helps us to attain spiritual maturity, he reveals the full meaning of the truth of the body because he is the full revelation of the mystery of the Father, and he is the full revelation of the truth about man. Let us return to Genesis, to which Christ refers in his conversation with the Pharisees, in order to see what the Father inscribed on man and woman from the beginning.

In the second creation account, before the creation of woman Adam is not specified as male. He is does not have an awareness of being male because he is not yet in the presence of the other sex. He is alone with regard to God's animal creatures, and we read that this aloneness is "not good" (Gen 2:18). It is then that "the LORD God caused a deep sleep to fall upon the man, and while he slept took one of his ribs and closed up its place with flesh; and the rib which the LORD God had taken from the man he made into a woman and brought her to the man" (Gen 2:22–23). In the presence of the woman, Adam "wakes up" male, exclaiming, "This at last is bone of my bones and flesh of my flesh; she shall be called woman because she was taken out of man" (Gen 2:23). This account of woman coming from the rib of Adam contains some important anthropological and theological truths. According to the second chapter of Genesis, it is not that the first man or first woman each have their own human sexual identity, established independently of the other, and then come together to form a union of one flesh. On the one hand, man and woman share a common humanity, "bone of my bones," "flesh of my flesh." On the other hand, Adam becomes himself as man, as masculine, only in the presence of the woman. In order for Adam to say "I" as man he must look to Eve as woman. Likewise, the woman, having come from the rib of man, only finds herself, her femininity, in the presence of man. Eve must take into account Adam as man before she can say "I" as woman. Neither Adam nor Eve is intelligible without the other. Even the Hebrew words of the text express something of this truth as man is *'is* and the woman' *issah*. Thus, Pope John Paul spoke of an original unity of man and woman.

There are two ways of being in a body that at the same time complete one another. In his apostolic letter *Mulieris Dignitatem* (*MD*) the Pope writes, "In the 'unity of the two,' man and woman are called from the beginning not only to exist 'side by side' or 'together,' but they are also called to exist mutually 'one for the other' " (*MD* 7). The human body, whether masculine or feminine, expresses this spousal meaning. God called the first man to accept the woman as willed "for her own sake," and reciprocally, woman is called to accept man as willed for "his own sake" by the Creator.[4] Sexuality here is not a mere attribute of the embodied person, the way that ethnicity or race is, but a constituent part of the person because of how femininity and masculinity are determined in the presence of one another.

Asymmetrical Complementarity

It is important to be clear about the nature of this reciprocity between man and woman that the spousal meaning of the body shows forth. Angelo Cardinal Scola has observed that sexual reciprocity is not a simple complementarity in the sense that the opposite sex is a missing part of the other sex. The sexual reciprocity that is at the heart of human existence is "asymmetrical," to use the words of Cardinal Scola.[5] Let me explain.

Now there is a complementarity between the sexes to be sure, but not in the sense that the sexes are understood as two fractional parts that can somehow be overcome in a kind of higher unity. Sexual difference in humanity and the orientation to the opposite sex is not about a frantic seeking of the other half of one's self and the recovery of a lost whole. Such a view would involve an androgynous understanding of humanity. Common human experience shows this to be false. Sexual difference is not transcended in our basic human relationships. A woman's feminine "I" is a point of reciprocity when she relates to persons of the opposite sex, every one of whom has a different status in relation to her. So, for instance, a woman is immediately related to her father, her brother, her male friend, and so on. Every man or woman lives in a plurality of relationships with different persons of the opposite sex, and in doing so we are not at all on a quest to find "the other half" of ourselves.[6]

The androgynous view of humanity, which understands the highest form of unity to be one where sexual difference is transcended and eliminated, is

[4] John Paul II, General Audience of January 16, 1980, in *TOB*, 187.

[5] See Angelo Cardinal Scola, *The Nuptial Mystery*, trans. Michelle K. Borras (Grand Rapids: Eerdmans, 2005), 92.

[6] Ibid., 94.

actually very old, and it is widespread in many quarters in our own time and not just among non-believers. Some Christians, even some theologians, understand Galatians 3:28—"There is neither Jew nor Greek, there is neither slave nor free, there is neither male nor female; for all are one in Christ Jesus"—to mean that the risen Christ has overcome sexual differences and that there will be an absence of sexuality in heaven. The good creation in Genesis speaks of something entirely different. The reciprocity between man and woman is not some sign of cosmic alienation, but is at the center of the good creation and therefore is not some negativity to be overcome.[7] Far from meaning that man and woman are two fractional halves of humanity, sexual reciprocity means that there are two ways of being an embodied human person that complete one another and therefore do not overcome one another. Writing on this subject, Angelo Cardinal Scola helps us to understand the point:

> My existence as a sexual being means, in some sense, that I am placed from the beginning in relation to another. The other is present to me as being identical in her own being as a person, but at the same time, because of sexual difference, she reveals to me a radical difference that distinguishes her from me at all levels. Thus if my way of embodying the identity of the person is masculine, the feminine that stands before me is a different way of being a person. The reciprocity that springs from sexual difference thus shows that the "I" emerges into existence from within a kind of constitutive polarity.[8]

Moreover:

> Anthropologically speaking, human sexuality is the "high road" along which man experiences differences as internal to the "I" itself. This is so not because the "I" lacks its own autonomous ontological consistency, made up, as Maritain writes, of constitutive elements and necessities. Rather, the polarity of the other at the same time constitutes the "I." There is not *first* a wholly autonomous "I" which *then* enters into relation with an other. The relation is not extrinsic and accidental, but intrinsic and constitutive.[9]

So a woman is more than just the "other" but is the "other" sex that makes the masculine "I" grow and become. In the presence of the "other"

[7] What androgyny and homosexuality have in common is the canceling out or elimination of sexual difference.

[8] Scola, *Nuptial Mystery*, 93–94.

[9] Ibid., 121. Scola cites J. Maritain, "La personne et le bien commun," in Maritain, *Oeuvres 1940–1963* (Paris, 1978), 287ff.

sex, who is different yet like me, there is a movement toward a greater possession of my own humanity. Adam must take Eve into account before he can say "I" in the fullest sense, at least in the sense of his masculine identity. God created a sexual reciprocity in which the opposite sex, the other sex, always remains "the other" for me. "Sexual difference always presents itself in terms of difference."[10] It is in this way that sexual reciprocity is understood to be "asymmetrical." The otherness of the opposite sex can never be overcome or transcended, and seeking to do so would harm one's own identity as man or woman polarized, as it were, toward the opposite sex. As Cardinal Scola observes, to try to overcome the duality of the sexes would be the death of love itself.[11] It would involve necessarily a refusal to accept the opposite sex for what he or she is as a person. Now we can gain a little better insight into why Pope John Paul claimed that affective maturity requires an awareness of love that is expressed in the spousal meaning of the body. Love requires a complete acceptance of the "otherness" of the person who is different from me. This truth is manifested in a very clear way in the spousal meaning of the body, whereby man and woman are oriented to one another and called to accept one another as creatures willed for their own sake precisely as embodied masculine and feminine creatures. A sound theological anthropology must inform how we understand affective maturity.

This reciprocity of the "unity of the two" has a deep foundation. Pope John Paul constantly taught in many of his writings (for example, his catechesis on Genesis and in *MD*) that human persons image the Triune God most fully and completely as a communion of persons, especially in the spousal relation between man and woman. The Pope pointed out that the revelation that God is the loving communion of the Father, Son, and Holy Spirit sheds much light on human persons created in the image of God. To exist as a person in the image and likeness of the Triune God involves existing as a person who is in relation, as man or woman, to another "I." Here again, we see how constitutive sexuality is for being a person. We stand in relation to others not in a generic way but as a woman or man. Our creation in the image of God not only means that all persons image God because they are free and rational creatures, individually, but also because man and woman, in the words of the Pope, "created as unity of the two in their common humanity are called to live in a communion of love, and in this way to mirror in the world the communion of love that is

---

10 Scola, *Nuptial Mystery*, 119.

11 Ibid., 94n38. On this point Scola cites G. Zuanazzi, *Temi e simboli dell'eros* (Rome: Città Nuova, 1991), 76.

in God, through which the Three Persons love each other in the intimate mystery of the one divine life" (*MD* 7). To speak of human persons, male and female, as existing in the image and likeness of God means that human persons are called to exist "for others, to become a gift" (ibid.). But this means too that just as man and woman exist for each other as gift, so their communion of love is not turned in on itself but exists for another, for a third someone, a child. The "unity of the two" is taken up into a dynamic that opens them up to procreation. Called to image and mirror the communion of love that is God, a communion characterized by fruitfulness, the communion between man and woman must itself be open to and marked by fruitfulness.

The Fall: A Limit on the Spousal Meaning of the Body

Of course this spousal meaning of the body has a limit placed on it because of the Fall of our first parents. The words of Jesus in Matthew 19—"it was not that way in the beginning"—instructs both the Pharisees and us that something changed for the worse. The consequences of the tragic disobedience of Adam and Eve include not only death and corruption but the burden of lust as well. The first letter of the Apostle John (2:16–17) tells us that this lust is not from the Father's good creation of the world, but from the knowledge of the tree of good and evil: "For all that is in the world, the lust of the flesh and the lust of the eyes and the pride of life, is not of the Father but is of the world." Adam and Eve found themselves naked and ashamed, which manifested the "uneasiness of conscience connected with lust." Fearing that they might be looked on by the other as an "object" rather than a creature willed for his or her own sake, Adam and Eve hid their nakedness, removing from one another's sight their visible femininity and masculinity.[12] Now ironically, they find themselves alienated on account of it. Genesis 3:16 testifies to this break and threat to the "unity of the two" with the words "Your desire shall be for your husband, and he shall rule over you." With the entrance of concupiscence into the human race, Adam and Eve and their descendants bear within themselves the constant "inclination to sin," the tendency to go against the moral order corre-

[12] John Paul II, General Audience of May 28, 1980, in *TOB*, 242–46. The Pope explains that man's original spiritual and somatic unity is ruptured. The body has ceased drawing on the power of the spirit that raised him to the level of the image of God. The body is no longer capable of expressing the person as it had been created to do. The body could now obscure the person as well as reveal him or her. Now the body could play into the selfish desire to consume and manipulate as well as to give oneself away in love.

sponding to the truth of the body and the dignity of man and woman as persons called to communion. All of this involves a certain diminishment of the divine image and likeness of God in humanity.

Pope John Paul, reflecting on the meaning of concupiscence, observed that concupiscence involves the loss of an interior freedom to give, to make a gift of self, because concupiscence reduces the other person to an object of satisfaction or enjoyment. In the words of the Pope, "[c]oncupiscence brings with it the loss of the interior freedom of the gift. The spousal meaning of the human body is linked exactly to this freedom. Man can become a gift—that is, man and woman exist in the relationship of the reciprocal gift of self—if each of them masters himself."[13]

In other words, genuine freedom is such that a person has the spiritual maturity to be master of herself in the sense that she is in possession of herself and so is able to freely give herself. It is precisely this kind of freedom that is lost in the Fall. With the loss of this freedom, this loss of the mastery of self, it is no longer possible to make a complete and sincere gift of self. The relationship between the sexes is distorted and the original communion is violated. The human heart now becomes a battlefield between lust and love. In this way, the subjection of man and woman to lust puts a limit on the spousal meaning of the body. This meaning is not just a conceptual reality. It is, at the same time, the way of living in the body in real concrete interpersonal relations. While it remains true objectively that the body manifests the truth that men and woman are created for one another and are called to communion, in the fallen state, the interior spiritual condition of man and woman makes it difficult for them to live according to this objective truth.[14] All of this involves a diminishment of the divine image and likeness in Adam and Eve who, as we have seen, were created as a "unity of the two" in their common humanity, "called to live in a communion of love and in this way to mirror in the world the communion of love that is in God," Father, Son, and Holy Spirit (*MD* 7).

Christ the New Adam

It is, of course, this condition of humanity after the Fall that the Son is sent by the Father to reverse and overcome. In becoming man the Son assumes our human condition burdened by sin and death. His perfect self-giving on the Cross obtains for us the forgiveness of sins and our freedom. In his encyclical *Veritatis Splendor* (*VS*) the Pope points out that true freedom is won and disclosed for us on the Cross. True freedom is the ability to make

[13] John Paul II, General Audience of July 23, 1980, in *TOB*, 259.
[14] Ibid, 257.

a sincere gift of self in service to God and one's brothers and sisters. Christ is the new Adam who gives himself up and unites himself to the second Eve, the Church. The one-flesh union of the new Adam and new Eve is the restoration of the fullness of the divine image and likeness that was defaced by the first Adam and the first Eve. In Christ's union of communion with his Bride, the Church, the call of humanity, as a unity of the two, to live in a communion of love, mirroring that communion of love that is in God, is realized in a way that is even greater than was possible in the first Adam and Eve. The Father's intention from the beginning for man and woman is fulfilled in Christ, the second Adam, and the Church, the second Eve. It is fulfilled in a way that is permanent and can never be lost because the Christ, the Son of God made man, has perfectly given himself to the Church and has made his Bride holy. The spousal meaning of the body is realized and its full meaning is revealed in the one-flesh union of Christ, the Bridegroom, with the Church, his Bride. A new kind of fecundity is inaugurated, and the fruitfulness of Eden is surpassed. The children of God are born, not of blood, nor of the will of the flesh, but by the Holy Spirit of God. No wonder the Church speaks of Christ's virginal love for the Church. With the transforming nature of the redemption there begins a new relationship between sexual difference, love, and procreation. Of course, the Church awaits that final day when, in the words of the Second Vatican Council, "that mystical marriage established by God" will be "fully manifested" in the future resurrection (*Presbyterorum Ordinis*, number 16). The call to virginity for the sake of the kingdom is directed to this reality. Those who answer this call are closely united to Christ's new way of loving and therefore anticipate for all members of the Church the full manifestation of the marriage of Christ with the Church.

Living the Mystery of the New Covenant and Virginity

As we have seen, Pope John Paul spoke of an affective maturity that has an awareness of love expressed in the spousal meaning of the body. This affective maturity will grasp both of these things about the spousal meaning of the body: the spousal reciprocity where masculinity and femininity is discovered in the presence of one another, and the loving, fruitful communion that the human person is called to precisely as a man or woman. Both of these things apply to the state of perfect continence because virginity for the sake of the kingdom is a way of living the mystery of the new covenant of Christ, the second Adam, with his Church, the second Eve.

An authentic living of this mystery requires an affective maturity where there is disciplining of sexual desire and affection. It requires the consolidation of a person's passions and emotions into stable patterns that are congruent with and cooperate with moral virtue. So, a heterosexual woman who has reached affective maturity and is ready for the state of consecrated virginity is serenely chaste, and the stable pattern of her passions and emotions does not spontaneously and precipitously bring her to the brink of immoral action: she not only wants to be chaste, but her sexual desires and emotional responses are chastened—disciplined, schooled, if you will—and therefore are well ordered. They cooperate with her moral decision to be chaste.

Virginity for the sake of the kingdom requires a kind of redirection of a woman's natural sexual orientation and desire for motherhood to the service of Christ, and to spiritual maternity. In this, the heterosexual woman does not have to suspend or abstract from what would be her felt and conscious choice of the masculine and of motherhood were she sexually active. The consecrated virgin has renounced something that nonetheless, on a different plane of the symbolic and the Christological, finds expression; she has embraced someone—Christ, the Bridegroom of the Church—in a unique way that is in harmony with what she has renounced in marriage and earthly motherhood. In *MD* 20 Pope John Paul made this very point:

> In order to understand this path, it is necessary to refer once more to the fundamental idea of Christian anthropology. By freely choosing virginity, women confirm themselves as persons, as beings whom the Creator from the beginning has willed for their own sake. At the same time they realize the personal value of their own femininity by becoming "a sincere gift" for God who has revealed himself in Christ, a gift for Christ, the Redeemer of humanity and the Spouse of souls: a "spousal" gift. One cannot correctly understand virginity—a woman's consecration in virginity—without referring to spousal love. It is through this kind of love that a person becomes a gift for the other.

The choice of virginity, in the response to Christ the Bridegroom, is in complete harmony with how woman was created from the beginning. It supposes the very spousal reciprocity between man and woman disclosed in Genesis but as resituated in relation to its perfection in the risen Christ. Thanks to the action of the Holy Spirit the consecrated virgin finds her feminine identity in her special relationship with the Lord. The Pope called attention to this in *MD* 20:

> Women, called from the very "beginning" to be loved and to love, in a vocation to virginity find Christ first of all as the Redeemer who "loved until the end" through his total gift of self; *and they respond to this gift with a "sincere gift"* of their whole lives. They thus give themselves to the divine Spouse, and this personal gift tends to union, which is properly spiritual in character. Through the Holy Spirit's action a woman becomes "one spirit" with Christ the Spouse (cf. 1 Cor 6:17).

Given the symbolic meaning of their own virginity, women in the state of consecrated virginity can say, "It is precisely because we are women that our virginity and celibacy is religiously important; it is our virginity, womanly virginity, which we bring to the representation of redeemed humanity, of the Church, the bride." Authentic representation, of course, requires the kind of feminine maturity where there is no discord but a harmony between a woman's own identity, affectivity, and sexuality—and her representation of the Church, the Bride of Christ.

In the bishop's homily for the Rite of Consecration to the life of virginity we are reminded that Christ "desired [the Church] to be a virgin, a bride, and a mother: a virgin, to keep the faith whole and entire, a bride, to be one with him for ever; and a mother, to raise up the family of the Church."[15] Women joined to Christ in consecrated virginity manifest the spiritual and supernatural fruitfulness of the virginal love between Christ and the Church.

Virginal Love and Spiritual Fruitfulness

We have seen that the union of the second Adam with the second Eve has brought about a new fruitfulness that surpasses that of creation. This fruitfulness of the Spirit is the birth of the children of God and their growth in the divine life. While consecrated virginity involves the renunciation of earthly marriage and the procreation of children, it participates in this new form of fruitfulness, that of spiritual motherhood. The exemplar of this spiritual motherhood, of course, is the Blessed Virgin Mary. She accepted God's word in faith and allowed the Holy Spirit to overshadow her and became the Mother of the Redeemer who is the firstborn among many brethren, that is, among the faithful, who in the Son, are the adopted sons and daughters of God. In her maternal love the Virgin Mary cooperates with the birth and growth of the faithful. Mary's divine maternity is a revelation of the fruitfulness of the Holy Spirit. A hymn from the Eastern liturgy expresses beautifully Mary's exemplarity of virginal and spiritual motherhood:

---

[15] "Consecration to a Life of Virginity for Women Living in the World," no. 16, in *The Rites of the Catholic Church as Revised by the Second Vatican Ecumenical Council*, vol. 2 (Collegeville, Minnesota: The Liturgical Press, 1991), 164.

Hail, mother and nurse of virgins!
Hail, you who lead souls to the Bridegroom!
Hail, Virgin Spouse![16]

Looking to the Blessed Virgin Mary we see that a consecrated virgin's spiritual motherhood is directed to the nurturing and growth of the children of God, leading them to the Bridegroom. The apostolic exhortation on the consecrated life, *Vita Consecrata*, takes up this very point:

> This virginal love is the source of a particular fruitfulness which fosters the birth and growth of divine life in people's hearts. Following in the footsteps of Mary, the New Eve, consecrated persons express their spiritual fruitfulness by becoming receptive to the Word, in order to contribute to the growth of a new humanity by their unconditional dedication and their living witness.[17]

This spiritual fruitfulness, of course, takes place in many different forms, but like the Blessed Virgin it often happens in a hidden way in prayer, silent faith, and love for others. So the bishop's homily for the Rite of Consecration instructs consecrated virgins to pray for the spread of Christian faith, for the unity of all Christians, and for the welfare of the married and poor sinners who have forgotten their Father's goodness and have abandoned his love.[18]

There is always a readiness in spousal love to be emptied out for those who are within the realm of one's activity and work. For those in earthly marriage this readiness, although open to others outside the immediate family, is focused primarily in the love that mothers and fathers give to their children. In virginity, there is a special readiness to be open to all people who are held close by the love of Christ the Spouse, "so that a great family of children might be born, or reborn to the life of grace."[19]

Consecrated Virginity and the Life of the World to Come

Those who are united to the risen Christ in consecrated virginity become a prophetic sign of the future life to come in the resurrection. In his theology of the body, Pope John Paul presented the prophetic witness of the life of perfect continence in terms of witnessing to the fulfillment of the spousal meaning of the body. We know from the reply of Christ to the Sadducees on

---

16 "Akathistos" hymn, as cited and translated in Raniero Cantalamessa, O.F.M. Cap., *Virginity*, trans. Charles Serignat (Boston: Alba House, 1995), 89.

17 John Paul II, *Vita Consecrata*, no. 34.

18 "Consecration to a Life of Virginity," no. 16.

19 Ibid.

the question of the resurrection (Mk 12:25) that "when they rise from the dead, they neither marry nor are given in marriage." Earthly marriage and procreation are not the eschatological future of humanity. In the risen life they lose their raison d'être, which was to bring forth, through bodily conjugal unity, human creatures made in the image and likeness of God, so that they might subdue the earth.[20] With the passing away of this world there is the quantitative closing of this process of the good creation. On the other hand, we know that the creation of man and woman belongs ontologically to the good creation. We will not cease being men and women in the resurrection, nor will the spousal relationship of men and women and the call to communion cease. Christ does not come to deliver us from what God created as good from the beginning; he comes to save the whole human person. Our identity as men and women together with the spousal meaning of the body is destined to be transformed and fulfilled.[21] If it were otherwise, if we were asexual in heaven, then it would be meaningless to talk about the resurrection of our bodies. Such a condition would not be the resurrection of *our* earthly bodies. Those who share in the future world of the resurrection will be in perfect communion with God in knowledge and love and will enjoy a perfect masculine or feminine subjectivity in their glorious risen bodies. Sexuality will be fulfilled in the resurrected body, which is to say that the spousal meaning of the sexually determined bodiliness of human persons is fulfilled in heaven. In this condition there will be the fullness of personal self-donation and an intersubjective communion with the whole world of persons who are in an eternal union with God, Father, Son, and Holy Spirit. As the Pope puts it: "We should think of the reality of the 'other world' in the categories of the rediscoveries of a new, perfect subjectivity of each person and at the same time of the rediscovery of a new, perfect intersubjectivity of all. In this way this reality means the true and definitive fulfillment of human subjectivity and, on this basis, the definitive fulfillment of the 'spousal' meaning of the body."[22]

This union of the perfect masculine and feminine subjectivity of all those in heaven is nothing less than the union of men and women in the communion of saints. In a manner beyond our present understanding all that is masculine in humanity in the risen state will be in a union of communion

---

20 John Paul II, General Audience of December 2, 1981, in *TOB*, 387.

21 On this point see Augustine, *City of God*, 22.17; Congregation for the Doctrine of the Faith (CDF), "Letter to Bishops of the Catholic Church on the Collaboration of Men and Women in the Church and in the World" (2004), no. 12. Also see my essay included in the present work, chapter 9 above, "The Augustinian Foundations of the Theology of the Body: He Who Created Both Will Restore Both."

22 John Paul II, General Audience of December 16, 1981, in *TOB*, 396.

with all that is feminine. This communion of saints will form the one Bride of Christ who through her eternal union with Christ her Bridegroom will live in eternal union with the Blessed Trinity in knowledge and love. In heaven the ancient rupture in humanity between body and soul, and on earth the alienation between man and woman because of lust, will be overcome. The absolute and eternal spousal meaning of the glorified body will be revealed and realized in union with God face-to-face in the communion of the saints. The Pope calls this future condition of humanity (male and female) in heaven "the eschatological virginity of the risen man."[23]

Existing as it does between the tension of the kingdom of heaven, which has arrived but not yet fully, continence for the sake of the kingdom is a prophetic sign and anticipation of the future anthropology of the resurrection. The state of consecrated virginity serves as a reminder that marriage and family is not the final end of humanity no matter how noble as a state of life, no matter how holy its communion. The consecrated virgin testifies that there awaits us a communion more comprehensive than what we know from marriage and family life. Consecrated virgins who renounce earthly marriage for the sake of Christ the Bridegroom are a sign and witness to the truth that human sexuality does not pass away in the kingdom and that the final lasting goal of masculinity and femininity is a spiritual fruitfulness. This is so because the consecrated virgin is waiting in a bodily way for that heavenly marriage of Christ with the Church by giving herself completely to Christ in the hope "that he may give himself to the Church in the full truth of eternal life."[24]

Consecrated Virginity Can Be a Service to Married Couples

All of this is to say that the consecrated virgin, who steps into that state in which women and men no longer marry or are given in marriage, witnesses to the fulfillment of the spousal meaning of the body in heaven, and hence to the future anthropology of the resurrection. It remains true, of course, that those in the state of consecrated virginity live deeply in the reality of earthly life and must struggle against concupiscence and the weakness of human nature just like any other woman who has not made a similar commitment and whose choice is that of matrimony. The difference is the kind of responsibility for the different type of good that is chosen. The consecrated virgin must be faithful to the interior dynamism of virginity that bears a likeness to Christ himself. It involves remaining faithful to that special readiness and openness to all persons and living a

---

[23] John Paul II, General Audience of March 24, 1982, in *TOB*, 419.

[24] John Paul II, *Familiaris Consortio*, no. 16.

detachment that teaches true love. This detachment looks upon other persons not as how we might make them out to be by our own lights or want them to be for some reason of self-interest, but as they really are, as they have been created by God and in view of the kingdom of heaven. Without this kind of detachment there can never really be true love of the other person. It is how Christ lived every human relationship.[25] Cardinal Scola describes this state of living as a "possession in detachment." He observes:

> Therefore virginity can be understood neither as only a specific vocation within the church, nor primarily as a renunciation of something. It is rather a manner of love characteristic of Jesus Christ, which all Christians, even spouses, are therefore called to live. The virginal charism, as a specific vocation for some in the church, literally bears witness to this.[26]

In this way we can see too how the state of consecrated virginity lived in happiness can be of service to couples and families. It can be an unmistakable reminder of how family members are intended to relate to one another as unique persons called to follow Christ and destined for the kingdom of heaven. The spiritual motherhood of consecrated virgins reminds Christian parents their motherhood and fatherhood must become a spiritual motherhood and fatherhood in order to respond to the whole truth of the humanity of their children who are a union of body and soul (see *MD* 21). The witness of virgins who are consecrated to Christ the Bridegroom can come to the aid of young couples. One of the things that threatens healthy marriages today is the unrealistic and disproportionate expectations that our culture places on couples. They invite disillusion-

---

25 On this point see the helpful discussion in Scola, *Nuptial Mystery*, 270.

26 Ibid. What Walter Ong, S.J., observed about how the Blessed Virgin Mary is represented in Michelangelo's Pieta is most relevant here. "In the Pieta the Virgin Mother has freed herself of all possessiveness, transmuted all eros (love involved in its own need) into agape (love as self-giving, involved with the other). She has done so by lovingly acquiescing to her now adult Son's doing what he was called to do, his Father's will. She leaves her Son completely free, though doing so returns him dead to her arms. And when she takes him dead to her arms, she does not clutch him, but leaves her arms open. The statue tugs at the hearts of women and men alike, but its subject matter is supremely feminine. And it is supreme human freedom: Mary has deliberately chosen to let her Son to be about his Father's business. If she had the choice once more, knowing what it would cost, she would do it again. No regrets. Total courage. Her youthful choice is still part of her. Hence her youthful face, often commented on, despite her mature age. Her arms are open and relaxed. She is completely free, for she is fully aware of what she has chosen." See Walter Ong, *Fighting for Life* (London: Cornell University Press, 1981), 101.

ment and despair when the inevitable happens and unrealistic expectations are not met. Consecrated virginity is a powerful reminder that earthly marriage is not our final fulfillment and that our hearts our restless until they rest in God. It can help free husbands and wives from the unbearable burden of having to be "everything" for the other, of taking the place, in effect, of God. Consecrated virginity can also come to the help of those marriages that are troubled in part because husbands and wives use their happiness or lack of happiness as the supreme measure of their lives.[27] Virgins consecrated to Christ the Bridegroom remind married couples that their loving communion will not dissolve into an abyss of nothingness but will be transfigured and spiritualized in heaven, in a communion that is greater than anything we know here on earth.

---

[27] See the discussion in Cantalamessa, *Virginity*, 8.

CHAPTER 13

Revelation, Natural Law, and Homosexual Unions*

AT A CONFERENCE celebrating the twenty-fifth anniversary of the Holy Father's pontificate, Cardinal Ratzinger recalled the aim of *Veritatis Splendor* (*VS*) to help moral theologians bring together the metaphysical and biblical sources of moral theology.[1] Both are necessary. A pure biblicism set free from the appreciation of the natural law founded in creation cannot address contemporary questions, while confining the Bible to providing inspiration to do good and avoid evil empties Christian morality of its specific ethos. On the other hand, inattention to creation means inattention to the creation that the Lord God found good and even very good. We end with a rationalism that, divorced from both the Bible and the order of creation, can do nothing but calculate the consequences of acts.

It is easy to see that limiting the Bible in the way Cardinal Ratzinger laments means limiting Christ himself, who is the fullness of revelation and the only adequate referent of the Scripture, to the role of a moral motivator or cheerleader. Truly to found moral theology in the Bible would be, contrariwise, to take Christ as the One who in the concreteness of his life, death, and Resurrection conveys to us the content of the moral law.[2]

---

* A version of this essay appeared in *Nova et Vetera* 2 (Fall 2004) 337–66.

1 Joseph Cardinal Ratzinger, "Intervention by Joseph Cardinal Ratzinger at the Symposium of the Pontifical Lateran University on the 25th Anniversary of the Pontificate of His Holiness John Paul II" (May 9, 2003). For the full text of Ratzinger's remarks, see www.vatican.va/roman_curia/congregations/cfaith/documents/rc_con_cfaith_doc_20030509_ratzinger-simposio_laterano_ge.html.

2 *VS* 15: "Jesus himself is the 'fulfillment' of the Law inasmuch as he fulfills its authentic meaning by the total gift of himself: he himself becomes a living and personal

It must be said, unfortunately, that the call of *VS* has not been entirely met. If there has been positive reception of the encyclical, there has also been non-reception. An especially good example of its non-reception, we think, is to be found in Professor Stephen Pope's recent treatment of homosexuality. It is a good example, not only because Dr. Pope seems content with the consequentialism the Holy Father reproves, but also because although he seems to see what *VS* is offering by way of a properly Christian apprehension of the natural law, where nature is illumined by revelation, he rejects it. It is this second issue we would like to take up. We would like to show both the unsatisfactory character of Dr. Pope's approach and as well indicate what the road not traveled might look like. In other words, we want to show how the revelation of Christ—Christ himself—provides the "content" of the moral law relative to sexuality and marriage.[3]

Stephen Pope on Natural Law on Homosexual Unions

Dr. Pope characterizes the Magisterium's rejection of same-sex relations as a position based on what he calls "revealed natural law."[4] The seemingly contradictory nature of this term is calculated and is meant to indicate that the position holds not only that grace is necessary to keep the Law but also that revelation—supernatural revelation—is necessary even to know the Law. This is to say that *supernatural* revelation teaches and is required for us to know the *natural* law. *Veritatis Splendor* is an expression of this, according to Dr. Pope, and we may well agree.[5] Dr. Pope seems at one point to recognize that this position has the support of St. Thomas.[6] Subsequently, however, he wants to distinguish it from St. Thomas's position, and he criticizes the idea that we need revelation to know the natural law on the ground that it is not the position of St.Thomas.[7] So to speak, the difference between Dr. Pope and us is wholly and entirely over this

Law, who invites people to follow him; through the Spirit, he gives the grace to share his own life and love." For a particularly vigorous statement of this view, see Hans Urs von Balthasar, "Nine Theses in Christian Ethics," in *International Theological Commission: Texts and Documents 1969–1985*, ed. Michael Sharkey (San Francisco: Ignatius Press, 1989), 105–20. The theses first appeared in 1974.

3 For an overview of the problem of Christocentricism and moral theology as well as a summary of moralists who approach Christ as a motivator, see Livio Melina, "Christ and the Dynamism of Action: Outlook and Overview of Christocentrism in Moral Theology," *Communio* 28 (2001): 112–39.

4 Stephen J. Pope, "Scientific and Natural Law Analyses of Homosexuality," *Journal of Religious Ethics* 29 (2001): 89–126.

5 Ibid., 104.

6 Ibid., 105.

7 Ibid., 108.

term—"revealed natural law." For Dr. Pope, the paradox invites dismissal. For us, the paradox leads to some important truths.

Dr. Pope thinks the Magisterium's rejection of same-sex relations is not really a rejection based on the natural law, but a rejection based on revelation. He thinks that when the Magisterium takes the procreative finality of sexual relations to be evident and evidently constitutive of such relations, such that it is immoral to take steps to thwart this finality, this is based on a "certain interpretation" of such passages as Genesis 1:27–28 and not a straightforwardly factual claim. He thinks the Magisterium's rejection relies too much on such passages as Leviticus 18:22, 20:13, and Romans 1:26, and is therefore unsuccessful, since the meaning of such passages is controversial.[8] Further, Dr. Pope considers that the "revealed natural law" position "attends too narrowly to the ultimate [supernatural] end [of man] and does not give sufficient attention to the inclusive end of human desire, encompassing body as well as soul."[9] Allied with this, the position too much "isolates" the theological understanding of man from modern empirical scientific interpretations of man.[10]

In the absence of a natural law argument against same-sex unions, and on the supposition that biblical revelation does not speak clearly on the issue, Dr. Pope wants to listen to the experience of homosexual couples. If they report happiness and fulfillment and flourishing within the context of such unions, then this should count heavily for their moral legitimacy. The happiness of stable gay unions is an empirical question,[11] and we will find out whether such unions contribute to the human flourishing of couples and communities by both psychological and sociological investigation.[12] Dr. Pope seems to recognize that the sciences cannot determine issues of virtue and vice;[13] still, if human flourishing is an empirical question, and is to be settled by psychological and sociological survey, it is hard to see that this will entail anything much more sophisticated than asking couples whether they are "happy," and neighbors whether such couples are good citizens.[14] It is

[8] Ibid., 107n13.

[9] Ibid., 109. How it is that risen life in Christ is not sufficiently "inclusive" is not explained.

[10] Ibid., 109.

[11] Ibid., 118.

[12] Ibid., 120.

[13] Ibid., 119.

[14] Ibid., 112. Exactly what Dr. Pope thinks science contributes to ethics is in fact hard to say, nor does it seem any clearer in his *Evolution of Altruism and the Ordering of Love* (Washington, DC: Georgetown University Press, 1994), where an elaborate deployment of sociobiological machinery somehow gives intelligibility to the ethical obligation of parents to love their own children more than other children.

this approach, moreover, that Dr. Pope thinks congruent with St. Thomas's way to the discovery of ethical principles.[15]

Dr. Pope's position is in fact hard to summarize. Whatever he seems to give with one hand he takes away with the other. So, St. Thomas agrees with "revealed natural law" on what it takes to know the natural law easily and accurately, and he does not; the question of the morality of sexual unions cannot be settled by science, and then it can be so settled; appeals to lived experience in settling matters moral are inadequate and treacherous,[16] and on the other hand reports of such experience are a font of theology.[17] He is apparently evenhanded in criticism of both the "revealed natural law" and "revisionist" positions. But this is a mere appearance. The only thing he brings to the revisionist discussion is a call for more "science," which quickly devolves into a call to listen to the experience of homosexuals as reported by homosexuals.

Initial Criticism of Stephen Pope's Position

First Criticism

In the first place, it has to be said that the natural law argument for the immorality of same-sex relations has been made several times and that, in its own order, it is very strong. We return to the qualifying phrase shortly. The argument has been made by the Congregation for the Doctrine of the Faith (CDF) in 1975 and again in 1986.[18] As Dr. Pope recognizes in a note, John Finnis has addressed at length the natural law argument that same-sex relations are immoral.[19] Martin Rhonheimer is alert to the natural law's declaration of the "truth" of the sexual inclination in stable and permanent marriage ordered to procreation.[20] The natural law argument for the immorality of

[15] Pope, "Scientific and Natural Law Analyses," 112.

[16] Ibid., 116.

[17] Ibid., 111–12.

[18] CDF, Declaration on Certain Questions concerning Sexual Ethics, *Persona Humana* (1975), no. 8; CDF, "Letter to the Bishops of the Catholic Church on the Pastoral Care of Homosexual Persons" (1986), no. 7.

[19] John Finnis, "Natural Law and Unnatural Acts," *Heythrop Journal* 11 (1970): 365–87. In this article, Finnis is especially aware of the relation of the natural law to revelation in the area of sexual morality. Finnis returns to the topic of same-sex relations in "Law, Morality, and 'Sexual Orientation,'" *Notre Dame Law Review* 69 (1994): 1049–76, and "The Good of Marriage and the Morality of Sexual Relations: Some Philosophical and Historical Observations," *The American Journal of Jurisprudence* 42 (1997): 97–134.

[20] Martin Rhonheimer, "Excursus: The Natural Law and Contraception," in his *Natural Law and Practical Reason: A Thomist View of Moral Autonomy* (New York: Fordham University Press, 2000), 109–38.

same-sex unions is already made in principle by *Humanae Vitae* (*HV*) and its many able apologists.[21] Among these should be mentioned John Paul II in *Familiaris Consortio* (*FC*).[22] It should be clear that the natural law exclusion of contraception found there is equally exclusive of homosexual acts, and this is indicated briefly in *VS*, where it restates the principle of *HV*.[23]

One will think the argument has not been made only if one is persuaded that natural law arguments, if made, must be found persuasive by any man of good sense, whatever his religious persuasions or lack thereof. Russell Hittinger charts the course by which it came to be supposed that the truth of a natural law argument can be "measured by its success in garnering assent" and that appeal to the natural law is an appeal to "what every agent is supposed to know according to what is first in cognition."[24] If this is erroneous, it should not surprise us that what Hittinger characterizes as "the thin strands of argument about natural functions" in *HV* did not carry the Western world.[25]

Three reasons especially may be given why the argument against same-sex relations and same-sex unions is unconvincing to modern men. First, there is no argument from a natural finality or the procreative meaning embedded in human persons and their sexually differentiated bodies to a moral obligation of law unless one thinks nature, including human nature, is created, and its finalities capable of speaking the mind of a Lawgiver.[26] Apart from creation, we may speak of natural right but not of natural law.[27] But non-existent babies have no rights, and the rights of spouses can easily be supposed freely and morally renunciable.

Second, and even granted that all natural finalities are created, such finalities may, but again may not, bespeak a moral obligation. The natural finality

---

21 One can start with Janet E. Smith, *Humanae Vitae: A Generation Later* (Washington, DC: Catholic University of America Press, 1991).

22 See John Paul II, *Familiaris Consortio*, no. 32.

23 Read *Veritatis Splendor*, no. 47 and 50 together.

24 Russell Hittinger, "*Veritatis Splendor* and the Theology of the Natural Law," in *"Veritatis Splendor" and the Renewal of Moral Theology*, ed. J. A. DiNoia, O.P., and Romanus Cessario, O.P. (Princeton, NJ: Scepter Publishers, 1999), 108, 111. A fuller statement of this material can be found in chapters 1 and 2 of Hittinger's *The First Grace: Rediscovering the Natural Law in a Post-Christian World* (Wilmington, DE: ISI Books, 2003).

25 Hittinger, "*Veritatis Splendor* and the Theology of the Natural Law," 107.

26 Lawrence Dewan, O.P., "St. Thomas, Our Natural Lights, and the Moral Order," *Angelicum* 67 (1990): 297–98.

27 Ernest Fortin, "Natural Law," in *Human Rights, Virtue, and Common Good: Untimely Meditations on Religion and Politics*, ed. Brian J. Benestad (New York: Rowman & Littlefield, 1996), 160.

of the hair follicles on masculine faces does not forbid shaving. The natural finality of sex to procreation forbids contraception and homosexual acts. For in the first place, this finality is not realized apart from an exercise of the properly human agency, informed by thought and presupposing freedom (even where freedom is pressured by passion), of a man and a woman. In the second place, this finality terminates in the instantiation of another agent similarly endowed with intelligence and freedom—a person. Part of our appreciation of the difference between the finalities of hair follicles and of sex, in both the realization of the finality and its term, therefore, will be a function of apprehending human persons as the only personal reality within a material world created by a transcendent personal agency (see *Evangelium Vitae* [*EV*], number 83). Our ability to respond to the good of persons, in other words, is conditioned according as we think them the product of the chances of evolution, or the product of the choice of a transcendent Person.[28] Where there is nothing above it, the universe itself and everything in it too easily gets flattened out, and in a time when all our bodily functions are increasingly under technological control, it can be hard to see why any finality should escape our own direction of it by our own choice to good ends, even where such direction is contrary to what is given prior to our choice.

A third reason the natural law argument seems weak, a reason with ties to the first, is that even supposing one has the greatest respect for the procreative meaning of sex, and wants children, it can still be hard to see why every single act of sexual intercourse must be open to procreation. Why must union and fecundity go together in every act? Even if they do so "naturally," in a sexual practice unconditioned by interventions ranging from *coitus interruptus* to the use of condoms to an orally ingested contraceptive, why must they? It is not that there is no good natural law argument here, but only, we are saying, that at this point especially, an unreligious man of goodwill will most easily fail to be moved.

Even so, there is one thing in the argument of *HV* as well as in the argument against same-sex unions that really should be taken as obvious, and that is the procreative finality of sexual acts. If this is obvious, *and* if we see the rightness of never impeding this finality because of the dignity and fundamentality of the good it is ordered to, *and* if we take the world as created, then the moral obligations themselves become "obvious" as a matter of "natural law." What, however, of the first and foundational obvi-

[28] See Robert Sokolowski, "The Christian Understanding of the Person," chap. 10 in *Eucharistic Presence: A Study in the Theology of Disclosure* (Washington, DC: Catholic University of America Press, 1994). The New Testament brings a further light, according as our personal agency is now to be a participation in the personal agency of Christ.

ousness? Is not such a characterization of the procreative finality or meaning of sexual acts as "obvious" a polemical one and, as well, something that begs the question Dr. Pope addresses?[29] Kevin Flannery nicely expresses the way in which such a thing may be said to be obvious.

> Consider the type of acts characteristic of homosexual activity: acts in which one of the partners penetrates the body of the other or somehow simulates such penetration (as even a masturbator can do). If one is to give a complete account of such acts, one must acknowledge that they belong properly to heterosexuality. Why this desire to *penetrate*? And why penetration with that organ from which is discharged semen? Homosexual advocates prefer to look away from these facts and limit their account of what homosexuals do to talk about providing pleasure or intimacy or about giving expression to their true selves.[30]

This account is noteworthy for its calm insistence, first, that the heterosexual and therefore procreative finality of sexual acts is nothing except the intelligibility of facts (penetration, discharge of seed) universally available to every human being.[31] Moreover, if the intelligibility of a fact is part of the fact, then the procreative finality of sexual acts is also a "fact."[32] Second, the sort of fact or insight that is determinative of the issue of the morality of sexual acts is something available to common experience. It is not something for which one needs the refined, specialized experience of the modern empirical sciences.[33] It is not something for which we need modern chemistry, biology, or psychology. Third, the heterosexual and procreative meaning of sexual acts is nonetheless something that one can ignore. One turns away from such givens as the desire to penetrate, and the capacity of semen,

29 See Pope, "Scientific and Natural Law Analyses," 99, for a dutiful reportage of the sociobiological assessment that homosexual behavior is "normal, "beneficent," and related to altruism.

30 Kevin L. Flannery, S.J., "Homosexuality and Types of Dualism: A Platonico-Aristotelian Approach," *Gregorianum* 81 (2000): 363–64. Is this physicalism? Then so is the recognition of the eye as the organ of sight.

31 See St. Augustine, *City of God* 14.22: "sicut evidentissime apparet in diversi sexus corporibus, masculum et feminam ita creatos, ut prolem generando crescerent et multiplicarentur et implerent terram, magnae absurditatis est reluctari." (As appears most evidently in bodies of diverse sex that masculine and feminine were so created that they might increase and multiply by generating offspring and fill the earth, it is a great absurdity to deny it.)

32 See Bernard J. F. Lonergan's discussion of "data" and "facts" in *Method in Theology* (New York: Herder and Herder, 1972), 201–3.

33 For the notion of "common experience," see Henry B. Veatch, "Some Suggestions on the Respective Spheres of Science and Philosophy," *The Thomist* 3 (1941): 177–216.

and changes the subject. To say that something is "obvious" does not mean one does not have to look. The "obvious," therefore, is not the "undeniable." It might also therefore be the case that we need help to see the obvious.

To conclude this first criticism: if deliberately to destroy the procreative meaning of heterosexual acts is immoral, if it is to act against the truth of the language of the body, in John Paul II's way of putting things, then it must be likewise so for homosexual acts.[34] Even though intended to signify a sincere gift of the self, the homosexual act cannot of itself bear that meaning, because the meaning of the body that is part of one's "self" has been ignored.[35] The "proper and primordial nature" of man, "which is the person himself in the unity of soul and body, in the unity of his spiritual and biological inclinations," has been ignored (see *VS* 50).

Second Criticism

There is a second initial criticism of Dr. Pope to be made. The kind of grounds upon which he thinks same-sex unions could be seen to be legitimate would also legitimate polygamy. There are men and women in polygamist families in Utah and Arizona, so-called "fundamentalist Mormons," that will readily assert that their form of marriage is an active ingredient in their human flourishing and felt satisfaction.[36] The reports of the lived experience of such families, the narrative of their own lives such as they can give them, will be filled with accounts of the warmth of the affective exchanges and loyalties such families foster among the adults, man and women, and of the advantages for the children of many caregivers, and all this quite independently of the special satisfaction such families take in living according to the will of God as they hold is revealed to them by the teaching and example of Joseph Smith.

That We Need Revelation Even for What We Can Know by the Natural Light

The above criticisms are easily made. What is more vexing about Dr. Pope's essay is its failure to understand the relation between reason and revelation, nature and grace, in the Church's apprehension of the immorality of same-sex relations and unions. In the first place, this is indeed a matter of seeing

34 See John Paul II, General Audience of August 22, 1984, in *Theology of the Body* (*TOB*), no. 631.

35 John Paul II, *FC* 32.

36 For an instance with regard to the experience of women see Janet Bennion, *Women of Principle: Female Networking in Contemporary Mormon Polygyny* (New York: Oxford University Press, 1998).

in general that we need revelation to strengthen our grasp of the natural law. In the second place, it is a matter of beholding the quite explicit light that revelation sheds on the immorality of same-sex relations and unions. This is in fact what *VS* invites us to do.

Our ordinary apprehension of the natural law needs to be strengthened by the light of revelation. Dr. Pope's rejection of previous natural law arguments concluding that same-sex relations are immoral is itself a kind of proof of this. The inability of people to see the immorality of such relations on natural grounds is not extraordinary or remarkable but is not evidence that the argument has not been made.

St. Thomas, Revelation, and Natural Law

First, just what is St. Thomas's position as to whether we need revelation to strengthen our grip on the natural law? Denis J. M. Bradley has recently addressed this question. After noting that the love of neighbor is a primary and self-evident principle of the natural law for St. Thomas, he reports his position on how evident the Ten Commandments are.

> It should be . . . apparent that killing, committing adultery, bearing false witness, and stealing are not beneficent acts to one's neighbor. These acts clearly violate the first-order principle that one should not harm or do evil to any person. Yet ordinary men, because of passions and evil habits, can ignore what is obviously just and what is obviously unjust.[37]

This is an accurate summary. Can the natural law be removed from the heart of man according to St. Thomas? In the abstract, the first principles of the natural law cannot not be known; they cannot be expunged from the human heart, St. Thomas says.[38] Concretely, even they can, as it were, be suspended by passion. As for the secondary principles, such as are to be found in the Decalogue, they are even more fragile. St. Thomas says:

> [A]s to the secondary precepts, the natural law can be blotted from the human heart, either by evil persuasions, just as in speculative matters errors occur in respect to necessary conclusions; or by vicious customs and corrupt habits, as among some men, theft, and even unnatural vices, as the Apostle states, were not esteemed sinful.[39]

---

[37] Denis J. M. Bradley, *Aquinas on the Twofold Human Good: Reason and Human Happiness in Aquinas's Moral Science* (Washington, DC: Catholic University of America Press, 1997), 321.

[38] *ST* I–II, q. 94, a. 6.

[39] Ibid.

Therefore, St. Thomas expressly remarks the "fittingness" of the assistance provided by revelation for our apprehension of the secondary principles of the natural law, conclusions from the first principles. Reason can err, and sinful habits corrupt our grasp of these principles. Therefore, he concludes, "there was need for the authority of the divine law to rescue man from both these defects."[40] There is a lapidary summary of St. Thomas's thought in his late conferences on the Ten Commandments: "Because the law of nature had been destroyed by the law of concupiscence it was necessary that man be brought back to the works of virtue and withdrawn from vice: for which needful things there was the law of Scripture."[41] Man still desires the good, but "the law of concupiscence frequently corrupts the law of nature and the order of reason."[42]

Dr. Pope does not accurately reflect this teaching when he says that for St. Thomas "human reason is more or less adequate for understanding the natural law per se," and that the competence of reason is "unnecessarily diminished in revealed natural law" as measured by the teaching of St. Thomas.[43] It is not quite clear what the "per se" is doing here. But, yes, St. Thomas's position is that human reason is "more or less adequate," that is, in itself or "per se" competent to understand the natural law since the natural law means especially the first principles of practical reason. These principles of the Law, such things as that life is to be preserved, remain always in the habit of synderesis, which can be styled a natural habit, which is to say a natural faculty of the intellect whereby we understand and assent to the truth of these principles.[44] Since the first principles are correlative to the fundamental inclinations of human nature, and human nature is wounded but not destroyed by sin, they must always be able to be formulated.[45] These are but

---

40 *ST* I–II, q. 99, a. 2, ad 2. See q. 100, a. 5, ad 1. See for the same position St. Augustine, *The City of God* 18.41 and 22.22. On the problem of the naturally unknowable character of the natural law, see Ernest Fortin, "Augustine, Thomas Aquinas, and the Problem of the Natural Law," *Ernest Fortin: Collected Essays II: Classical Christianity and the Political Order*, ed. J. Brian Benestad (New York: Rowman & Littlefield, 1996), 199–222, for an examination of the role of revelation in knowing natural law.

41 *Expositio in duo praecepta caritatis et in decem legis praecepta*, in *Opuscula Theologica* (Rome: Marietti, 1954), Prologus I, no. 1131. Or see the new edition by Jean-Pierre Torrell, *Collationes in Decem Preceptis*, I, line 27, in *Revue des sciences philosophiques et théologiques* 69 (1985): 5–40, 227–63.

42 Ibid., no. 1130. See the discussion in Hittinger, "*Veritatis Splendor* and the Theology of the Natural Law," 102–4.

43 Pope, "Scientific and Natural Law Analyses," 108.

44 See the detailed treatment in Bradley, *Aquinas on the Twofold Human Good*, 296–313.

45 *ST* I–II, q. 94, a. 1, and q. 109, a. 2.

seeds, however; to get a crop requires more.[46] The first principles must grow into prudence and the moral virtues, and are themselves as little sufficient for human action as is seed just broadcast in the field for a harvest. Moreover, human reason does not exist in itself, abstractly, and it does not operate unconditioned by history, culture, sin, grace. Especially as to those last, reason operates conditioned by either sin or grace or both. Dr. Pope makes St. Thomas out to be some Enlightenment *philosophe* for whom "reason" is ever the same, has always the same prospects, sees always clearly and distinctly.[47]

Revelation and the Knowledge of God

Further, our cognitive situation relative to the natural law is not unique. It is very like our cognitive situation relative to the knowledge of God. God is naturally knowable, and knowable as Creator. But as St. Thomas notes, the natural knowledge of God is difficult, restricted to those fortunate enough to have the leisure required for the philosophic life, and commonly mixed with error.[48] Chapter 2 of *Dei Filius* follows St. Thomas here.[49] So also does *Fides et Ratio*, expressly attributing to sin our difficulty in coming to know God by the natural light.[50] *Veritatis Splendor* recognizes an analogous cognitive situation in the moral order (see *VS* 12).

The supposition that since something is contained in or follows strictly from the natural law, it ought therefore to be acknowledged by all men is reminiscent of the naïve supposition that since St. Paul says truly that God can be known from the things that have been made and the First Vatican Council repeats him, therefore his existence and the character of his transcendence are generally acknowledged by all men in every state and condition. But these implications by no means follow. If there is a nation that does not know God, the teaching of St. Paul is not falsified, and if there is a nation that does not recognize the immorality of contraception, the claim that contraception is contrary to the natural law is not invalidated. For our ignorance of first things, whether they be metaphysical or moral, the Catholic tradition has always supposed, with St. Augustine, that the condition and orientation of our will affects what we can see.

---

46 See *ST* I–II, q. 61, a. 1, for naturally known first principles of both knowledge and action, first principles that are seeds (*seminalia*) of both intellectual and moral virtue.

47 See the discussion of what is called "Encyclopaedia" in Alasdair MacIntyre's *Three Rival Versions of Moral Enquiry: Encyclopaedia, Genealogy, and Tradition* (Notre Dame, IN: University of Notre Dame Press, 1990).

48 *ST* I, q. 1, a. 1; cf. Aristotle, *Metaphysics* I, 1, 981b19–22.

49 DS 3005. See Norman Tanner, ed., *Decrees of the Ecumenical Councils* (Washington, DC: Georgetown University Press, 1990), vol. 2, 806.

50 John Paul II, *Fides et Ratio*, nos. 21–23.

And for the deformation of our appetite and the wounding of our will itself, we know of the presence of sin, both original and actual, and of the absence of original justice. Apart from grace, we will not keep the moral law; not keeping the moral law, we shall soon be unable to see it.

Now, just as Christ is the Author of grace, so is he the fullness of revelation who perfects it in both word and deed, in the personal history that leads from cradle to Cross and from death to risen life. Just as we should not expect to keep the moral law apart from his grace, so we should not expect to know it in any detail apart from his light.

What most of all one misses in Dr. Pope's article, therefore, is any awareness of the context, cognitive and affective, in which we both act morally and think about our moral action. It is awareness of this context, however, the context of sin and grace, that in part constitutes Catholic moral theology as Catholic.

Revelation and the Knowledge of the Nature and Properties of Marriage

In the third place, our cognitive situation relative to same-sex relations and unions is not unique even within our knowledge of the nature and properties of marriage.

There is a natural law argument for the unity and indissolubility of marriage, as required for the successful prosecution of the ends of marriage. One would never learn from Dr. Pope that it is just as strong (or for him, just as weak) a position as the natural law argument against same-sex unions, for both depend on the procreative meaning of sexual relations.

But revelation, in providing further grounds for the unity and indissolubility of marriage, also enables that natural law grounding to be more easily and confidently seen. It is admitted by theologians that otherwise this grounding is difficult to perceive. After all, for hardness of heart Moses permitted divorce even though from the beginning and by the nature of marriage as fashioned by the Creator's hand it was not so. Michael Schmaus, who can stand for the traditional theological sensibility here, readily acknowledges this: "As the history of marriage shows, not only has it been difficult for man, in the course of his development, to preserve the unity and indissolubility of marriage; *it has been difficult for him even to recognize it.*"[51]

If there were no natural grounding for the unity and indissolubility of marriage, then a revealed requirement of these things would be a deformation of marriage, a deformation of something natural or at best a burden

---

[51] Michael Schmaus, *Dogma*, vol. 5, *The Church as Sacrament* (London: Sheed and Ward, 1975), 289, emphasis mine.

imposed on marriage extrinsic to its nature. What revelation provides is rather, as John Finnis puts it, a more "intense grasp" of the basic value of life, since human life is now ordered to share in the divine life.[52] But it is the same value, life, that is grasped both naturally and supernaturally.

Revelation on Same-Sex Unions

The Exemplarity of the Moral Agency of Christ

It is usually taken for granted that the revelation of the immorality of same-sex relations is confined to a few pieces of Old Testament legislation or New Testament condemnation. In fact, it is much more massive and, one can even say, central to revelation as a whole and especially as completed by Christ. Also, this revelation is such as to bring out the natural law prohibition itself more plainly, and make it easier for us to see it.[53]

Veritatis Splendor invites us to see this more massive witness of the New Testament to the immorality of same-sex unions where, in affirming the immutability of the natural law, it remarks that according to St. Thomas moral norms maintain a "determinate content" in the New Law because of "the assumption of human nature by the Word."[54] The encyclical directs us to the *Prima secundae* of the *Summa*, question 108, the first article, on whether the New Law ought to proscribe or prohibit any exterior acts. The question arises because, according to question 106, article 1, on whether the New Law, the law of the New Testament, is a written law, we learn that "the New Law is chiefly the grace of the Holy Spirit." And in the reply to the first objection, we read that "the gospel writings contain only such things as pertain to the grace of the Holy Spirit, either by disposing us to it, or by directing us to its use." They dispose us, for example, by manifesting the divinity of Christ and so inviting us to faith, whereby we receive grace. As to directing the use of grace, "this consists in works of virtue to which the writings of the New Testament exhort men in various ways." And in question 107, article 1, the New Law is again first of all grace poured into our hearts. However, as the reply to the third objection has it, the New Law

---

52 Finnis, "Natural Law and Unnatural Acts," 384.

53 In what follows, we will take St. Thomas as a guide; for a brief exposition of St. Bonaventure on this theme, see Livio Melina, *Sharing in Christ's Virtues: For a Renewal of Moral Theology in the Light of "Veritatis Splendor,"* trans. William E. May (Washington, DC: Catholic University of America Press, 2001), 128–34.

54 *VS* 53, note 98. Nor, as the letter tells us, at no. 37, note 63, is this a question touching theological opinion alone, since the Council of Trent reproves those who deny a moral teaching to the New Testament and see Christ only as Redeemer and not also as Lawgiver; see the Sixth Session, canons 19–21 of the Decree on Justification. For these canons see Tanner, *Decrees of the Ecumenical Councils*, vol. 2:680.

of which Christ is the Author "consists secondarily in certain moral and sacramental acts." So, regarding these acts, are new or different exterior acts prescribed? That is the question of the *Summa*, question 108, article 1.

In addressing the question whether the New Law prescribes external acts, article 1 of question 108 determines the basis upon which it does so. The New Law is grace; but grace is from the incarnate Word, whose humanity grace filled first. Hence, it is fitting that the grace that comes from the incarnate Word "should be given to us by means of certain external sensible objects," "and that from this inward grace, whereby the flesh [our flesh] is subjected to the Spirit, certain external works should follow."

The external sensible objects are the sacraments; the external works concern acts that are necessarily either in keeping with or opposed to internal grace: so, for example, the confession of faith is prescribed, and the public denial of faith is forbidden. Above, in article 1 of question 106, however, the external acts are acts of the virtues.

This last point finds more complete expression in article 2 of question 108, on whether the New Law made sufficient ordination about external acts. "The New Law had to make such prescriptions or prohibitions alone as are essential for the reception or right use of grace." So, Christ instituted the sacraments, and they are for the reception of grace; but, the article continues, "the right use of grace is by means of works of charity," and these "insofar as they are essential to virtue, pertain to the moral precepts, which also formed part of the Old Law. Hence, in this respect, the New Law had nothing to add as regards external action."[55] "Accordingly, the New Law had no other external works to determine, by prescribing or forbidding, except the sacraments, and those moral precepts which have a necessary connection with virtue, for instance, that one must not kill, or steal, and so forth."[56]

Now, although St. Thomas does not belabor the idea here, we perceive that just as the sensible and bodily Incarnation makes it fitting that grace be given through sensible and bodily sacramental forms, so the exercise of grace in Christ himself is according to the moral precepts of the New Law, which repeat the Decalogue. The Giver of the Law on Sinai gives it again, and—mystery of condescension—obeys it perfectly as a man.[57]

---

[55] See *ST* I–II, q. 108, a. 3, ad 3: "[T]he moral precepts necessarily retained their force under the New Law, because they are of themselves essential to virtue."

[56] *ST* I–II, q. 108, 2.

[57] Recall the Great Antiphon for the Magnificat of December 18: "O Adonai, et Dux domus Israel, qui Moysi in igne flammae rubi apparuisti, et ei in Sina legem dedisti: veni ad redimendum nos in brachio extento." (O Adonai and Leader of the house of Israel, who appeared to Moses in the fire of the burning bush and who gave him the

He gives it again in giving the New Law, most obviously in his teaching, preeminently the Sermon on the Mount. St. Thomas has it in question 107, article 2, that "Christ fulfilled the precepts of the Old Law both in His works and in his doctrine," where by "works" is meant the ceremonial precepts and by "doctrine" the moral precepts. Christ fulfills the sense of the moral precepts by teaching that the true sense of the Law regards not just the exterior act of the moral precepts but the interior act as well.[58] The New Law adds to the Old Law the interior disposition of charity.

He obeys the Law, both Old and New, as a man. For in addition to Christ's role as teacher, there is his example. In question 108, article 1, St. Thomas does not dwell on the point that the incarnate Word not only institutes the sacraments but himself also exercises the very external acts we are called upon to exercise, and with the right interior disposition. Elsewhere, however, he takes it up quite explicitly. So, in the *Tertia pars* of the *Summa*, question 7, article 2, he asks whether Christ possessed the virtues. The answer is yes, that all the virtues were in Christ. As powers flow from the essence of the soul, so virtues from grace.[59] Here, evidently, it is a question of the infused supernatural moral virtues.[60] In fact, Christ possessed them "most perfectly" and "surpassing the common mode."[61] So, as Michele Schumacher says: "Christ, the new Moses, giver of the New Law, is the first to obey its precepts and, in so doing, he sets the standard of its perfection."[62]

Further, the exercise of the virtues depends on knowledge, practical knowledge, which must be the case in Christ, too, a man like us in all things but sin. St. Thomas recognizes such knowledge in Christ in two places. First, presenting the reasons for acknowledging created knowledge in the soul of Christ, he gives as the third reason the existence of a knowledge natural to man: "[S]ome created knowledge pertains to the nature of the

---

Law on Sinai, come to redeem us with your powerful arm.) His redemption of us includes keeping the Law he gave to Moses.

58 For an extended treatment of Christ's fulfillment of the Law according to St. Thomas, see Matthew Levering, *Christ's Fulfillment of Torah and Temple: Salvation according to Thomas Aquinas* (Notre Dame, IN: University of Notre Dame Press, 2002), 15–30, 51–79.

59 The same argument appears in *In III Sent.*, d. 13, q. 1, a. 1, and a. 2, q. 1, a. 1.

60 Though different in species from the acquired moral virtues, since they enable acts that move us to our final and supernatural end, the infused virtues perfect action with regard to the same matter as the acquired virtues; see *ST* I–II, q. 63, a. 4, and ad 2. Infused temperance does not, for instance, permit the agent any indulgence forbidden by the standard of acquired temperance.

61 *ST* III, q. 7, a. 2, ad 2. Christ possesses the gifts, too: q. 7, a. 5.

62 Michele M. Schumacher, "An Inseparable Connection: The Fruitfulness of Conjugal Love and the Divine Norm," *Nova et Vetera* 1 (2003): 389–90.

human soul, namely, that whereby we naturally know first principles."[63] Therefore, we must acknowledge the naturally known first principles of practical reason in Christ, too, which are first principles of the natural law, the habit of which is synderesis. Second, St. Thomas acknowledges in Christ the virtue of practical wisdom itself, prudence: "[S]ince Christ had the fullness of prudence by the gift of counsel, he consequently knew all singular things—present, past, and future."[64]

Beholding Christ, we see that human nature, its exercise within a human history, is the fitting and adequate expression of a divine Person, a divine identity, that of the Son. This means also that the humanly natural knowledge of the natural law, and the virtue of prudence, which knows what is right in the sensibly perceived here and now, and the moral virtues properly so called—it means that all these things are fit instruments of the expression of the moral agency of the Son of God within the economy of salvation. By the Incarnation, there is therefore a sort of seal stamped on the moral principles with which we are endowed by nature, as well as their development in prudence, and of the virtues that we know by the natural light are the excellences of man. What were once the instruments of the expression and a part of the expression in time of the moral agency of a divine and eternal Person remain for all time models for the moral agency of us who are created in the image of that eternal Person. Christ is the incarnate Word in whom and according to whom all things, including our freedom and its exercise, were created. His moral agency must be the expression of the norm of our own.[65] Furthermore, we see in Christ's agency not only the beginning and pattern but also the end of our own. We can say that his agency is the norm of our own because our very "person" is now to be included in his Person; we are to have the same mind as was in Christ Jesus (Phil 2:5), and our mission is an extension of his mission.[66] Because we act in the power of the grace of Christ, moreover, we can say with Livio Melina that the moral acts of a Christian are "a participation in the action of Christ," and for that reason are they beatifying and a foretaste of beatitude.[67]

It is by both grace and revelation, therefore, that Christ conforms us to the moral law in conforming us to himself. We find inspiration in his example; also, he inspires the Holy Spirit in us. Nor is it the case that his exemplarity is merely illustrative of a moral knowledge we already possess.

---

63 *ST* III, q. 9, a. 1.

64 *ST* III, q. 11, a. 1, ad 3.

65 Melina, "Christ and the Dynamism of Action," 126.

66 See here Hans Urs von Balthasar, *Theo-Drama*, vol. 3, *Dramatis Personae: Persons in Christ*, trans. Graham Harrison (San Francisco: Ignatius Press, 1992), 263ff.

67 Melina, "Christ and the Dynamism of Action," 138.

Yes, the seeds of virtue remain in us, but by them and by the first precepts of the natural law we recognize only that the supernaturally graced moral agent is in continuity with, builds on, and perfects the naturally constituted moral agent. This continuity is presupposed in beholding Christ as the standard of human moral agency than whom no greater could be conceived. But the content of that agency, beyond the fulfillment of the rudiments of the natural law, is difficult for us to see in our postlapsarian condition, and impossible for us to anticipate insofar as it bespeaks action inspired by charity. So, without his example, we could not really see, clearly and effectively, what human life should look like. As the Holy Father puts it: "The crucified Christ reveals the authentic meaning of freedom; he lives it fully in the total gift of himself and calls his disciples to share in his freedom" (*VS* 85).

To ask "WWJD?" ("What would Jesus do?") is therefore an entirely appropriate question, a necessary question, for a morally earnest Christian. One of the motives of the Incarnation is to promote us in the good, and in particular, "with regard to well-doing, in which he set us an example."[68] It is therefore wholly right and just to ask what a divine Person operating through human senses, mind, synderesis, prudence, and moral virtues would do. Just so, St. Paul tells the Corinthians, "Be imitators of me, *as I am of Christ*" (1 Cor 11:1, emphasis mine).

The Exemplarity of the Chastity of Christ

If we say with question 108, articles 1 and 2, that by his Incarnation Christ confirms the material content of the natural law, he must do this also relative to the sixth and ninth commandments. Again, if we say that Christ had all the virtues, then he had also the virtue of chastity, and his chastity is an example and norm for ours.[69]

The vice opposed to chastity is lust, a species of which is "unnatural vice." When St. Thomas discusses it in due course, he purports to show the immorality of same-sex relations by saying simply enough that they are pursued for erotic pleasure but without being able to be procreative.[70] This, it will be said, is a mere statement of the natural law exclusion of such relations; it does not add anything to what we know from the natural law or strengthen it by an appeal to the example of the chastity of Christ.[71] Where is that given to us?

---

68 *ST* III, q. 1, a. 2.

69 This is not to say that Christ's is the only chastity the New Testament presents.

70 *ST* II–II, q. 154, a. 11.

71 *Lectura super epistolam ad Ephesios* 5.8.321.

The example and manner of Christ's chastity is communicated to us in what the New Testament says about Christ and the Church. Commenting on chapter 5 of the Letter to the Ephesians, St. Thomas notes that the chastity of the husband is a matter both of the precept of Genesis (2:24) and of the example of Christ. It is in contemplating this example that we can perceive a revealed judgment of the immorality of same-sex unions. St. Paul, it will be remembered, says that he betrothed the Corinthians as a chaste bride to Christ (2 Cor 11:2). The Lord styles himself a Bridegroom in Mark 2:19, something said also by the Baptist in the Gospel according to John (3:29). Ephesians 5:25, 28–32, however, is the great text:[72]

> Husbands, love your wives, as Christ loved the church and gave himself up for her. . . . Even so husbands should love their wives as their own bodies. He who loves his wife loves himself. For no man ever hates his own flesh, but nourishes and cherishes it, as Christ does the church, because we are members of his body. "For this reason a man shall leave his father and mother and be joined to his wife, and the two shall become one flesh." This mystery is a profound one, and I am saying that it refers to Christ and the Church.

The teaching about Christ's relation to the Church in Ephesians calls on our acquaintance with marriage. Also, it reveals something about marriage, and speaks normatively about marriage.[73] We would not know of the extent to which a husband is to love his wife by looking to our already known and measured human experience of marriage; we know of it by looking to Christ. Of course, there is a circle, and Ephesians presupposes a prior acquaintance with marriage just as did Isaiah before him speaking of the relation of Israel to God. The point is that we can and ought to argue from the Christological-ecclesiological reality to the nature and structure of marriage. This is completely classical. So for instance Michael Schmaus says that husband and wife "re-enact" the relation of Christ and the Church.[74] "Husband and wife play the roles of Christ and the Church."[75] Christ is the perfect revelation of the man who abandons all to cling to his wife, and so gives Christological concreteness to Genesis 2:24, "therefore a

[72] See also Mt 22:1–14, the parable of the wedding feast, and Mt 25:1–13, the parable of the wise and foolish virgins, and the characterizations of Christ and the Church in Rev 19:7, 9, and 21:2.

[73] Rudolf Schnackenburg, *The Epistle to the Ephesians: A Commentary*, trans. Helen Heron (Edinburgh: T. & T. Clark, 1991), 154, 241, 257.

[74] Schmaus, *Dogma*, 5:269.

[75] Ibid., 272.

man leaves his father and his mother and cleaves to his wife."[76] The same mutual illumination of marriage and the relation of Christ and the Church is pursued by the Holy Father.[77]

Others, however, are wary of such argument. Elizabeth J. Picken, for instance, warns us against making too much for sacramental theology of the nuptial imagery the Bible uses in speaking of the relation of God to Israel, of Christ to the Church. "A metaphor is a metaphor. God is not married to Israel any more than God is a shepherd of sheep."[78] The appeal to the relation of Christ to the Church, however, is not an invocation of a purely symbolic reality. Truly, the Old Testament characterization of the relation between God and Israel in nuptial terms can be called figurative. However, as Louis Ligier says, the New Testament is "the passing from figures to the time of reality."[79] The Incarnation makes of the Word a quite concrete and historically apprehensible man of the male sex. "For this reason," Ligier says, "his nuptial relations with his people take on a sacramental value which goes beyond that of the symbols of the first covenant."[80] The surplus sacramental value he alludes to is spelled out by Michele Schumacher, who points out that the relation signified by marriage, that of Christ and the Church, is also shared in and fostered by marriage: The grace of the sacrament is a participation in the life-giving grace Christ gives to the Church as a whole in sanctifying each of her members.[81] Therefore we may expect that the resources for thinking about the sacrament of marriage offered by the nuptial characterization of Christ and the Church are a little richer than Picken allows. Especially, to characterize Christ, a man like us in all things but sin, as "spouse" of the Church is to direct us to the determinate moral character of a quite concrete human being. If we then say that Christ is "personally" chaste, therefore, we are saying that it is the chastity of the Son of God displayed, as chastity perforce must be, since it is a virtue whose formality presupposes both the body and sexual differentiation, in the flesh and blood, the passions and prudence and practical wisdom that are part of the perfection of the assumed humanity of Christ.

It may be rejoined that, although Christ is not figuratively a man, but concretely and literally so, the Church remains figuratively a Bride just as

---

76 Ibid., 270.

77 John Paul II, *TOB*, 465–77.

78 Elizabeth J. Picken, "If Christ Is Bridegroom, the Priest Must Be Male?" *Worship* 67 (1993): 274.

79 Louis Ligier, "Women and the Ministerial Priesthood," *Origins* 44 (April 20, 1978): 698.

80 Ibid.

81 Schumacher, "An Inseparable Connection," 385, 387–88.

much as Israel in the Old Testament. Does not the symbolic character of the Church as Bride destroy the inference from the theological to the anthropological level? No, it does not. First, it is enough that one pole of the relation be concretized and take historical form. We see that the chastity of Christ, which is a determination of reason in his passional nature, and the self-gift he makes of his entire being are both turned to and specified by a femininely characterized personal subject, and this is enough to indicate what must be true when both poles are concrete, historical individuals.[82] Moreover and second, the contours of the nuptial chastity of the Church are concretized for the Christian, as is the very person of the Church herself, in Mary.[83] Third, the extreme density of the symbolic value of the nuptial imagery follows from the Eucharist. The relation of Christ and the Church is not indeed sexual, but it is consummated in a "one flesh" union, really and not figuratively, in virtue of the Eucharist.[84]

To repeat, it is not, then, as if Christian spouses are told to imitate some purely figuratively heavenly or theological reality when we read Ephesians. The heavenly and theological has become the earthly and anthropological. That is the point of the Incarnation. Here, we have the chaste Jesus who takes the Church for his spouse, a Church styled as Bride, and this shows us something about chastity. Moreover, if the relation of Christ to the Church is normative for marriage, what Christ's chastity shows us is something normative for the virtue of chastity that marriage, every marriage, calls on. Furthermore, if every sacrament depends on a natural sign, then we can deduce what the parameters of the sign are from the nuptial relation of Christ and the Church. To quote Ligier again, "the sacraments are not only instruments of a purely spiritual grace; they are also natural signs of it because they symbolize it in their natural structure."[85] Symbolizing grace in its natural structure, the sacrament of marriage as kept in the Church, and even more the great sacrament of Christ and the Church, both declare what the "natural structure" of marriage is and that it is constituted by sexual distinction. If in a period of cultural and moral confu-

---

[82] Ibid. For the same teaching, see *Gaudium et Spes*, (*GS*), no. 49.

[83] See, for instance, among many, many examples, Hans Urs von Balthasar, "Who Is the Church?" in *Church and World* (New York: Herder, 1967), 112–65, and "The Marian Principle," *Communio* 15 (1988): 122–30.

[84] Schumacher, "An Inseparable Connection," 396. Earlier, see Yves Congar, *Lay People in the Church*, trans. Donald Attwater (Westminster, MD: Newman Press, 1967), 128: "[T]he body God has fashioned [Heb 10:5] is at the same time Christ's personal body, his fellowship body—the body of which we are the members—and, making a living bond between these two, his sacramental body." Congar appeals to St. Augustine for this point.

[85] Ligier, "Women and the Ministerial Priesthood," 698–99.

sion we have forgotten this, revelation comes to the aid of what we should see, and used to see more readily, by the natural light.

The Content of the Exemplary Chastity of Christ

The Chastity of Christ and the Chastity of Christians. What then does the chastity of Christ, as displayed relative to the Church, his Bride, teach us about sexual morals and marriage? The relation of Christ and the Church implies the duty of faithfulness. Christ is faithful to the Church unto his death, giving himself up for her (Eph 5:25). It implies exclusivity or "unity," for the Bride is the Body, and there is only one Body of Christ just as there is only one Christ (Eph 4:4). The relation of Christ and the Church implies indissolubility. For again, the Bride is the Body, and the members of the Body are one person in Christ. Further, as the Church is the fullness of Christ (Eph 1:23), so a man comes to the fullness of his personal reality when he makes the gift of himself as husband. It is therefore well said in Ephesians that "he who loves his wife loves himself" (Eph 5:28).[86] Last, the relation implies fruitfulness. The bridal bath in which Christ washes the Church is the bath at once of his Passion and of his baptism, in which we are made to die to self and live in Christ.[87] The laver is the womb of the Church, making Christ the firstborn among many brethren.[88]

So, the relation of Christ to the Church teaches us that marriage excludes adultery, polygamy and polyandry, divorce, and the separation of the marital act from its reproductive possibilities, which separation would be like celebrating baptism without the baptized, keeping the bath water without the baby.

But does the relation of Christ to the Church also imply that marriage must be between a man and a woman, and so exclude same-sex unions? Most obviously and certainly, for how can the couple be a sign of the relation of Christ to the Church if in the absence of their sexual distinction they would more naturally be taken to be an image of the relation of Christ to Christ or Church to Church?

As was said above, the distinction between Christ and the Church is more than "symbolized" by styling Christ as the husband and the Church as the wife. Christ really is male. The differences between male and female here help to show the identities of the differentiated. We come to know Christ and the Church across the distinction. So also, and in the same way, we come to know man and woman, which is to say man and woman

86 Also see Schnackenburg, *Ephesians*, 257.

87 Ibid., 249–51.

88 See here John Paul II, "Letter to Families" (1994), 19.

come to know themselves as male and female, and in those ways human, across and through the distinction. Man as such is shown in the distinction of male and female, and male and female themselves only appear within their distinction from one another, a distinction that allows for marital union and that marital union is uniquely privileged to bring to light. "The encounter of man and woman presupposes their diversity," Schmaus says, commenting on Genesis 2.[89] Moreover, "the fullness of being-human, according to the testimony of Genesis, is achieved only in the encounter of man and woman."[90] As the Holy Father says, commenting on the expostulation "bone of my bones and flesh of my flesh": "The man uttered these words, as if it were only at the sight of the woman that he was able to identify and call by name what makes them visibly similar to each other, and at the same time what manifests humanity."[91]

Writing in 1952, Schmaus says that the diversity of the partners of the marital encounter is "not only external" but determines the whole reality of the spouses.[92] Writing today, one supposes, he might be tempted to reverse the emphasis and say that the diversity of the spouses is not only "internal," a matter of the mind and freedom of the person, but also somatic and "external." The Holy Father asserts both kinds of diversity, both kinds of complementarity. These are, as it were, two "incarnations" of the same metaphysical solitude before God and the world. They are two ways of "being a body" and at the same time a man, which complete each other. They are two complementary dimensions of self-consciousness and self-determination and, at the same time, two complementary ways of being conscious of the meaning of the body.[93]

It might be objected that the symbolic structure of marriage is in fact more complicated than has been represented above. Each spouse, after all, is conformed to Christ.[94] Both spouses together form a domestic church that images the great Church.[95] While the latter may be granted, it should be recalled that the conformation to Christ that the grace of the sacrament

---

89 Schmaus, *Dogma*, 5:265.

90 Ibid.

91 John Paul II, *TOB*, 164.

92 Michael Schmaus, *Katholische Dogmatik*, IV/1: *Die Lehre von den Sakramenten* (Munich: Max Hueber, 1952), 609: "Die Bestimmtheit als Frau bzw. als Mann haftet dem Menschen nicht nur äußerlich an, sondern prägt ihn vom Innesten her. Der Mensch ist ganz Mann oder ganz Frau." This is repeated in Schmaus, *Dogma*, 265.

93 John Paul II, *TOB*, 165. See the whole of the eighth, ninth, and tenth catecheses in *TOB*, 156–68.

94 Schmaus, *Dogma*, 5:282.

95 Ibid., 283.

works is interior, a conformation in charity. The sexual difference of the spouses, on the other hand, both bodily and personal, belongs to the exterior, sensible, and natural sign the sacrament presupposes. Within and on the basis of imaging Christ and the Church visibly and publicly, each is interiorly conformed to Christ by grace.

Each sacrament is built on a natural sign. The signification of grace in marriage is built on the difference of man and woman, which recalls the relation of Christ and the Church, wherein Christ purifies and sanctifies the Church. Marriage is like the sacrament of orders in that both require sexually determinate subjects: male and female for marriage, male for priestly orders. It is no accident that those who do not see the relevance of maleness for priestly orders do not see the relevance of sexual diversity for marriage. A reading of Ephesians that suppresses its implied rejection of homosexual unions was first produced by those who wished to suppress its implication for orders.

Objection: An Alternative Reading of Ephesians. Ephesians 5, in helping us see the content of Christ's exemplary chastity, is directing us at the same time to what Catholic tradition has always said the natural law also teaches us. Those who do not see what is inscribed in the relation of Christ and the Church for our moral instruction predictably do not perceive the law that is written on our heart, and vice versa. Just as predictably, failure to hear the word about orders spoken by the relation of Christ and the Church silences it for marriage as well.

Elizabeth Picken is concerned not to restrict priestly orders to men. She sees no grounds for such restriction in the nuptial imagery of the Bible. She wishes to reduce the content of the Bible's nuptial imagery to fidelity. For Picken, "sexuality and marriage are not the model on which Christ fashions his relationship to the Church," and marriage does not tell us anything about this relationship.[96] This relationship rather tells us of something about marriage, but what it tells us is only that spouses should be faithful to one another. "What is the point of the comparison?" she asks. "Is it not the loving fidelity of the covenant relationship?"[97]

In this reductive reading of the data of revelation, Picken is preceded by David Power and Carroll Stuhlmueller and followed by Susan Ross. So Power, also writing about the ordination of women, reduces the meaning of the nuptial symbolism to unity. "It is doubtful that prevailing importance needs to be given to the sexual side of this imagery in configuring

[96] Picken, "The Priest Must Be Male?" 276.

[97] Ibid., 276–77.

the Christ-Church or Christ-humanity relationship. Indeed, that would risk undermining the unity that has been established between Christ and the Church through the work of reconciliation."[98]

In other words, the imagery cannot be used to argue that the distinction of the male Christ from the femininely figured Church is significant, and calls for male priests. Stuhlmueller concludes his study of the image with the judgment that "the Yahweh-Spouse or Jesus-Bridegroom image does not stress sexual differences but intimate, joyful and fruitful union of all persons."[99]

Susan Ross's immediate concern is likewise ordination. She does not see quite the same thing in the "spousal/nuptial imagery" that Picken does. Where Picken sees fidelity, Ross sees what she thinks is the same thing, namely, "intimacy": "the close relationship between God and Israel, and between priest and faithful, as it is also found in the relationship between husband and wife."[100] Ross sees something Power and Picken do not, however, and that is the extension of the implication of this reductive reading of Ephesians to the question of same-sex relations. She reproves the Magisterium for adverting to the differentiation of Christ and Church as inscribed in the difference of man and woman, husband and wife, and alleges the deleterious consequences of such a focus on differences, not only for women within marriage, and not only for the prospect of the ordination of women, but also for same-sex relations. The implications of "Vatican theology," she says, "for men and women in same-sex relations are at least as severe as they are for women in heterosexual relationships."[101]

What shall we make of these other ways of reading the nuptial theme of revelation whose climax is found in Ephesians? In the first place, the unity that Power rightly sees established between Christ and the Church and that is enacted in the Eucharist does not mean the Church is absorbed into Christ. The Mass is indeed the sacrifice of Christ himself, as Congar observes, but it is also the Church's sacrifice, first, "in as much as Christ's sacrifice is offered by the Church," and second, "in as much as the Church offers her own sacrifice in and through Christ's."[102] Thus it makes sense

[98] Power, "Representing Christ in Community and Sacrament," 120.

[99] Carroll Stuhlmueller, "Bridegroom: A Biblical Symbol of Union, not Separation," in *Women Priests*, ed. Leonard Swidler and Arlene Swidler (New York: Paulist Press, 1977), 283.

[100] Susan A. Ross, *Extravagant Affections: A Feminist Sacramental Theology* (New York: Continuum, 1998), 114–15. She makes no distinction between her "intimacy" and Power's "unity."

[101] Ibid., 115n67.

[102] Congar, *Lay People*, 216.

for Congar to say: "The worship of the Church as such, considered not simply as Christ's worship sacramentally celebrated but as her own worship, is worship as bride, and in this respect a theology of liturgy must learn from an ecclesiology of the Church as bride."[103]

In the second place, let us note that Ross, with her "intimacy," sees even less there than Picken's "fidelity." There can be plenty of intimacy, sexual and personal, without fidelity. Can that really be the only thing that Scripture has to say to married people? In order for women to be ordained, and in order for same-sex marriage to be blessed, the word of God is prevented from speaking to genuinely married couples about anything except "intimacy." But of course, we do not need the Scripture to speak to us about intimacy. That is one of the watchwords of the modern desacralized world. Sexual intimacy and sexual self-definition together make one of the chief things modernity recognizes as sacred, and worthy of worship and sacrifice.[104] We can learn about intimacy from watching *Friends*. There really is a slippery slope. Get rid of the procreative meaning of sexual relations, and the whole ensemble of the properties of marriage dissolves. In the third place, the reductive readings, as a group, seem not to reckon with the overwhelming testimony of the Bible to the Lord God's interest in life and in fostering life. He is the God not of the dead, but of the living (Mt 22:32); he is the God of life, who gives life—and this is arguably the most characteristic description of God in the Old Testament.[105] Does this interest in life and the production of life turn up expressly every time the nuptial imagery is used? No, just enough to see that it is most certainly co-intended whenever the symbolism is used, something that therefore can go without saying. Particularly fine and express, on the other hand, is Isaiah 54:1:

> Sing, O barren one, who did not bear;
>   break forth into singing and cry aloud,
>   you who have not been in travail!

103 Ibid., 209.

104 See Jacques Ellul, *The New Demons*, trans. C. Edward Hopkin (New York: Seabury Press, 1975), 70–80. Ellul also points out the convergence of technology, another object of modern absolute reverence, with sex. This book is too early for an appreciation of "deep ecology," but we see how things shape up: the nature that man is not is the nature that is to be preserved pure and inviolate from technological alteration and manipulation; the nature that man is, is open to every such possible manipulation. This is because, really, modern man no longer has a nature, but is only a locus of rights and the freedom to exercise them; see Pierre Manent, *The City of Man*, trans. Marc A. LePain (Princeton, NJ: Princeton University Press, 1998), 133–55.

105 Cf. Alfons Deissler, "Gottes Selbstoffenbarung im Alten Testament," in *Mysterium Salutis*, vol. 2, ed. J. Feiner and M. Löhrer (Einsiedeln: Benziger, 1965), 238–39.

For the children of the desolate one will be more
than the children of her that is married, says the LORD.

And with regard to Ephesians itself, it is an uncontroversial exegesis to see the bridal bath as also the laver of baptism, the teeming womb of the Church. What this Great Mystery tells us of marriage, then, beyond "intimacy" and even beyond fidelity, is that marriage is to be fruitful, for which procreative end there is required the congress of two distinct but complementary principles of sexual fecundity.

A same-sex union, on the other hand, can neither look back to the origins of Genesis nor forward eschatologically to the Bride and the Lamb of Revelation. Marriage passes away, according to that saying whereby there is no marriage or giving in marriage in heaven (Mk 12:25), but in what it figures and in what it finds its norm does not. In that respect, therefore, it is not just an "earthly" reality, but "an element" of the kingdom, in Schmaus's words, and this is shown by the very fact that Jesus spoke of it in the first place.[106] The Holy Father says the same when he speaks of the nuptial meaning of the body finding its fulfillment in heaven.[107]

The Fundamentality of Fecundity. We said that orders and marriage are alike in depending on sexual distinction. They are alike in this, too: that as marriage passes away into eschatological fulfillment, so also an ordained priest's priesthood passes, in the sense that it is no longer exercised in the eschaton, because in heaven everyone has immediate access to what the ministerial priesthood imitates and is a participation of, Christ the High Priest. Both in their various ways are signs of the eschatological goods of the last age.

Priestly orders and marriage are alike in a third way, too. Both are ordered to fecundity. Priestly evangelization and catechesis should be fruitful in drawing new Christians from the laver of baptism. As was briefly noted above for marriage, the unity and indissolubility of marriage were classically seen to follow from its procreative end. The friendship enacted within marriage is also served by exclusivity and permanence (see *GS* 50). It is the good of children, however, that demands a stable and permanent union of man and wife so that a child can have both a father and a mother available. Finnis puts it this way: "[W]hat, in the last analysis, makes sense of the conditions of the marital enterprise, its stability and exclusiveness, is not the worthy and delightful sentiments of love and affection which

[106] Schmaus, *Dogma*, 5:268.

[107] John Paul II, the catecheses entitled "The Resurrection of the Body," in *TOB*, 233–61, esp. 243–45.

invite one to marry, but the desire for and demands of a procreative community, a family."[108]

That the procreative good of marriage calls for stability and permanence is a matter of justice rendered to children.[109] Of course, pursuing this procreative good, remaining open to it, is a matter of justice to one's spouse as well. It is a matter of the justice of spousal love, in that one does not render the complete gift of oneself to one's spouse if one withholds one's fecundity, nor does one receive the complete gift of one's spouse if one refuses to receive his or her fecundity. Nor is justice rendered to the sacrament, to the Great Mystery of which the sacrament is a sign, if the procreative meaning of marriage is abrogated. Certain it is that the *bonum prolis* is not the only good of marriage. But it is foundational. Getting in its way wrecks all the other goods of both nature and grace in Christian marriage.[110] This priority of fecundity, this foundational role that fecundity plays in the natural law intelligibility of the traditional form of marriage, is true also for the relation of Christ and the Church, which in turn enables us to discern the natural order more clearly. That is to say, the unity and indissolubility of the relation of Christ to the Church in the supernatural order is a function of the good of the life—but here, the supernatural life—of the children of this union, the members of the Church, Christians. They need the constant availability of both the Church and her Head, and so the promise of Christ to be spouse must be unbreakable, and the Church's cleaving to Christ indefectible.

The Inseparability of Procreative and Unitive Meanings. There is, finally, the issue of the inseparability of the procreative and unitive meanings of sex for each sexual act. Does the symbolic force with which the Church is Bride, and the denial that the relation is, in fact, sexual, mean that revelation finally deserts us, and has nothing to say here in order to strengthen the natural law assertion of this inseparability? Michele Schumacher offers two resources here.

> Because . . . the conjugal act is considered . . . as an act of love, it is necessarily governed by the love of Christ. Thus the same logic applies: because the divine love is so fully generous not merely in itself (as a mutual gift of Persons, bearing fruit in a third, divine Person)

108 Finnis, "Natural Law and Unnatural Acts," 383.

109 See, for instance, John Paul II, "Letter to Families," no. 10.

110 See Bernard J. F. Lonergan, "Finality, Love, Marriage," in *Collection*, ed. F. E. Crowe (New York: Herder and Herder, 1967), 22, 49: "While the supernatural goods of marriage are more excellent, children are the more essential good of marriage."

> but also in the economy of creation and redemption . . . the spousal love of Christians, and more specifically the conjugal act itself, ought to be generous.[111]

But then, second, there is also the Trinitarian gift of Persons that is fecund. While marriage finds its exemplar, an exemplar in which it participates, in the Christ-Church relation, that relation itself is a sign and a function of a yet higher relation, that of Father and Son in the Trinity. Here, union and fecundity coincide.[112] That the three Persons are one eternal God means, Schumacher says, that "neither the 'union' nor the 'fruit' is subsequent to the real distinction of Persons within the Trinity."[113]

Both as to the kinds of goods and the ordering of these goods in marriage, revelation gives us to see in the relation of Christ and the Church the natural order writ more clearly, more largely. Just as one cannot look at the nuptial relation of Christ and the Church and ask whether there could be such a thing as Christian polyandry, or a sacramental marriage that was "open" and "non-exclusive," so little can one look at the Great Mystery and ask whether same-sex unions could be blessed in the Church. But, and this is the point, in showing us these holy things, the Great Mystery also and at the same time shows us the natural things of marriage, the structure and requirements of marriage such as can in principle, "per se," be made evident to us by the natural light.

Conclusion

That we should expect not to need revelation in order to know the natural law with the completeness required to direct our action betrays a twofold forgetfulness, dogmatic and historical. First, we are forgetting the ignorance that is a result of original sin and the enfeeblement of our sight by passion and vice. Second, we forget how much of the intellectual effort of modernity is devoted systematically to obscure the very idea that man has a nature. If Pierre Manent is correct in this characterization of the modern project, then there can be no argument for modernity, from the nature of sexuality as concerned with the good of new human life to such things as the immorality of contraception and homosexual unions.[114] There can be

---

[111] Schumacher, "An Inseparable Connection," 399.

[112] Ibid., 399–402.

[113] Ibid., 391. The Trinity means that "God is 'always-already' fruitful" (ibid.).

[114] For a brief expression of Manent's view, see his "Christianity and Democracy: Some Remarks on the Political History of Religion, or, on the Religious History of Modern Politics," in *Modern Liberty and Its Discontents*, ed. and trans. Daniel J. Mahoney and Paul Senton (New York: Rowman & Littlefield, 1998), 97–115.

no invocations of bodily distinction as by nature fitted to signify the altereity of persons in marriage, or as expressing anything about the person except what the person says it expresses. Neither can there be any argument from the nature of child-rearing to a requirement of permanence and promise. All there can be are persons—not necessarily inclined to respect the antecedent givenness of their bodies—who are subjects of rights. Then we shall very easily construct the sexual culture and mores of modern America. But this is not to say it will have anything to do with the civilization of love, or the culture of life.

Understanding Stephen Pope's article as an instance of the non-reception of *VS* shows some important things. It lays bare the possibilities: either a Christ that speaks to the moral life as empowering us to enter into him and the moral pattern that he lived and revealed to us as the full revelation of man's true identity; or, a Christ understood as one who inspires us to do the good, whatever that is, and avoid evil, however we may make it out by our own lights—a Christ who can be the truth and the life, but who cannot be the way. Such a view of Christ is far from the view of St. Thomas and, indeed, from the experience of the Church.

Selected Bibliography

Aquila, Samuel. *The Teaching of Vatican II on "In Persona Christi" and "In Nomine Ecclesiae" in Relation to the Ministerial Priesthood in the Light of the Historical Development of the Formulae*. Rome: Licentiate tessina, Pontificium Athenaeum Anselmianum, 1990.

Augustine, St. *The Works of Saint Augustine: A New Translation for the 21st Century* (*WSA*). 15 vols. Edited by John E. Rotelle. New York: New City Press, 1990–.

———. *Letters*, vol. 2. Trans. Sister Wilfrid Parsons. Fathers of the Church 18. New York: Fathers of the Church, 1989.

Barth, Markus. *Ephesians: Introduction, Translation and Commentary*. Garden City, NY: Doubleday, 1974.

Becker, Karl. "The Church and Vatican II's *'Subsistit in'* Terminology." *Origins* 35 (January 19, 2006): 514–22.

Boyle, John. "The Ordinary Magisterium: Towards a History of the Concept." *Heythrop Journal* 20 (1979): 97.

Bradley, Denis J. M. *Aquinas on the Twofold Human Good: Reason and Human Happiness in Aquinas's Moral Science*. Washington, DC: Catholic University of America Press, 1997.

Brown, Raymond. *The Virginal Conception and the Bodily Resurrection of Jesus*. New York: Paulist Press, 1970.

Butler, Sara. "Priestly Identity: 'Sacrament' of Christ the Head." *Worship* 70 (July 1996): 290–306.

———. "The Priest as Sacrament of Christ the Bridegroom." *Worship* 66 (1992): 511.

Cantalamessa, O.F.M. Cap., Raniero. *Virginity*. Translated by Charles Serignat. Boston: Alba House, 1995.

Coffey, David. "The Common and the Ordained Priesthood." *Theological Studies* 58 (June 1997): 209–36.

———. "Priestly Representation and Women's Ordination." In *Priesthood: The Hard Questions*. Edited by Gerald P. Gleeson. Newtown, New South Wales, Australia: E. J. Dwyer, 1992, 79–99.

Congar, Yves. *Lay People in the Church*. Translated by Donald Attwater. Westminster, MD: Newman Press, 1967.

———. Vraie et fausse Réform dans l'Église. Second edition, revised. Paris: Cerf, 1968.

Congregation for the Doctrine of the Faith (CDF). Commentary on the Document "Responses to Some Questions regarding Certain Aspects of the Doctrine of the Church." See *Origins* 37 (2007): 134–39.

———. Declaration on Certain Questions concerning Sexual Ethics. *Persona Humana*. 1975.

———. Declaration on the Question of the Admission of Women to the Ministerial Priesthood. *Inter Insignores*. 1976.

———. Instruction on the Ecclesial Vocation of the Theologian. See *Origins* 20 (July 5, 1990): 118–26.

———. Letter to Bishops of the Catholic Church on the Collaboration of Men and Women in the Church and in the World. 2004.

———. Letter to the Bishops of the Catholic Church on the Pastoral Care of Homosexual Persons. 1986.

———. Letter to the Bishops of the Catholic Church on Some Aspects of the Church Understood as Communion. See *Origins* 22 (June 25, 1992): 108–12.

———. Notificação sobre o livro *Igreja: Carisma e Poder: Ensaios de Eclesiologia Militante* de Frei Leonardo Boff, O.F.M. (Notification on the book *Church, Charism, and Power: Essays on Militant Ecclesiology* by, Leonardo Boff, O.F.M.) March 11, 1985. See AAS 77 (1985): 756–62.

———. Responses to Some Questions regarding Certain Aspects of the Doctrine of the Church. June 29, 2007. See *Origins* 37 (2007): 134–36.

———. *Quaecumque Sterilizatio*. March 13, 1975. See AAS 68 (November 1976): 738–40. English translation: *Origins* 6 (June 10, 1976): 34–35.

"Consecration to a Life of Virginity for Women Living in the World." No. 16, in *The Rites of the Catholic Church as Revised by the Second Vatican Ecumenical Council*, vol. 2. Collegeville, Minnesota: The Liturgical Press, 1991.

Dictionary of Fundamental Theology. Edited by René Latourelle and Rino Fisichella. New York: Crossroad, 1994.

DiNoia, J. A. "Communion and Magisterium: Teaching Authority and the Culture of Grace." *Modern Theology* 9 (1993): 403–15.

Documents of Vatican II. Edited by Walter Abbot. Baltimore: America Press, 1966.

Dulles, Avery. *Catholicity of the Church*. Oxford: Oxford/Clarendon, 1985.

Finnis, John "Natural Law and Unnatural Acts." *Heythrop Journal* 11 (1970): 365–87.

Flannery, S.J., Kevin L. "Homosexuality and Types of Dualism: A Platonico-Aristotelian Approach." *Gregorianum* 81 (2000): 353–72.

Fortin, Ernest. "Natural Law." In *Human Rights, Virtue, and Common Good: Untimely Meditations on Religion and Politics*. Edited by Brian J. Benestad. New York: Rowman & Littlefield, 1996.

Gaillardetz, Richard. "The Ordinary Universal Magisterium: Unresolved Questions." *Theological Studies* 63 (2002): 447–71.

———. *Witnesses to the Faith: Community, Infallibility, and the Ordinary Magisterium of Bishops*. New York: Paulist Press, 1992.

Geyer, Christian. "Ratzinger on *Dominus Iesus*." *Inside the Vatican* 9 (2001): 112–18.

Greshake, Gisbert. *The Meaning of Christian Priesthood*. Translated by Peadar MacSeumais. Westminster, MD: Christian Classics, 1989.

Grisez, Germain. "The Ordinary Magisterium's Infallibility." *Theological Studies* 55 (1994): 721–32.

Heim, Maximilian. *Joseph Ratzinger: Life in the Church and Living Theology*. San Francisco: Ignatius Press, 2007.

Hellín, Francisco Gil. *Lumen Gentium. Constitutio Dogmatica de Ecclesia Concilii Vaticani II Synopsis in ordinem redigens schemata cum relationibus necnon patrum orationes atque animadversiones*. Vatican City: Libreria Editrice Vaticana, 1995.

Hittinger, Russell. "*Veritatis Splendor* and the Theology of the Natural Law." In *"Veritatis Splendor" and the Renewal of Moral Theology*. Edited by J. A. DiNoia, O.P., and Romanus Cessario, O.P. Princeton, NJ: Scepter Publishers, 1999.

John Paul II, Pope. *God, Father, and Creator: A Catechesis on the Creed*. Translated by *L'Osservatore Romano*. English ed. Boston: Pauline Books and Media, 1996.

———. *The Original Unity of Man and Woman: Catechesis on the Book of Genesis*. Boston: Daughters of St. Paul, 1981.

———. *A Theology of the Body*. Translated by Michael Waldstein. Boston: Pauline Books and Media, 2006.

Johnson, Elizabeth. *She Who Is*. New York: Crossroad, 1993.

Kasper, Walter. "Theological Anthropology." *Communio* 26 (Winter 1996): 129–40.

Keefe, Donald. "Sacramental Sexuality and the Ordination of Women." *Communio* 3 (1978): 228–51.

Keenan, James. "Institutional Cooperation and the Ethical and Religious Directives." *Linacre Quarterly* 64 (August 1997): 53–76.

———. "Not an Excessive Claim, Nor a Divisive One, But a Traditional One: A Response to Lawrence Welch on Immediate Material Cooperation." *Linacre Quarterly* 67 (November 2000): 83–88.

Keenan, James, and M. Cathleen Kaveny. "Ethical Issues in Health-Care Restructuring." *Theological Studies* 56 (March 1995): 136–50.

Keenan, James, and Thomas Kopfensteiner. "The Principle of Material Cooperation." *Health Progress* 76 (April 1995): 23–27.

Ligier, Louis. "Women and the Ministerial Priesthood." *Origins* 44 (April 20, 1978): 694–701.

Lonergan, Bernard J. F. "Finality, Love, Marriage." In *Collection*. Edited by F. E. Crowe. New York: Herder and Herder, 1967.

McCormick, Richard. "Medicaid and Abortion." *Theological Studies* 45 (December 1984): 715–21.

Melina, Livio. "Christ and the Dynamism of Action: Outlook and Overview of Christocentrism in Moral Theology." *Communio* 28 (2001): 112–39.

———. "The Role of the Ordinary Universal Magisterium: On Francis Sullivan's Creative Fidelity." *The Thomist* 61 (1997): 605–15.

National Conference of Catholic Bishops (NCCB). Ethical and Religious Directives for Catholic Health Care Services (ERD). Washington, DC: USCCB, 1995.

———. "NCCB Statement on Tubal Ligation." *Origins* 10 (August 28, 1980): 175.

O'Rourke, J. "Some Considerations about Polygenism." *Theological Studies* 26 (1965): 407–17.

Philibert, Paul. "Issues for a Theology of Priesthood: A Status Report." In *The Theology of Priesthood*. Edited by Donald Goergen and Ann Garrido. Collegeville, MN: The Liturgical Press, 2000.

Picken, Elizabeth J. "If Christ Is Bridegroom, the Priest Must Be Male?" *Worship* 67 (1993): 269–78.

Pope, Stephen J. "Scientific and Natural Law Analyses of Homosexuality." *Journal of Religious Ethics* 29 (2001): 89–126.

Power, David. "Representing Christ in Community and Sacrament." In *Being a Priest Today*. Collegeville, MN: The Liturgical Press, 1992.

Rahner, Karl. *Sacramentum Mundi*. 6 vols. New York: Herder, 1968.

Ratzinger, Joseph Cardinal. "The Ecclesiology of the Constitution *Lumen Gentium*." In *Pilgrim Fellowship of Faith: The Church as Communion*. San Francisco: Ignatius, 2005, 123–52.

———. "Pastoral Constitution on the Church in the Modern World." In *Commentary on the Documents of Vatican II*. Vol. 5. Edited by Herbert Vorgrimler et al. New York: Herder and Herder, 1968, 115–63.

———. *Principles of Catholic Theology*. Translated by Sr. Mary Frances McCarthy. San Francisco: Ignatius Press, 1987.

Rausch, Thomas. "Priestly Identity: Priority of Representation and the Iconic Argument." *Worship* 73 (March 1999): 169–79.

Schindler, David. "Christology and the *Imago Dei*: Interpreting *Gaudium et Spes*." *Communio* 23 (Spring 1996): 156–84.

Schlier, Heinrich. *Theological Dictionary of the New Testament*. Vol. 3. Edited by Gerhard Kittle. Translated by Geoffrey W. Bromiley. Grand Rapids, MI: Eerdmans, 1964–1976.

Schmaus, Michael. *Dogma*. Vol. 5, *The Church as Sacrament*. London: Sheed and Ward, 1975.

Schnackenburg, Rudolf. *The Epistle to the Ephesians: A Commentary*. Translated by Helen Heron. Edinburgh: T. & T. Clark, 1991.

Schumacher, Michele M. "An Inseparable Connection: The Fruitfulness of Conjugal Love and the Divine Norm." *Nova et Vetera* 1 (2003): 381–402.

Scola, Angelo. " 'Claim' of Christ, 'Claim' of the World: On the Trinitarian Encyclicals of John Paul II." *Communio* 18 (Fall 1991): 322–31.

———. "The Nuptial Mystery at the Heart of the Church." *Communio* 25 (1998): 630–62.

Scola, Angelo Cardinal. *The Nuptial Mystery*. Translated by Michelle K. Borras. Grand Rapids: Eerdmans, 2005.

A Select Library of the Nicene and Post-Nicene Fathers (*NPNF*). Reprint. Edited by P. Schaff and H. Wace. Vol. 2/5. Grand Rapids, MI: Eerdmans, 1994.

Smith, William B. "Catholic Hospitals and Sterilizations." *Linacre Quarterly* 44 (May 1977): 107–16.

"Sterilization Policy for Catholic Hospitals." *Origins* 7 (December 8, 1977): 399–400.

Sullivan, S.J., Francis A. *The Church We Believe In*. New York: Paulist Press, 1988.

———. *Creative Fidelity*. New York: Paulist Press, 1996.

———. "The Doctrinal Weight of Evangelium Vitae." *Theological Studies* 56 (1995): 560–65.

———. "Further Thoughts on the Meaning of *Subsistit in*." *Theological Studies* 71 (March 2010): 133–47.

———. "Guideposts from the Catholic Tradition." *America* (December 9, 1995): 5–6.

———. "Infallible Teaching on Moral Issues? Reflections on *Veritatis Splendor* and *Evangelium Vitae*." In *Choosing Life: A Dialogue on* Evangelium Vitae. Edited by Kevin W. Wildes, S.J., and Alan C. Mitchell. Washington, DC: Georgetown University, 1997, 77–89.

———. *Magisterium*. New York: Paulist Press, 1983.

———. "The Meaning of *Subsistit in* as Explained by the Congregation for the Doctrine of the Faith." *Theological Studies* 69 (2008): 116–24.

———. "Reply to Germain Grisez." *Theological Studies* 55 (1994): 732–37.

———. "Reply to Lawrence J. Welch." *Theological Studies* 64 (2003): 610–15.

———. "A Response to Karl Becker, S.J., on the Meaning of *Subsistit in*." *Theological Studies* 67 (2006): 395–409.

———. *Salvation Outside the Church: Tracing the History of the Catholic Response*. New York: Paulist Press, 1992.

———. "The Secondary Object of Infallibility." *Theological Studies* 54 (1993): 536–50.

Tanner, Norman, ed. *Decrees of the Ecumenical Councils*. Washington, DC: Georgetown University Press, 1990. Vol. 2.

Vanneste, Alfred. *Dogma of Original Sin*. Translated by Edward P. Callens, SS.CC. Brussels: Vander; Louvain: Nauwelaerts, 1971.

Vaughn, Austin. "Magisterium on Mary's Virginity." *Marian Studies* 21 (1971): 75–90.

Von Balthasar, Hans Urs. *Theo-Drama*. Translated by Graham Harrison. Vols. 2–3. San Francisco: Ignatius Press, 1990, 1992.

Waldstein, Michael. *Man and Woman He Created Them: A Theology of the Body*. Boston: Paulist Press, 2006.

Weigel, George. *God's Choice: Pope Benedict XVI and the Future of the Catholic Church*. New York: HarperCollins, 2005.

Welch, Lawrence. "Direct Sterilization: An Intrinsically Evil Act: A Rejoinder to Fr. Keenan." *Linacre Quarterly* 68 (May 2001): 124–30.

Zizizoulas, John. *Being as Communion*. Crestwood, NY: St. Vladimir's Seminary Press, 1985.

1

Index

CPSIA information can be obtained at www.ICGtesting.com
Printed in the USA
BVOW032351030412

286780BV00003B/3/P

9 781932 589597